The Corporation
of the 1990s

THE CORPORATION OF THE 1990s

Information Technology and Organizational Transformation

Edited by

MICHAEL S. SCOTT MORTON

New York   Oxford
OXFORD UNIVERSITY PRESS
1991

Oxford University Press

Oxford   New York   Toronto
Delhi   Bombay   Calcutta   Madras   Karachi
Petaling Jaya   Singapore   Hong Kong   Tokyo
Nairobi   Dar es Salaam   Cape Town
Melbourne   Auckland

and associated companies in
Berlin   Ibadan

Copyright © 1991 by Sloan School of Management

Published by Oxford University Press, Inc.,
200 Madison Avenue, New York, New York 10016

Oxford is a registered trademark of Oxford University Press

Library of Congress Cataloging-in-Publication Data
The Corporation of the 1990s : information technology and organizational transformation
edited by Michael S. Scott Morton.
p. cm.   Includes bibliographical references and index.
ISBN 0-19-506358-9
1. Management—Data processing.   2. Information technology—Management.
3. Organizational change.   I. Scott Morton, Michael S.
HD30.2.C66   1991   658.4′038—dc20   90-37886

5 7 9 8 6

Printed in the United States of America
on acid-free paper

Foreword

This book is one result of the pioneering efforts in a new form of collaborative research. The Management in the 1990s Research Program, from its beginning in 1984, was conceived as a close collaboration between academic researchers at the MIT Sloan School of Management and representatives of major corporations to do research on a set of issues of mutually agreed upon importance. Though it is primarily the academic researchers who have written this book—they have the time and expertise for the task—each chapter is the fruit of an active dialogue between its nominal authors and the representatives of the sponsoring organizations. For it is the organizations themselves that know the nature of the problems and the opportunities they face better than any outsider, no matter how wise.

The Management in the 1990s Research Program was charged with the task of investigating the *impact* of the new information technologies (IT) on organizations with the goal of determining how the organizations of the 1990s—and beyond—will differ from those of today. This book can be thought of as the "Final Report" of the research program; the authors discuss the full range of issues studied, from the changing nature of the work done by individuals to the changing competitive dynamics of whole industries. While each chapter was written by different authors, working from the perspective of their own discipline and informed by the research studies, care has been given to shaping the total into a book that can be read from cover to cover. A companion volume is also available, also from Oxford University Press, containing articles by individual researchers which provide some of the detailed supporting evidence for the conclusions presented in this book.

It is important to understand that the Management in the 1990s Research Program used a very broad definition of IT, including computers of all types, both hardware and software; communications networks, from those connecting two personal computers to the largest public and private networks; and the increasingly important integrations of computing and communications technologies, from a system that allows a personal computer to be connected to a mainframe in the office to globe-spanning networks of powerful mainframe computers. A major finding of the program is the importance of understanding and utilizing this broad array of new capabilities. This book, therefore, is not about office automation (OA), computer-integrated manufacturing (CIM), or fiber optic communication networks (ISDN). It is about how these new technologies can change—and are changing—the way people work, the way society's major organizations are structured, and the way corporations will collaborate and compete in the years to come.

Information technologies, for example, are the very means whereby the financial service industry creates, markets, and distributes its products. Today's world capital markets could not exist without information technologies. The menu of products they offer would be very different. Information technologies are not a means for corporate managers to monitor what their financiers are doing but a means for financiers to produce and sell new products more effectively.

Similarly the new electronic checkout counters at the supermarket are only secondarily an inventory management information system. Their primary purpose should be to allow firms to better market their products.

Out-of-date views of what information technologies are, and perhaps the word *information* itself, may lie behind what is a major economic mystery. Thinking of these new technologies as something that should be used to produce information has led them to be used wrongly. But that is to jump ahead of the story.

Organizations have invested enormous sums of money in the hardware and software of the new electronic technologies. There are many examples of extraordinarily useful systems that now exist that could not have existed only a few years ago. Specific cases in which the new technologies have permitted huge increases in output or decreases in costs can be cited, but when it comes to the bottom line there is no clear evidence that these new technologies have raised productivity (the ultimate determinant of our standard of living) or profitability.

In fact, precisely the opposite is true. There is evidence, in the United States at least, that the investment in the new technologies has coincided with lowered overall productivity and profitability. America's productivity growth rate is far below that of other countries whose investments in the new information technologies have been much less, and those industries that have invested the most have some of the worst productivity improvement performances in the United States—often negative. Similarly, profitability rates have been falling in U.S. industry in the last decade despite the new investments in information technologies.

If one looks at the conventional explanations for the lack of payoff, they all point to the need for learning how to change organizations faster than humans naturally want to change. Analysis indicates that technological change is simply moving much faster than humans are changing, and as a consequence the benefits of technological change are not what they should be.

Some say that the problem is a generational one. Today's senior executives just aren't comfortable with the new technologies. They feel threatened and therefore do not use them to their full potential. According to this argument, Western countries will just have to wait for a new generation of senior executives who feel comfortable with and not threatened by the new technologies before the potential productivity of the new information technology investments can be harvested. The first part of this argument may or may not be true, but, if it is true, the right answer is not the passage of time or a sharp reduction in new investments in the new technologies until the next generation of executives comes along. The right answer is a strategy that removes the threatening nature of the new technologies and enables executives to employ them as they should be employed.

Others have argued that the problem is exemplified by the American belief in "management by numbers." To reap the promised payoff of the new technologies requires knowledge of what should *not* be known just as much as they require a knowledge of what *should* be known. For example, I am often shown the computer on an executive's desk and proudly told that the chief executive could use that computer to get the inventories in his Singapore facility if he wished or recover some other kind of remote and detailed information. I am always tempted to ask four questions. First, when did you last ask for the inventories at your Singapore facility? Second, if you have to ask, don't you have the wrong person managing your Singapore facility? Third, if you did ask, is there any way that you can use the answer to make your company run better? And fourth, how much does it cost to have the capability of moving inventory information from Singapore to headquarters? The effective solution is, of course, not a worldwide inventory control information system but a just-in-time inventory system in which only the workers in the Singapore factory have the detailed inventory information. They make the right decisions, and no expenses have to be incurred moving inventory information around the company to inventory control experts.

The problem is knowing when to change to using new capabilities and knowing when new capabilities should not be employed even though they exist. The problems are management problems and not hardware or software problems.

Automate the office is a popular phrase, but to automate the office is to misuse the new information technologies. The office in some very real sense needs to be reinvented and redesigned given what are radically new capabilities and needs. As MIT's Management in the 1990s Research Program has shown, just to automate what is today being done is to grossly misuse the potential of the new technologies. But nothing is more sensitive than changing today's office with all of its inherited sociological relationships. Those skilled in organizational change know that satisfactory substitutes for today's relationships have to be designed into the new systems if those working in our offices are not to sabotage the potential of the new technologies. Judging by hardware and software investments, the American office has been automated, but the productivity of white-collar office workers has fallen. Office workers are being added to organizations at a much faster rate than output is growing and are a major source of lower productivity growth and lower profitability.

The Management in the 1990s Research Program has shown that it may take different forms of organization to fully exploit the new information technologies. At the level of the individual firm, the problem will be to overcome the resistance to change, both by individuals who feel threatened by such changes and by those who doubt the potential returns available from the large investments necessary in the new technologies. At the national level, countries may become laggards if, for example, they fail to provide an IT infrastructure adequate to enable their firms to take advantage of the new ways of doing business, ways that shrink the effects of time and distance.

This book explores these issues and seeks to define the shape of the corporation of the 1990s. In this collaborative effort, the Management in the 1990s Research Program reflected an essential mission of the MIT Sloan School of Management. That mission is to understand the technological world in which we live and to have an impact on the way managers and their organizations will cope with accelerating technological change.

Lester C. Thurow

Contents

Acknowledgments

This book is the result of the collective effort of a large number of people, too many to mention by name. It is important, however, to acknowledge their contributions.

First, I wish to thank the sponsor senior executives for their willingness to enter into a novel, long-term working relationship with a group of academic researchers and a diverse set of other companies. The Management in the 1990s Program was the largest collaborative research activity undertaken by the MIT Sloan School of Management as of that time. The close working relationship we envisaged was untested in practice. The sponsors' willingness to commit their financial and people resources to the effort was critical.

Next, I wish to recognize the contribution of the sponsors' managers who served as their organization's working representative to the Program. These managers became true working partners with the faculty and Program staff, participating in the selection of research projects, helping locate field sites for research, and contributing their personal expertise in workshops. In two cases sponsor representatives went well beyond what was originally expected. James A. Hernon, the original sponsor representative from Eastman Kodak, served as sponsor coordinator during the entire course of the Program. K. Hugh Macdonald of ICL became so deeply involved in Program content that he authored one chapter of this book.

I owe a special debt to my colleague Alvin Silk, then Deputy Dean of the Sloan School of Management, for his active support in getting the Program launched and to the more than forty Sloan School faculty members who became involved, in various ways, with the 1990s Program. Their willingness to participate in a large scale experiment, in a multidisciplinary framework, is sincerely appreciated. My faculty colleague Thomas Allen, who served as Research Director for the Program, deserves my special thanks for helping keep the research appropriately rigorous.

Finally, I wish to acknowledge the contribution of the Program's staff, initially under the direction of Diane Wilson, and then for the majority of the time under the direction of Roger Samuel. Roger's willingness and ability to assist me in nearly every aspect of the Program has contributed in a major way to the success of the Program; his help has definitely made my task much more manageable—often even fun. Without a smoothly functioning Program office the working relationship between MIT and the sponsors would not have developed. Of particular importance were the development of the joint governance process, the organizing of workshops and conferences, the production and distribution of working papers, and of course the production of the manuscript for this book. Special thanks are due Patricia White, Program Administrator, and Pamela Spencer, Administrative Assistant, for keeping on top of the myriad of details involved in an undertaking of this magnitude. Their always cheerful response to a never-ending stream of requests has earned my heartfelt gratitude.

Cambridge, MA   *M.S.S.M.*
June 1990

Contributors

ROBERT I. BENJAMIN is a visiting scientist at the Massachusetts Institute of Technology Sloan School of Management. He is engaged in the research activities of the school's Center for Information Systems Research and in the Management in the 1990s Research Program.

K. HUGH MACDONALD has been with ICL, the major British computer systems company, for more than thirty years and has worked with computers, computer systems, and applications since 1957. He served as the ICL sponsor representative for the whole of the MIT90s Research Program.

ROBERT B. MCKERSIE is currently codirector of the Industrial Relations Section as well as chair of the faculty committee for the Sloan Fellows Program at the Massachusetts Institute of Technology Sloan School of Management. His research interests have been in labor-management relations with particular focus on bargaining activity. He continues to do research on strategies being pursued in different industries to bring about more effective organizational arrangements.

STUART E. MADNICK is the John Norris Maguire Professor of Information Technology and Leaders for Manufacturing Professor of Management Science at the Massachusetts Institute of Technology Sloan School of Management. His current research interests include connectivity among disparate distributed information systems, database technology, and software project management.

PAUL OSTERMAN is associate professor of human resources and management in the Sloan School of Management, Massachusetts Institute of Technology. His particular specialty is labor economics and human resource management.

JOHN F. ROCKART is the director of the Center for Information Systems Research and a senior lecturer of Management Science at the Sloan School of Management, Massachusetts Institute of Technology. His most recent research interests are the "critical success factors" concept, the use of information by top management, the management of data resources, line management, systems delivery, and the management of interdependence.

JULIO J. ROTEMBERG is currently professor of applied economics in the Sloan School of Management at the Massachusetts Institute of Technology. He is an associate editor of *Econometrica* and the *Quarterly Journal of Economics*. His broad research interests include macroeconomics, industrial organization, and issues pertaining to the internal organization of firms. His particular interest is in the effect of the structure of the markets in which firms operate on both macroeconomic and organizational levels.

GARTH SALONER was professor of management and economics at the Massachusetts Institute of Technology during the course of the Management in the 1990s Program. He is currently professor at the Stanford Graduate School of Business. His research focuses on issues in competitive strategy and industry analysis. He has authored or co-authored more than 20 books and publications.

MICHAEL S. SCOTT MORTON is the Jay W. Forrester Professor of Management at the Sloan School of Management, Massachusetts Institute of Technology, and is chairman of the faculty for the Senior Executive Program. He served as program director of the schoolwide Management in the 1990s Research Program.

JAMES E. SHORT is research associate, Center for Information Systems Research, Massachusetts Institute of Technology, Sloan School of Management. He studies the impact of information technology on organizational structure, process, and managerial behavior. He is interested in how technology has enabled organizations to execute differential strategies through enhanced integration and flexible, problem-focused teams and task forces.

LESTER C. THUROW is dean of the Massachusetts Institute of Technology's Sloan School of Management. A prolific writer, Thurow is the author, coauthor, or editor of several books. He has served on the editorial board of the *New York Times* and was a contributing editor for *Newsweek* and a member of the *Time* Board of Economists. He currently writes articles for the *Boston Globe*.

N. VENKATRAMAN is Richard S. Leghorn Career Development Associate Professor of Management at the Sloan School of Management, Massachusetts Institute of Technology. His current research focuses on the emerging impact of information technology on sources of firm-level competitive advantage and on the organizational interlinkages between strategic planning and information systems and technology planning.

RICHARD E. WALTON is Jesse Isador Strauss Professor of Business Administration at the Harvard Graduate School of Business Administration. He consults with industrial firms and labor unions and is a member of the board of directors of Champion International Corporation.

JOANNE YATES is senior lecturer and coordinator of management communication in the Sloan School of Management at the Massachusetts Institute of Technology. Her primary area of research is the historical evolution of communication and information systems within firms in the late nineteenth and early twentieth centuries.

The Corporation
of the 1990s

CHAPTER 1

Introduction

MICHAEL S. SCOTT MORTON

The Management in the 1990s Research Program was created in 1984 to examine the profound impact that information technology (IT) is having on organizations of all kinds. Its mission was to explore how IT will affect the way organizations will be able to survive and prosper in the competitive environment of the 1990s and beyond. This book is the "final report" of the program. The program began with two basic premises:

1. The business environment is and will remain turbulent.
2. IT will continue its rapid evolution over at least the next decade.

A closer look at these premises and at the way the program was organized will help in understanding what follows in this book.

TURBULENT BUSINESS ENVIRONMENT

Turbulence in the business environment puts pressure on organizations to be sure they can effectively meet the fundamental changes that are occurring. The program identified four kinds of changes with which organizations must contend.

Social

The heightened expectations of people in Western Europe and North America are giving rise to pressures to improve the quality of working life and the quality of the environment. This is resulting in a changing concept of what constitutes *value*. This is particularly true of the prices people are willing to pay for products and services and the amount of damage to the environment that they will tolerate.

Political

The changing regulatory and governmental roles of the Western governments have resulted in a new competitive climate and a new set of rules for competition. This is also happening in other parts of the world (Gorbachev's *glasnost* is an example) and is typified by the coming together of the European Economic Community as an active force, with the symbolic 1992 "deadline."

Technical

There is obviously technical change in the IT area, a subject raised later in this book, but there are significant changes in other areas such as materials, with advances in superconductivity, ceramics, and advanced composites, to name just three. There are also major changes in the biosciences and bioengineering, where major technical breakthroughs are likely to continue to evolve rapidly.

Economic

The twin deficits in the United States, in the budget and in trade, will continue to cause economic turbulence for some years. The fact of considerable global trade, particularly among the "Triad" (EEC, North America, and Japan), will merely exacerbate the uncertainty surrounding firms. This trade results in shifting benchmarks for acceptable product quality, and it places new demands on corporations and nations.

THE RAPID EVOLUTION OF INFORMATION TECHNOLOGY

The second premise behind the management in the 1990s Research Program is that information technology now consists of a powerful collection of elements that are undergoing change and have wide and significant applicability. These elements go well beyond what has been available during the last thirty years, in what might be termed the data processing era. In the 1990s we expect organizations to experience the effects of the integration and evolution of a set of elements collectively termed *information technology*. The research program considers these elements to consist of the following:

1. *Hardware.* This ranges from large-scale mainframe computers to small-scale microcomputers.
2. *Software.* This ranges from traditional languages such as COBOL and their fourth-generation equivalents to expert systems that have emerged from developments in artificial intelligence.
3. *Networks.* These telecommunications networks range from public to private, broadband to narrowband.
4. *Workstations.* These range from those designed for engineers, with large computational capabilities and the ability to display dynamic, three-dimensional color graphics, to professional workstations used by bank lending officers or a market analyst in a consumer goods company. The latter rely on models, heuristics, and simple graphics and often have very large databases included in the system.

5. *Robotics.* These range from robots with "vision" and "hands" used on the factory floor to a variety of devices familiar to the average person on the street, such as automatic teller machines.
6. *Smart chips.* "Intelligent" chips are used in products to enhance functionality or reliability. For example, they are used in automobile braking systems to prevent skidding and in elevators to improve response time and to detect impending failures. In simpler forms they now appear in products such as the "active card" used to track via satellite the movement of shipping containers.

The continuing evolution and integration of these six elements of IT have now reached a threshold of cost and ease of use that is having widespread organizational impact.

CHANGE

Both premises—business turbulence and technological change—imply potential organizational change. The external forces associated with environmental turbulence must be reacted to for survival. IT offers the opportunity for organizations to react constructively. Because of the combined effect, there is no reason why organizations will necessarily continue in their present form.

These challenges suggest that it will not be possible to survive as a company just by working harder within existing organizational structures and using conventional practices and tools. Given what IT now allows an alert organization to do, an organization that merely works faster and harder will become uncompetitive in the global marketplace of the 1990s and beyond.

THE MANAGEMENT IN THE 1990s RESEARCH PROGRAM

A group of faculty at the MIT Sloan School of Management came together in 1984 to address the consequences of this turbulent and changing environment. These faculty members approached a number of organizations with the request to fund a multiyear cooperative research program. The researchers wanted a reality-based business perspective on framing the problems to study and on the interpretation and responses to the research findings. Thus, the sponsors were asked to contribute more than money; they were asked to support the program with time and effort.

The initial ten sponsors that agreed to participate were American Express Company; Arthur Young and Company; British Petroleum; BellSouth Corporation; Digital Equipment Corporation; Eastman Kodak Company; General Motors Corporation; International Computers Ltd.; MCI Communications Corporation; and the U.S. Internal Revenue Service. This group of faculty and sponsors became the Management in the 1990s Research Program. During the course of the study, the original ten sponsors were joined by two additional supporting organizations: CIGNA Corporation and the U.S. Army.

Program Objectives

The faculty and sponsors agreed that the effort would have two principal objectives:

1. To help managers throughout the world understand the kinds of impact IT will have on business missions, organizational structures, and operating practices.
2. To provide contributions to the theories of management that grow from our understanding of the impacts of IT, and to develop new curricula for the MIT Sloan School of Management.

The partners also agreed that research findings would be shared initially with the sponsors and later published and shared with others. In addition, the Sloan School had the goal of learning how to do cooperative research in ways that would benefit both sponsors and MIT. This goal has become vital since research funding for management schools has not kept up with the flood of important new issues that require investigation.

The cooperative character of the program extended to the governance structure, the critical element of which was the Joint Steering Committee (JSC). This committee, comprised of equal numbers of MIT faculty and sponsor representatives, provided a forum for major decisions affecting the research.

The Research

The program was conceived in very broad terms; the central question is, by its nature, broad. There is no one discipline or research methodology that could yield "truth" on a problem of such complexity. Therefore, the program was designed to bring together researchers from many disciplines to focus on a common issue. Interestingly, this mirrors what has been found necessary in many corporate settings, namely, that the IT function has become so important that it must be managed by a line executive. Multiple faculty and research methods were used to shed light on the basic questions. More than thirty research projects were undertaken by twenty-five faculty members. Appendix A presents a list of all research projects. The range of research methodologies was extensive and demonstrates the breadth of inquiry:

Prototypes. Professor Thomas Malone built a prototype that incorporated an expert filter in an electronic mail system. This combination of artifical intelligence concepts coupled with the use of electronic communication in a real organization yielded a rich prototype that has evolved and is now being tested in several organizations.

Experiments. Professor N. Venkatraman designed a number of controlled experiments. In one of these, one set of insurance agents had professional workstations with new functionality while a second set of similar agents proceeded to do their work in the traditional way. This design allowed for very robust findings.

Instruments. Professor Thomas Allen developed a questionnaire instrument to measure communication patterns among members of an organization. Measuring precise communication paths before and after the introductions of new IT-based communication tools made it possible to analyze the impact of IT in specific situations.

Surveys. Professor Edgar Schein is one of several faculty members who conducted surveys of practicing managers. With the support of Dr. Diane Wilson, he was able to identify attitudes, values, and approaches to the use of IT by CEOs.

Theory. Professors Garth Saloner and Thomas Malone developed, or extended, economic and organizational theory to shed light on the program's central research question.

Empirical data collection. Professors John Carroll, Lotte Bailyn, John Henderson, and Jack Rockart, among others, spent time in organizations collecting empirical data to begin to identify some of the issues and approaches that are emerging as organizations attempt to effectively employ IT.

Theory testing. Professor Eric von Hippel's project was designed to test whether theories that have been developed to explain the diffusion of innovation hold true in light of the new IT-based capabilities.

This list of research types and representative projects illustrates the wide variety of research questions addressed and the breadth of discipline-based effort required. The results of such research contributed in a major way to the foundation of knowledge upon which this book is based. Each of these approaches has shed some light on the central question and suggests that the challenge of exploiting the power of IT is not the provenance of any one point of view, function, or person. Among both the faculty and the sponsors a broader view of the important dimensions of the 1990s research evolved as the various individual projects were completed.

Results were discussed in seminars and workshops and published as working papers (See Appendix B). Other formal products of the research program, in addition to this book, are a book focusing on the organizational implications of the overall findings, a book containing a collection of articles presenting findings by individual researchers, and a series of conferences.

STRUCTURE OF THIS BOOK

This book draws on all the program research. Its structure emerged from a series of working conferences involving sponsors and the faculty starting in 1987. These conferences used the research work, seminars, and discussions that had gone on for the first three years of the program and created an outline of a book that was responsive to the original objectives. This was refined in subsequent meetings with the faculty members who agreed to write the various chapters. The sponsors formed small groups by chapter to help the faculty by responding to early drafts. The organization and content of this book is a result of their combined efforts.

"The Information Technology Platform" by Stuart Madnick makes explicit assumptions about the technological capabilities that will be widely available to most organizations by the mid-1990s.

"The Past and Present as a Window on the Future" by Robert I. Benjamin and JoAnne Yates first establishes that history has lessons to teach us; in particular, the introductions of the telegraph and telephone provide powerful analogies to current IT implementations. Benjamin and Yates demonstrate that as the level of integration of IT increases, so does the impact of the technology on the organization.

Part II of the book—"Interfirm Competition and Collaboration" by Julio J. Rotemberg and Garth Saloner, "IT-Induced Business Reconfiguration," by N. Venkatraman, and "Business Strategy Development, Alignment, and Redesign" by K. Hugh Macdonald—describes how the widespread adoption of IT leads to the reshaping of firm boundaries and the characteristics of whole industries, which in turn gives rise to new patterns of competition between organizations. Similarly, for a particular organization the opportunities for competition and collaboration (for example, joint ventures, strategic alliances) are changing. This chapter develops frameworks for examining an organization's strategic choices in light of these expanded opportunities. "The Networked Organization and the Management of Interdependence" by John F. Rockart and James E. Short examines the major impact of IT on the organization's internal operations and management systems, on the nature of the management practices and processes that can be used to deal successfully with the turbulent business environment.

Paul Osterman contributed "The Impact of IT on Jobs and Skills." As IT changes work, it affects the kinds of skills required by an employee and the location where work can be done. This, in turn, affects training and education as well as management skills.

"Organizational Change" by Robert B. McKersie and Richard E. Walton is the final chapter of the book. The uses of IT described in previous chapters require significant changes in organizations' processes and the roles played by individual employees. These changes present major challenges. This chapter discusses what has been learned about the successful implementation of IT and ways to manage the associated organizational change.

IT IN PERSPECTIVE

Information technology has important general-purpose power to manipulate symbols used in all classes of work, and therefore, as an "information engine," it can do for business what the steam engine did in the days of the Industrial Revolution. It goes beyond this, however, as a technology that permits one to manipulate models of reality, to step back one pace from the physical reality. Such an ability lies at the heart of IT's capacity to alter work fundamentally.

The telegraph and telephone were the forebears of IT and were central to the rise of the modern industrial corporation. The application of those technologies resulted in the mass-production, vertically integrated hierarchial organization. But there is nothing sacred about such an organizational form. At a particular moment in time, around the turn of the century, the conditions in the marketplace of the newly industrializing Western world were conducive to the emergence of this form. The pressures of global competition and the enabling coordinative capabilites of IT

Table 1-1. Computing Cost-Performance Trends

	1980	1990	2000
Constant Functionality*	4.5 MIPS	4.5 MIPS	4.5 MIPS
Cost			
Original projection (1981)	$4.5 million	$300,000	
Modified projection (1988)		$100,000	$10,000
Number of people of equivalent cost			
Original projection (1981)	210	6	
Modified projection (1988)		2	0.125

*Metaphor for constant functionality is millions of instructions per second (MIPS)

have led to experimentation, and an evolution away from the traditional hierarchical organization can be expected.

Information is the lifeblood of any organization. Little can be done successfully without it. Hence, the cost of handling and processing information is important. In the data processing era this was also true, but it was less critical to organizational success, as data processing principally dealt with back-office clerical functions and the technology was still expensive. Technology costs have dropped, and one can go beyond numerical data for algorithmic processing and move to qualitative information and heuristic manipulation. This, in turn, can be combined with the ability to work with pictures and drawings, and then one can connect all this to virtually any location in the world. Such power is new in kind; it represents a step-function change from what was available before.

The economics of IT have changed both absolutely and relatively. At an absolute level, we are expecting to see IT cost-performance ratios continue to change in the range of 20 to 30 percent a year. Such change can lead to very considerable differences over relatively short intervals of time. Table 1-1, based on results of an earlier MIT study, illustrates the profound consequences of such a compounding change. In 1980 the cost of a computer with a processing power of 4.5 MIPS was $4.5 million, the cost equivalent of 210 employees of a certain skill level. The cost of a machine of this power was projected to decline to $300,000 in 1990, the cost equivalent of 6 workers of the same skill level. The actual 1990 cost will be closer to $100,000. The cost of such a machine in the year 2000 is likely to be no more than $10,000, the cost equivalent of only a fraction of a worker. Thus, organizations are faced with radically different trade-offs over time among processing power, human effort, and dollars with which to best meet the organization's objectives.

The relative costs are also changing. The cost of IT relative to the cost of other forms of capital equipment is widening. Thus, it is *relatively* cheaper today to invest in IT capital than in any other form of capital. This relationship, based on thirty years of data, is shown in Figure 1-1.

IT Is Different

Information technology exerts such a strong influence because it can affect both production and coordination. Production refers to the task of producing any good or

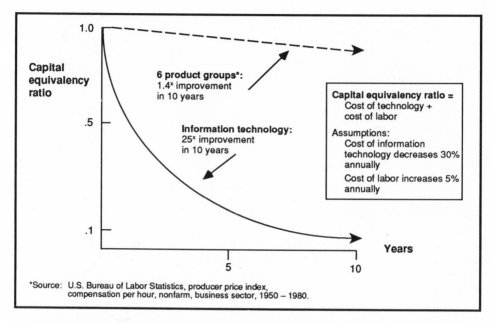

Figure 1-1. Capital equivalency ratio: Information technology vs. six product groups.

service that the organization is in business to sell. It is not limited to physical production but includes the intellectual production of things such as loans or other "soft" products. The production jobs that are most affected by IT are those in which information and/or knowledge makes a difference. We call such production workers "information workers" or "knowledge workers." The fraction of the work force that falls into this category has grown to be very large. In manufacturing industries it averages around 40 percent, and in service industries more than 80 percent. The information worker processes information without significant modification, a task that is typically classified as clerical, such as order entry. The knowledge worker category covers those who add value to the original information. This would include engineers and designers required to design new products, those who trade in the securities markets, those in financial institutions who lend money to companies or individuals, and all those who produce budgets, market research analyses, legal briefs, and so on. The use of IT to change the nature of both such categories of production work is widely recognized.

Just as important is the use of IT to change the ways in which coordination activites are carried out. Coordination tasks make up a large part of what organizations do. With IT the effects of both distance and time can shrink to near zero. For example, it is possible today to make financial trades in global markets anywhere in the world from any city. A similar activity is placing orders to a supplier's plant or accepting orders directly from a customer's site to one's own organization. The airline reservation systems are among the most visible and oldest examples of such coordination.

Organizational memory is another feature of coordination affected by IT. Corporate databases now provide an enormous reservoir of information that can be used for constructive management of the organization. Personnel records indicating who has had what job, at what salary, and with what training form the basis for understanding the skill mix in a company and help identify possible candidates for certain jobs. Thus, IT can be thought of as affecting coordination by increasing the organization's memory, thereby establishing a record that allows for the detection of patterns. Although this has been true for some time, the added power of heuristics and artificial intelligence provides important additional tools for using information.

In summary, the traditional organizational structures and practices do not have to stay the same as we move into the 1990s. All dimensions of the organization will have to be reexamined in light of the power of the new IT. The economics are so powerful and apply to so much of the organization that one has to question everything before accepting the status quo.

MAJOR FINDINGS OF THE RESEARCH

We see six major implications from the research. The first and most basic is that the nature of work is changing.

Finding 1. IT Is Enabling Fundamental Changes in the Way Work Is Done

The degree to which a person can be affected by the rapid evolution of information technology is determined by how much of the work is based on information—that is, information on what product to make or what service to deliver and how to do it (the production task), as well as when to do it and in conjunction with whom (the coordination task). In many organizations the people in these two categories account for a large proportion of the work force.

IT is available to radically alter the basic cost structure of a wide variety of jobs, jobs affecting at least half the members of the organization. IT is only an enabler, however; to actually change jobs takes a combination of management leadership and employee participation that is, thus far, extremely rare.

We saw change in three kinds of work being enabled by IT in ways that portend the kind of patterns we expect throughout the 1990s.

Production Work
The potential impact of IT on production work is considerable. This is most apparent when the nature of production work is broken up into three constituent elements:

1. Physical production affected by robotics (increasingly with "vision"), process control instrumentation, and intelligent sensors.
2. Information production affected by data processing computers for the standard clerical tasks such as accounts receivable, billing, and payables.
3. Knowledge production affected by CAD/CAM tools for designers; workstations for those building qualitative products such as loans or letters of credit; and work-

stations for those building "soft" products such as new legislation or new software (with CASE tools).

These forms of change are readily understood in the case of physical products and standard information processing but do not seem to be as easily grasped and exploited when it comes to knowledge work. As a result, organizations appear to be very slow in exploiting and utilizing technology to increase the effectiveness of knowledge production.

Coordinative Work

IT, as it has been defined in this research program, includes six elements, one of which is communications networks. These are currently being installed at a rapid rate by nations and organizations, and we expect this to continue throughout the 1990s. Such networks are being utilized within a building, within an organization, between organizations, and between countries. However, their use has been less than it might be, there is a lack of standards that permit easy connectivity. This situation has begun to improve, and we can expect this improvement to accelerate through the 1990s as the enormous economic benefits to industries and societies become more obvious.

The new IT is permitting a change in the economics and functionality of the coordination process. As a result we can see changes in three areas:

1. Distance can be shrunk toward zero, becoming increasingly irrelevant as far as information flow is concerned. Thus, the location of work can be reexamined, as can potential partners. Even in 1989 leading companies had design teams in different countries working together on a single product.
2. Time can shrink toward zero or shift to a more convenient point. Airline reservation systems are a leading example of IT in a time-critical setting. Organizations located in different time zones yet required to work together are utilizing store-and-forward and common databases as a way to shift time.
3. Organizational memory, as exemplified by a common database, can be maintained over time, contributed to from all parts of the organization, and made available to a wide variety of authorized users.

Beyond memory is the organization's ability to share skills. In a sense, such "group work," or the utilization of teams, combines the three aspects of coordination: distance, time, and memory. This combined effect has more impact than the three elements by themselves.

This change in the economics and functionality of coordination fundamentally alters all the tasks in an organization that have to do with coordinating the delivery of products and services to customers and the actual production of such goods and services. To the extent that an organization's structure is determined by its coordinative needs, it too is subject to potential change.

Managment Work

The third IT-enabled change in work is the work done by managers. The principal dimensions of management work that can be most affected are those of direction and control. *Direction,* as used here, is concerned with sensing changes in the external environment and also with staying in close touch with the organization its members' ideas and reactions to their views of the environment. Relevant, timely information from these two sources can be crucial input to the organization's direction-setting process. This is as true for a sophisticated strategic planning system as for an informal executive support system or customer feedback system.

The *control* dimension of management work has two key aspects for our purposes here. The first is the measurement task, that is, measuring the organization's performance along whatever set of critical success factors has been defined as relevant. The second aspect is to interpret such measures against the plan and determine what actions to take. Effective control is a critical dimension of organizational learning as it feeds back to future direction setting, and both of these can be fundamentally changed by the increasing availability of IT.

Finding 2. IT Is Enabling the Integration of Business Functions at All Levels within and between Organizations

The continuing expansion of public and private telecom networks means that the concept of "any information, at any time, anywhere, and any way I want to look at it" is increasingly economically feasible. The infrastructure to permit this is being put in place by different companies at different rates. Those organizations that have created a significant enterprise-level infrastructure will be able to compete effectively in the 1990s. Additionally, the ability to electronically connect people and tasks within and between firms will be increasingly available and affordable. Boundaries of organizations are becoming more permeable; where work gets done, when, and with whom is changing. This can be a difficult, often revolutionary, move whose impact is blunted by people's unwillingness to exploit the new opportunities. However, in a few situations components are being designed with suppliers in weeks, not months; parts are ordered from suppliers in hours, not weeks; and questions are answered in seconds, not days. This enormous speed-up in the flow of work is made possible by the electronic network. The integration it permits is showing up in four forms:

> *Within the value chain.* Xerox, among many others, connected design, engineering, and manufacturing personnel within its system of local area networks (LANs) and created a team focusing on one product. Such teams have accomplished tasks in shorter time with greater creativity and higher morale than with their previous tools and organizational structures. There is no part of an organization that, in principle, is excluded from the team concept.
>
> *End-to-end links of value chains between organizations.* A supplier's shipping department can be electronically connected to the buyer's purchasing department, and the sales force directly connected to its customers. This form of electronic integration is a powerful way of speeding up the flow of goods between organizations. It has been popularized in the press using various terminologies such as *electronic just-in-time* (JIT) or *electronic data interchange* (EDI). This can be thought of as the boundary of the organization being permeable to IT. It can also be thought of as shifting the boundary of the organization out to include elements of other organizations, thus creating a "virtual" organization.

Value chain substitution via subcontract or alliance. This occurs when an organization takes one stage in its value chain and subcontracts either a specific task
or the whole stage to another organization. A common example is when a firm
asks a supplier to design a component for it. Modern CAD/CAM environments
permit a supplier's designers to be electronically linked to the host team to allow
the data exchange needed to accomplish a joint design. Ford Motor Company's
agreement with Ryder Truck to handle Ford's new car shipments is an example
of a subcontracted task that would not work effectively without electronic integration. These collaborations are enabled by IT and would not be feasible without it. They lead to the host organization being able to take advantage of the
economies of scale and unique skills of its partner. To be of lasting value, of
course, there must be reciprocal benefits.

Electronic markets. This is the most highly developed form of electronic integration. Here, coordination within the organization or among a few organizations gives way to an open market. Travel agents, for example, are able to electronically reserve seats from all the major carriers and can look around for the
best price at which to complete the transaction. Electronic markets will be
increasingly prevalent in the 1990s as IT costs continue to drop and thereby
reduce transaction costs to the point where the "market" becomes economically
effective.

These four forms of electronic integration have, to varying degrees, the net effect
of removing buffers and leveraging expertise. Shrinking time and distance can have
the effect of allowing the right resources to be at the right place at the right time. In
effect, this removes the need to have people and other assets (such as inventory or
cash) tied up as unproductive buffers.

It should be noted that it appears an organization must have the necessary infrastructure of communications, data, applications software, and educated and empow-
ered users before any of these four forms of integration can be fully exploited.

We have found that each of these four forms of integration is visible in embry-
onic form in some organization. However, the real economic impact and rate of dis-
semination of the integration vary enormously, and in no case has there been a
clearly sustainable transformation. Some of the major reasons for this are discussed
below.

Finding 3. IT Is Causing Shifts in the
Competitive Climate in Many Industries

At the level of the industry, information technology has a unique impact on the competitive climate and on the degree of interrelatedness of products or services with
rivals. This can lead to unprecedented degrees of simultaneous competition and collaboration between firms. This effect of IT is spreading rapidly. For example, parts
suppliers that are linked electronically with purchasers for design and manufacturing
are not uncommon.

Another illustration is the creation of an electronic linkage between the U.S.
Internal Revenue Service (IRS) and tax preparation firms. The linkage was created
to enable the electronic filing of individual income tax returns prepared by those

firms. This has opened up opportunities for lending or borrowing what is, in aggregate, some $70 billion. This is causing the creation of new arrangements between multiple financial services firms (see Chapter 5).

The second unique impact of IT on competitiveness concerns the importance of standards. It is now important to know when to support standards and when to try to preempt competitors by establishing a proprietary de facto standard. Every industry has an example. For illustration here, we cite the attempt by the major insurance companies to tie agents to their systems. The general agents retaliated by using the industry association to grow their own network with its open standards to protect themselves.

Understanding the changed nature of one's competitive climate is important in an era of growing IT pervasiveness. A framework to help provide perspective is described in Chapter 4.

This framework adds a new dimension to the classic economic analysis of competition, a dimension we have termed *interrelatedness*. Such an expanded analysis has shown conclusively that as traditional economic forces (such as competitor actions) change, or as the economics and functionality of IT change, the position of an organization relative to competitive organizations will change. In both cases there is no technical or economic reason (such as ownership of patents) that can allow one organization to capture excess "economic rents" from the use of IT for any sustained period of time. Competitive and technological forces simply do not permit any single organization to enjoy a sustainable competitive advantage merely from its use of information technology.

It is possible, however, for an organization in the decade of the 1990s to capture benefits. This appears to come from being an early (or different) mover with a business benefit enabled by IT and then investing actively in innovations that continue to increase the benefits to the user of the innovation. In other words, the benefits do not flow from the mere use of IT but arise from the human, organizational, and system innovations that are added on to the original business benefit. IT is merely an enabler that offers an organization the opportunity to vigorously invest in added innovations if it wishes to stay ahead of its competitors.

The empirical fact that existing organizations constantly move—or are moved—to different points in the competitive matrix and that new organizations appear on the competitive horizon adds considerable importance to the functions of scanning and environmental monitoring. Effective scanning of the business environment to understand what is changing is critical if an organization is to proactively manage its way through an environment made additionally turbulent with changes in technology.

Finding 4. IT Presents New Strategic Opportunities for Organizations That Reassess Their Missions and Operations

A turbulent environment, the changing nature of work, the possiblities of electronic integration, and the changing competitve climate are all compelling reasons for the third stage in the evolution of the organization of the 1990s. In short, *automate* and *informate* set the stage for transformation.

Research during the 1990s program suggests that the three findings just discussed—new ways of doing work, electronic integration, and the shifting competitive climate—present an organization with an opportunity, if not a pressing need, to step back and rethink its mission and the way it is going to conduct its operations.

There appear to be three distinct stages that organizations are going through as they attempt to respond to their changing environments: automate, informate, and transformation.

Automate

IT applications in this stage are designed to take the cost out of "production." Savings are usually achieved by reducing the number of workers. For information handlers such as order entry clerks, this can result in effectively being eliminated from the work force. For other production workers, manual operations are replaced by machine actions under computer control. For example, an operator no longer has to change valve settings by hand but instead watches a computer screen and types instructions.

This requires fewer operators with consequent direct cost savings. Beyond process control and automation of traditional paper processing (for example, bank check clearing), IT is being used for automation with the scanner and bar code, the universal product code (UPC). This is now used not only for packaged goods but also for inventory in warehouses and a host of other tracking applications. These kinds of IT tools can give rise to enormous cost reductions.

The new IT tools, used by the "production" workers who are left after automation, often generate information as a by-product. This is clearly seen in the case of process control where the operators have information from multiple sensors and watch screens and type in instructions. In the automate stage, however, little or no use is made of this new information beyond direct control of the existing process.

Informate

Informate is a term (first coined by Shoshana Zuboff) that describes what happens when automated processes yield information as a by-product.

The informate stage as we saw it in the 1990s program has three distinguishing characteristics. The first is that production work involves new tools that provide information that must be used to get the job done; for example, the operator must read the screen to see if the process is within tolerance. This work can be farly "simple," as in monitoring machines, or it can involve complex new skills, such as using a 3-D dynamic color workstation for engineering design. Similarly, the foreign exchange trader working in several markets on a real-time basis has to use a set of computer-based tools that are quite different from the telephone and voice with which the job used to be done. At a more mundane level, a salesperson making a presentation to a potential customer uses financial models to demonstrate the savings on this month's "deal." All these knowledge workers are having to develop new skills to work with new information tools. These often involve new ways of thinking.

The second distinguishing characteristic of the informate state is that the new IT tools often generate new sorts of information as a by-product of the basic task. For example, the process control operator might notice that one limit is always exceeded when the weather is hot; the foreign exchange trader may notice that certain accounts are building a position in certain currencies; or the salesperson, by analyzing twelve months of sales data, notices buying patterns in some of the customers. Thus, the process of using the new IT tools develops some by-product information that in turn can require a different kind of conceptual grasp by the person concerned. Thus, "invisible" work is going on in the worker's mind. This kind of work may require changes in skills and managment practices if it is to be used successfully to improve the organization's performance. It requires an ability to see patterns and understand the overall process rather than just looking at controlling the information on the screen. In this situation the production worker becomes an "analyzer," a role involving a different level of conceptual skill from what was needed before as a "doer," or machine minder.

The third distinguishing characteristic of the informate stage is that the new skills and information are developed to the point where new market opportunities can be opened up. This may require a broader view of one's job and an identification with the whole organization rather than one's narrow piece of it. For example, American Hospital Supply (AHS) was able to sell the patterns of their customers' buying behavior, detected by the AHS sales force, back to the producer of the original product. The salespeople concerned had noticed that there were patterns with certain kinds of customers. They alerted their management to these patterns and in turn came up with the idea that this would be a valuable by-product that could be sold and thus form the basis for a new business.

Transformation

The changing nature of work does not stop with the informate stage but goes on to the transformation stage. The term *transformation* has been chosen deliberately to reflect the fundamental difference in character exhibited by organizations (or parts of organizations) that have been through the first two stages and have begun on the third.

This book contends that all successful organizations in the 1990s will have to pass through this stage, a stage characterized by leadership, vision, and a sustained process of organization empowerment so basic as to be exceptionally hard to accomplish. In a way, it can be thought of as the necessary follow-on to "total quality." The total quality programs are a uniquely American phenomenon of the late 1980s. They have served as a very useful rallying cry to energize organizations so that they could fix the woefully inadequate practices that had crept into their operations and managment procedures. The concept of transformation includes the broad view of quality but goes beyond this to address the unique opportunites presented by the environment and enabled by IT. A process to help accomplish this, the Strategic Alignment Model (SAM), emerged from the 90s research and is discussed in Section IV of this book.

Finding 5. Successful Application of IT Will Require Changes in Management and Organizational Structure

The 1990s program has shown that information technology is a critical enabler of the re-creation (redefinition) of the organization. This is true in part because it permits the distribution of power, function, and control to wherever they are most effective, given the mission and objectives of the organization and the culture it enjoys.

Organizations have always managed some form of matrix structure, a matrix involving functions, products, markets, and geography in some combination. With the new IT, unit costs of coordination are declining significantly. This means that over the next decade we can afford more coordination for the same dollar cost. In addition, IT is causing changing economies of scale. For example, flexible manufacturing permits smaller organizations to also be low-cost producers. Thus, IT is enabling a breakup, a dis-integration, of traditional organizational forms. For example, multiple skills can be brought together at an arbitrary point in time and location. In short, ad hoc teams are enabled by IT. Digital Equipment, among others, has all their engineers on the same network; thus an engineer anywhere in the world can share information, ask for help, or work on a project as needed. As these ad hoc teams become an effective way of working, they give rise to the "networking" organization. In such organizations, horizontal and vertical working patterns can be created as needed. This will not be the most appropriate organizational form for all tasks and all organizational cultures; however, it is increasingly an option. IT's ability to affect coordination by shrinking time and distance permits an organization to respond more quickly and accurately to the marketplace. This not only reduces the assets the organization has tied up but improves quality as seen by the customer.

Put another way, the 1990s research suggests that the "metabolic rate" of the organization, that is, the rate at which information moves and decisions are made, is speeding up and will get faster in the decade of the 1990s. This is partly because the external environment demands responsiveness and partly because of the way IT has enabled changes to be made in how work is done. In both cases the availability of electronic tools and electronic integration permits this responsiveness. Since global competitive forces do not permit an organization to ignore its competition, as one firm picks up the new options the others must follow. Thus, the managment of interdependence in the 1990s will take place in a dynamic environment. This requires new management systems and processes. The measurement systems, the rewards, the incentives, and the required skills all require rethinking in the new IT-impacted world. For example, the use of an electronically based JIT system obviously requires new production planning and control processes. The use of small autonomous product teams that combine design, engineering, and manufacturing raises issues of rewards, evaluation, and reassignment. The changes in work created by the use of new technology requires new skills and totally new ways of doing the job.

Management has the challenging task of changing the organizational structure and methods of operation to keep it competitive in a dynamically changing world. Research has shown that IT provides one set of tools that can enable such change. However, to think through the new systems and processes so that they can be exploited effectively is a major challenge for line management.

Finding 6. A Major Challenge for Management in the 1990s Will Be to Lead Their Organizations through the Transformation Necessary to Prosper in the Globally Competitive Environment

Before looking at the findings about organizational transformation, it is useful to provide some context. An organization can be thought of as comprised of five sets of forces in dynamic equilibrium among themselves even as the organization is subjected to influences from an external environment. This is represented in Figure 1-2. In this view, a central task of general management is to ensure that the organization, that is, all five "forces" (represented by the boxes), moves through time to accomplish the organization's objectives.

Within this context, it would appear that IT should affect the tasks in the organization and ultimately its strategy. However, the evidence at the aggregate level does not indicate any improvements in productivity or profitability. One sample data point from the United States is as follows.

Growth in number of white collar workers in 1985
Executives and managers	+5.6%
Support staff	+3.5%
Growth in U.S. output	+3.0%

Possible reasons for this lack of visible improvement are many, but they can be grouped into four broad categories. The first of these is that the benefits are there but simply are not visible. This could be true because the right data are not available or because there is a time lag between the impact of IT and the time when the benefits show up in the data. In addition, to some extent the nature of the impact may not be measurable. For example, the satisfaction derived from finding out one's bank account status without leaving home may be a very real benefit to some people, but it does not show up in the statistics on productivity that can be collected.

A second category of explanation is that the benefits from IT do in fact get created, but they are not capturable by the organization. Competition forces the improvement through to the consumer in the form of lower prices or better quality. In those cases the firm derives no direct financial benefit; investment in IT is necessary if they wish to continue in that business. This is clearest in financial services where there have been huge investments in IT, but the benefits have resulted in lower costs to the consumer, not in higher profits to the institutions. Heavy investment in IT is a cost of being in the business.

The third category of reasons stems from the fact that the external world is demanding more. For example, the consumer wants higher quality or more features, or the government has required more reporting or some other changed practice. In some cases the only practical way to comply is to use IT, but such an investment does not show up in economic returns, only in societal improvements in the quality of life or some similarly intangible dimension.

The fourth category is the most disturbing, namely, that there really is no bottom-line impact from IT investment in many firms. This may have happened for one or more of three reasons. The first is that many firms have applied IT to areas of low payoff. The literature is full of examples, such as elaborate refinements of financial accounting systems. The money invested in these cases has in fact produced no real economic payoff for the organization. A second reason is that too often IT is laid on top of existing practices. Thus, there was no real cost reduction, just cost displacement. People were removed as automation was implemented but were replaced by IT and other system costs. No one stepped back and rethought and

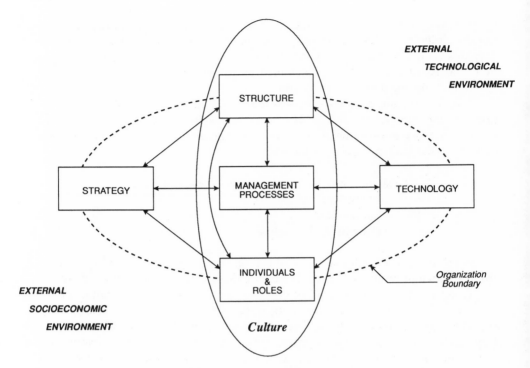

Figure 1-2. The MIT90s framework.

improved the overall process in such cases. The third reason is that the change was managed superficially and was not absorbed by the organization. In short, the organization did not make real changes in the way it worked or was organized.

The 1990s research has pinpointed some characteristics of the organizations that will be able to successfully go through the transformation process. The first, and obvious, fact is that none of the potentially beneficial enabling aspects of IT can take place without clarity of business purpose and a vision of what the organization should become. A clear mission visible to, and understood by, the organization is a well-known prerequisite for any major organization change. However, when the issue at hand is organizational transformation, enabled by technology, it appears particularly important to invest a large amount of time and effort in getting the organization to understand where it is going and why. This effort is further complicated by the lack of knowledge and skills, not to say fear, of new technology. There appear to be two other important preconditions of successful transformation. One is that the organization has been through a process of aligning its corporate strategy (business and IT), information technology, and organizational dimensions. The second precondition is that the organization have a robust information technology infrastructure in place, including an electronic network, and understood standards.

Given that there is a vision and an understood view of the business purpose, the challenge in the managment of transformation can be summed up in Figure 1-3.

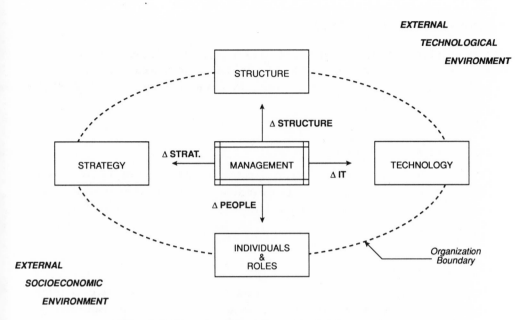

Figure 1-3. The role of management in the change process.

Research suggests that the "gray ellipse" in Figure 1-2 and the three forces included, which represent the "people issues," are critical in the transformation process. One root cause for the lack of impact of IT on the improved economic performance of organizations is an organization's unwillingness to invest heavily and early enough in human resources. Changing the way people work can be extremely threatening and therefore takes a great deal of investment. There must be investment in new skills, in psychological ownership of the change process, and in a safety net under the employee so that there is no fear of taking prudent risks. These investments are required throughout the organization as management itself is part of the required change.

The ultimate goal of this change is to give all employees a sense of empowerment. They need to feel that they can make a difference, that their efforts directly affect the organization's performance, and that they are able to take on as much responsibility and commensurate reward as they are willing to work for. Such a "Theory Y" view of an organization is a long way from our history of large hierarchically organized mass-production command and control organizations.

However, the economic realities engendered by IT and the nature of the business environment suggest that if the above factors are in effect the attributes needed by the successful organization of the 1990s, as has been suggested, moving from the present state of most large organizations to the next generation requires a transformation. Research has shown that if all the leadership and environmental conditions are adequate, then there are three stages—unfreezing, change, and refreezing (or embedding)—of successful organizational transformation. Chapter 9 of this book suggests how these steps may be undertaken.

SUMMARY CONCLUSIONS

This introduction has discussed the six major impacts of IT that have emerged from the research carried out by the 1990s program. These can be focused and regrouped to correspond to the five forces in an organization (shown in Figure 1-2) that can be influenced.

Technology

IT will continue to change over the next decade at an annual rate of at least 20 to 30 percent. This will lead to greater shrinkage of time and distance effects, greater inter-connectedness, and better organizational memory with greater capture of organization "rules" (heuristics).

Individuals and Roles

People will have new tools with which to work and increasing connectivity to information and other people. Much additional training will be needed to ensure effective use of the tools, and more education will be required to allow individuals to cope with the blurring of boundaries between job categories and tasks.

Structure

As the way work is performed changes, and as coordination costs drop enormously, new organizational structures become possible, as do new ways of working. Ad hoc teams will become more attractive as a way to get jobs done. IT will be a critical enabler of organizational restructuring.

Management Processes

Changes induced by IT will cause a redistribution of power and control. In addition, the shrinkage of distance and time effects can cause a speed-up in information flow. Thus, new methods of planning and control will be required, as organizations design ways to cope with a different kind of "management of interdependence."

Strategy

IT changes the nature and degree of interrelatedness within an industry and organization. As a result, boundaries blur and new collaborations are possible. However, IT by itself does not provide any sustainable competitive advantage. Such advantage comes from a sustained effort by line management to use IT to get closer to the customer's real needs. This constant flow of innovation and improvement requires vision and implementation skills if it is to be effective.

THE CHALLENGE OF THE 1990s

No impact from information technology is yet visible in the macroeconomic data available. A very few individual firms are demonstrably better off, and there is a larger group of isolated examples of successful exploitation in particular individual functions or business units. However, on average the expected benefits are not yet visible.

One major explanation of this lack of impact lies in the enormous strength of historical precedence. The Western economies have had more than half a century of doing business in a certain way. These ways are vey hard to discard, and it appears to be harder yet to learn new ones.

Understanding one's organizational culture, and knowing what it means to have an innovative culture, is a key first step in a move toward an adaptive organization. This in turn seems to require innovative human resource policies that support the organization's members as they learn to cope with a changing and more competitive world. To accomplish this successfully is one of the major challenges for an organization in the decade of the 1990s.

REFERENCE

Zuboff, S. 1988. *In the Age of the Smart Machine: The Future of Work and Power.* New York: Basic Books.

PART I

THE IT REVOLUTION

CHAPTER 2

The Information
Technology Platform

STUART E. MADNICK

The focus of this chapter is the shaded parts of the model shown in Figure 2-1. The information technology incorporated in the organization's platform must be in balance with the organization's structure and culture, processes, business and technology strategies, and human resources policies and practices. The organization, with its technology platform in place, must be in balance with its external environment—including the emerging external technology. In very broad terms we can say that there will be at least a factor-of-10 improvement in each of the six components of IT mentioned in Chapter 1. We can expect unusual progress in three areas, each of which is central to the ability of technology to change the way work in organizations is done. The first of these is an extensive communications ability. There will be continued expansion of public and private networks, but beyond this is the interconnect ability that will come from the continued adoption of standards and the spread of such things as integrated services digital networks (ISDN). Added to this is the continued development of our ability to combine voice, images, data, and computation. One small example of such new capabilities is represented by high-definition television (HDTV) and the opportunities that will follow in its wake.

The second area of unusual progress is represented by the availability of databases. The fact that relevant information can be identified and retrieved, manipulated, and made available to other appropriate individuals will be of enormous importance. The emerging technologies permit much lower costs, faster response time, and a more natural working style. The result will be that all organization members can be comfortable with the process of gaining access to relevant information.

The third area of unusual progress is that of enhanced workstations. Not only will these have software that powerfully leverages the particular production or coordination task, but they will also have a human interface that permits ready, "natural" use. An indication of things to come can be gained by watching a structural design engineer work with three-dimensional dynamic graphic shapes on a current CAD workstation. A less visually dramatic example is that of the foreign exchange traders buying and selling in markets around the world. The workstations that were once black and white "dumb" terminals with columns of numbers are now intelligent

27

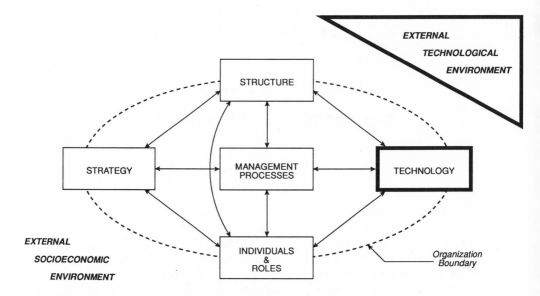

Figure 2-1. MIT90s framework—Chapter 2 emphasis.

terminals able to use models, filter data, and present ordered tables as well as color graphic representations. These powerful workstations will spread to a host of new areas in the 1990s; so also will simpler ones. The current portable lap-top machines and the newer "breast-pocket" equivalents will have their functionality extended and their cost reduced so that anyone anywhere could use such a device to do their information-based work. Some sales forces use such devices to enter orders from the field now; we expect this to be virtually universal by the end of the 1990s.

These three factors, when combined, generate some clear effects for all organizations. There are three in particular. We can expect to see increasing degrees of connectivity given the widespread nature of networks and the "standardization" of connections. This moves us toward the point where anyone, anywhere, can connect to anyone else. Although this is an extreme statement, from a practical standpoint there will be no serious barriers to low-cost communication vertically and horizontally within an organization and between it and its principal working partners (suppliers, collaborators, customers, etc.).

A second effect will be increasing organizational memory. This is a geometric effect; as more work gets done with workstations and more transactions take place electronically, it becomes possible to save patterns of product or service use and performance. These can then be accessed by the organization and used as a basis for resource allocation decisions and/or product, customer, or employee emphasis decisions.

The third effect we see is the ubiquitous availablity of these tools. By the end of the 1990s they will be in use throughout all organizations in the developed world. As they become easy to apply and increasingly affordable, more and more people can use them. This in turn increases the pool of those who can create new uses for the tools, through modifications of the software and hardware. It also increases the number of people and applications for which these tools are useful. Thus, it appears as though we will see the creation of a "virtuous spiral" in which new tools (and lower cost) enable new applications, which encourage wider use, thus further lowering cost and stimulating the creation of new tools, and so on.

Of course, such a virtuous spiral is not inevitable, and there are several forces that may severely inhibit its development. These inhibiting forces, and some enabling ones, are largely organizational and are spelled out in this chapter. These forces are very real, but they can also be directly influenced by the will and determination of the organization and, in turn, by the nation. There can be no question that the quality and nature of these information tools and the way they are used will have a powerful effect on the performance of organizations and nations in the global economic competition of the 1990s. They represent the next stage of organizational evolution following the industrial evolution of the mass-production organization of the late 1800s.

In surveying the trends that are most strongly influencing the evolution of information technology for the 1990s, a common theme has emerged from our research efforts, reasearch sponsors, and related literature: *Advances in information technology provide opportunities for dramatically increased connectivity, enabling new forms of interorganizational relationships and enhanced group productivity.*

This theme emerges as the end result of two forces at work: 1990s business forces and 1990s information technology opportunities, as depicted in Figure 2-2.

1990s BUSINESS FORCES

Although articulated many different ways, four business forces are exerting increasing influence and will, for many organizations, shape their destiny in the 1990s. The first of these forces is the rapidly increasing growth in globalization, whereby the scopes of organizations are expanding beyond their traditional geographic boundaries. In the case of current multinational firms, the entire corporation and all of its subsidiaries are finding needs to be increasingly coordinated to provide maximum impact, such as in manufacturing and supply activities, as well as in marketing and distribution. As a by-product of globalization, its inverse effect in the form of world-wide competition is also on the rise. This means that the number of competitors one must face in each marketplace and geographic region has increased through the entry of corporations that are expanding through their globalization activities. This puts increased pressure on the established organizations in these marketplaces and in many cases changes the entire nature of the competition.

In order to seize the opportunity of globalization and withstand the impact of worldwide competition, corporations are seeking ever-increasing levels of productivity improvement. These productivitiy requirements take many forms. They may involve better-coordinated manufacturing and purchasing so as to make maximum effectiveness in economies of scale and production, local efficiencies of labor force, and efficient purchasing and warehousing of components. Furthermore, by increasing the responsiveness to market trends and the requirements of customers, it is intended to gain sales volume and minimize wasted energy.

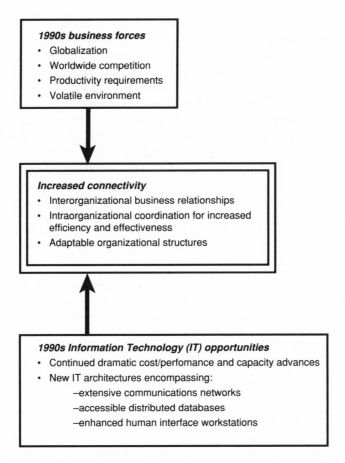

Figure 2-2. Advances in IT provide opportunities for dramatically increased connectivity, enabling new forms of interorganizational relationships and enhanced group productivity.

Attaining such improvements in productivity would be a significant challenge under normal circumstances, but the process is made significantly more complex by the volatile environment that is becoming more evident and is expected to continue to increase into the 1990s. This volatile environment emerges not only from the business forces described above but also through various governmental, sociological, and legal changes. As one example, the various steps being taken to form a boundary-free European community, targeted for 1992, represent a major change in the business map of the world, with implications for business in Europe and businesses dealing with Europe, as well as rippling effects throughout the world.

As a result of various governmental and legal actions encouraging deregulation and privatization, as well as desires for corporations to rapidly accelerate their globalization efforts, massive mergers, acquisitions, and divestitures are taking place. Thus, while one is attempting to coordinate for maximum efficiency the various plans and resources of a corporation, it is not clear which of those resources will be there tomorrow. Therefore, if a division is sold off or divested, it is necessary to adapt both marketing and manufacturing activities to replace any critical capabilities that were being provided by those facilities. On the other hand, if other organizations or divisions are acquired, it is desirable to assimilate these facilities as rapidly as possible into the total environment, eliminate unnecessary redundancies and duplication, and produce as efficient a marketing and production capability as possible. These two forces clearly represent a major challenge for the manager of the 1990s. In a highly stable environment, traditional approaches to optimization and productivity improvements can be used. But in this highly volatile and upredictable environment, novel approaches to attaining high levels of productivity must be pursued.

In almost every major industry, these business forces can be identified and in many cases are fairly advanced even at this time. Independent from these forces are various developments occurring in information technology that have a strong bearing upon the situation.

1990s IT OPPORTUNITIES

In reviewing the trends in information technology with key executives of the major vendors, as well as research colleagues, various trends can clearly be identified that are expected to continue and even increase into the 1990s. Continued advancement of both cost reductions and performance improvements in IT is almost taken for granted based on four decades of this process. As one colleague noted, although this progress seems continuous, in fact whenever a factor-of-10 improvement in cost and/ or performance occurs, major discontinuities usually follow. The rapid infusion of personal computer technology throughout society in recent years is one clear example, as is the current acceleration of local area networks (LAN). There are many simple explanations for this phenomenon, but in general they revolve around the fact that a 10-percent improvement merely allows existing applications and uses to be implemented somewhat more effectively or economically. A factor-of-10 change usually enables whole categories of applications to emerge that did not previously exist.

Although these advances in the individual components of IT are quite important, an even more significant impact will occur as a result of new IT architectures (i.e., new ways to organize and interconnect these components). Three particular trends in this direction can be identified: (1) extensive communications networks, (2) accessible distributive databases, and (3) enchanced human interface workstations. These trends in architecture will be elaborated upon later in this chapter. In brief, the development of high-performance, high-reliability, comprehensive communication networks, both intraorganizationally and interorganizationally, is occurring at a rapid pace. At the same time, both hardware and software technologies are evolving in ways that make it possible to maintain extensive amounts of information on line and to be able to access this information in conjunction with the communication networks from almost any location. Furthermore, the increased capability of advanced personal computers, often referred to as workstations, is providing many improvements in ease of use, enabling people to work with these systems with much less formal training yet accomplish much more complex tasks. This is similar to the way an automatic transmission is able to hide the detailed workings of an automobile's transmission system, involving multiple gears, with the actual selection of gear setting for optimal performance accomplished without being observed by the user. In fact, such enhancement in the human interface has been one of the many important aspects, besides the reduction in costs, that have enabled personal computers to be absorbed into society at such a rapid rate.

INCREASED CONNECTIVITY

At the intersection of the 1990s business forces and the 1990s information technology opportunities lie the need and the ability to provide increased and more flexible connectivity. Here we mean connectivity in a very broad sense that can be manifest in many forms. Three of the most critical are identifed below.

There have been dramatic increases in efforts to establish much more efficient and tightly coupled interorganizational business relationships. These take many forms. A major thrust is to increase productivity, reduce cost, and improve service by providing highly automated end-to-end electronic connectivity. In the most idealized case, all of the processes, from the entry of an order at the customer site, through its processing at the manufacturer's site, and on to the request for replenishment of necessary supplies, are handled through direct electronic connections among customers and suppliers, with minimal manual intervention or paperwork.

In addition to these "electronic" arm's-length transactions, there is an increasing emergence of "virtual corporations." This often occurs as the by-product of the agreement among two or more corporations to pool their resources for the purpose of pursuing a particular business opportunity. An example of this type of activity occurs in large-scale military projects, such as the development of the B-1 bomber. In that case, divisions or groups from as many as two thousand separate corporations are essentially working together as departments within a "virtual corporation" to accomplish the design and manufacture of this product. This type of activity is being seen at an increasing rate in the civilian manufacturing sector as corporations strive to take advantage of manufacturing economies and expertise available in other organizations, or particular cost advantages of labor and raw materials. In these situations it is desirable to set up an efficient management structure and information flow comparable to that which would be expected in a large, mature organization, but it is necessary to establish this infrastructure on a dramatically accelerated time scale.

Looking within a single corporation, we find various similar forces at work, driving toward attempts to provide intraorganizational coordination for increased efficiency and effectiveness. Because of corporate culture or the past limitations of IT, many corporations have run as a group of loosely coupled minicorporations, each running fairly autonomously from its siblings. Although this often simplifies the management structure, it has been found to incur various inefficiencies. For example, the designers are often removed from the concerns and needs of the manufacturing and purchasing groups. This has led some organizations to strive to develop task forces that consist of members from design, manufacturing, and purchasing working together on new products. Furthermore, in looking at the traditional regional separation or product separation within corporations, opportunities can exist to take advantage of the total corporation's resources, for example, by pooling

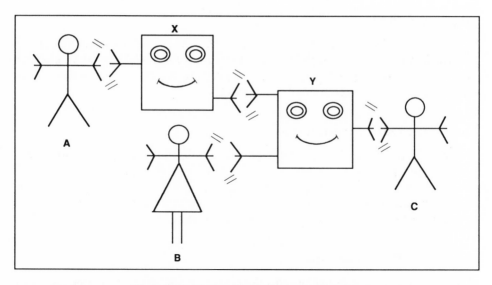

Figure 2-3. Cooperating information systems.

its purchasing activities to gain greater economies of scale or pooling its warehousing and distribution capabilities to accomplish higher utilizations and reduced costs.

As a by-product of these inter- and intraorganizational needs, we must also add forces identified as part of the volatile environment of the 1990s. Significant adjustments to an organization may need to occur on rapidly accelerated timetables, leading to the need to develop approaches to support highly adaptable organizational structures. It is not uncommon to read about an organization that has switched from being structured along regional divisons to being organized along product lines. At the same time, another corporation, often in the same industry, is undergoing the exact reverse reorganization. Furthermore, in this environment of acquisitions and divestitures, it is not uncommon to find two large corporations merging to form a megacorporation and spinning off various smaller divisions, either to operate as autonomous corporations or to be absorbed themselves into other corporations. There is a need to be able to rapidly restructure organizations in response to these changes and to provide all of the necessary IT infrastructure support. This is being made possible, in varying degrees, through the developments currently under way in information technology.

COOPERATING INFORMATION SYSTEMS

A key generalization arising out of our theme is that we can look for increased coordination and cooperation among both human and computer information systems. As Figure 2-3 depicts, most situations involve an ensemble of humans and computers. Based upon current day examples, we can illustrate various forms of cooperation.

Electronic Mail

In an electronic mail application, IT can provide a rapid and convenient means of communicating between two individuals. The connections might be fairly direct, as seen between individuals B and C, or they may involve multiple electronic intermediaries, as seen between individuals A and C.

Electronic Data Interchange

In electronic data interchange (EDI), information flowing between computing systems may take place with minimal, if any, human intervention. For example, if computing system X detects that the inventory for certain items has dropped below its predefined automatic order point, it can initiate a direct request for replenishment to its supplier's computer system, identified as computer system Y.

Electronic Conferencing

In looking at ways to improve the effectiveness of organizations, it is often necessary to combine and exploit the unique capabilites of both humans and computing systems. For example, in some experimental electronic conferencing or brainstorming systems, multiple humans interact. Rather than communication in the form of simple electronic transmissions, the computing systems help to organize, correlate, and structure the information flows, allowing more individuals to participate more effectively than would normally be possible in a noncomputer-enhanced environment.

As seen in these examples, we can improve the effectiveness of cooperating information systems consisting of a large array of humans and computers through more effective and increased capability for connectivity.

IT COMPONENTS

Before we attempt a detailed view of the trends in information technology capabilities that can be expected in the 1990s, it is necessary to identify the individual and critical components. Figure 2-4 depicts the four key components: (1) the workstations, (2) the shared-access distributed databases and knowledge bases, (3) the communications network, and (4) the specialized processors.

Workstations

For most users, the workstations are the most visible aspect of information technology. This entry point may be a simple terminal, often referred to as a "dumb" terminal, or, as is becoming more common, a personal computer (PC). Although the definition of a workstation is subject to various interpretations, for our purposes it can be thought of as a sophisticated PC. That covers significant territory, since current-day systems may range from a low-end PC costing less than $1,000 to an extremely sophisticated high-performance computer-aided design system costing in

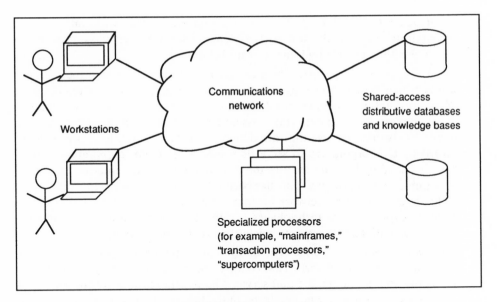

Figure 2-4. IT components.

excess of $100,000. One key aspect that differentiates a workstation in our context from the common view of a PC is that we are focusing on workstations that can be interconnected with other workstations and other IT resources through communication networks, as depicted in Figure 2-4.

Shared Access Distributed Databases and Knowledge Bases

The second key element is that of shared-access distributed databases and knowledge bases. As the cost of on-line storage technology, in the form of both magnetic disks and optical disks, continues to decline, and as the ease of use and sophistication of database management system software and knowledge-based systems software increase, the gathering and storage of vast amounts of information on line is increasing. Although Figure 2-4 depicts disk-type storage devices, these are actually controlled by computing systems that may range from traditional "mainframe" computers (running traditional database management systems software such as IBM's IMS) to newer local area network "file servers" or even the emerging "database machines" which are specialized computers optimized for maximum performance and minimum cost in supporting database and/or knowledge-based processing.

Communication Networks

As noted earlier, a key element in our notion of a workstation is the fact that it can conveniently communicate with other workstations as well as other corporate resources, most notably the shared-access database and knowledge bases, through communications networks. It is important to note that these communications networks may take many forms. Three common forms are:

Local area networks (LANs). These are communications networks internal to a corporation used to connect various systems within relatively close proximity, typically within a single building or plant location.

Internal wide-area networks. These are often called corporate information networks, which are used to tie together the various geographically distributed parts of the corporation. These corporate networks often provide both voice (that is, telephone) services and data transmission capabilities. These are referred to as internal networks because they are designed, managed, and, to a large extent, owned by the corporation to serve its needs. Most major corporations either have installed or have under way the development of such internal corporate communications networks. This has been driven by various forces, such as the ability to customize the network for maximum efficiency at minimum cost, the ability to exploit specific technologies, and the need and/or ability to circumvent various regulations that restrict or delay external public networks.

External wide-area networks. The traditional telephone network is an example of a public external network. That is, the equipment is owned by the telephone company and is maintained and serviced by it, and services are supplied on a fee basis to customers, who might be individual residential users or large corporate users. In the same vein, there are various services provided by both traditional telephone companies and specialized data communications corporations that provide similar data communications services.

Although these three types of networks have been listed separately, it is critical to be able to use them in combinations. For example, operating at a workstation one may be able to access and communicate with other workstations in close proximity via a LAN. In order to access a remotely located corporate database, it would be necessary to make use of a wide-area network, either internal or external. Furthermore, in order to communicate with workstations at a remote site, operating on a separate LAN, it is necessary to provide wide-area communications capability to couple these individual LANs together. In order to deal with members of other organizations not typically connected to the internal communication network of one's corporation, it would be necessary to operate through an external public network connecting individual corporate networks or, through prior arrangements, to have established appropriate agreements between the two corporations providing for direct means to link their internal corporate networks. Another example that has become increasingly popular is that of individuals who have workstations in their residences that communicate with their corporate counterparts and resources, accessed through external networks, typically using standard telephone services today.

Furthermore, there may be many variations of the three network types listed. As an example, metropolitan area networks (MANs) provide high-performance capabilities for linking individual LANs within a geographic area, such as a city. A MAN may be run as an internal service, an external service, or some intermediate form, such as linking all financial institutions in the city.

Thus, in many ways, Figure 2-4 greatly simplifies the issues involved in these communications networks. The depiction of a cloud is intended to indicate that the users of a network wish to have as little knowledge as possible about what actually goes on. In much the same way, a typical user of current-day voice telephone service is unaware that a telephone call from Boston to Los Angeles may go through various technologies such as copper wire, microwave, satellite, and fiber optics, and may undergo various transformations and switching at dozens of sites along the way. Unfortunately, this transparency that we have come to expect on the voice telephone has been a major challenge to duplicate in complex communications networks. A trend that will be elaborated on later is the need and capability to provide increased transparency and functionality for these communications networks, so as to make the resources of the corporation and all of its partners accessible to the user's work-station in a transparent, easy-to-use manner.

Specialized Processors

The components described above represent a vision of the IT capabilites and archi-tectures for the 1990s. Examples reflecting this structure can already be found emerg-ing in many organizations. One area that has attracted considerable controversy, and probably will represent differences in strategy, is represented in Figure 2-4 as "spe-cialized processors." Several issues are incorporated under this category.

One major issue involves the evolution of the traditional "mainframe." In many organizations today, the user is serviced through a "dumb" terminal, and all of the processing, for servicing the end users' interactions, the application, and the man-agement and manipulation of the data, is accomplished on a single, shared, large-scale computing system. From a strictly technological point of view, there is often a comparable amount of computing power available in current-day workstations. (There are actually specialized workstations, such as for computer-aided design, which by certain measures provide more computational power to that single user than is available on most commercial large-scale mainframe computers.) Further-more, to increasing degrees, the amount of processing in support of the storage and management of large databases on specialized "file server" or "database server" sys-tems effectively eliminates much of the need for traditional mainframes. On the other hand, there are at least two reasons why the traditional mainframes are expected to continue to play a major role in many organizations.

First, there is a tremendous investment in software and procedures that has been based and centered on the mainframe concept. Thus, it is expected that there would be a slow evolutionary movement of certain capabilities, such as the front end-user interface moving to the workstation and the data management moving to the shared-access database systems. In many organizations, the key systems, such as accounting and inventory control, were first developed twenty years ago and have been updated through incremental developments. As we will discuss later, the ability to evolve such systems at a much more rapid rate will be necessary to deal with the business forces of the 1990s, as well as the ability to exploit the information technology architecture depicted in Figure 2-4.

A second factor involves various needs for centralized control. Although the combined computing power of the workstations and shared-access database servers may be able to provide all the necessary processing ability, it is often desirable to have a central coordinating element. This is for processing that would not be partic-ular to an individual workstation but in fact would coordinate the activities of many throughout the organization. For example, in determining the optimal manufacturing policies or pooling and processing all of the purchasing needs, a system would be required that would scrutinize all of the appropate data gathered on the shared-access databases and make appropriate decisions for the organization. In addition, in certain areas such as financial transaction systems, there may be concern regarding the integrity of the user and/or the software that is operating on the workstation.

To meet these concerns, certain processors are designated as transaction processors or coordinators. They may stand as intermediaries between the workstation and the databases; that is, the transaction would be sent from the workstation to the transaction processor, which would validate the request and then perform the appropriate actions resulting in changes to critical database information. Alternately, the workstations may directly interact with the shared database (which enforces certain restrictions and security restraints). The central coordinating processor would periodically examine the information that had been deposited in the shared databases, take appropriate actions, and update the appropriate data in these databases.

In addition to the example of functionally specialized processors to provide a coordination function as described above, there is also the opportunity to make use of performance-specialized processors. Two particular examples would be ultra-high-speed performance processors and ultra-high-reliability processors. Although the processing power of workstations is continuously increasing and is likely to match or exceed that of the "mainframe" computers of the 1980s, there will be "top-of-the-line" mainframes and "supercomputers" whose performance might be tens, hundreds, or even thousands of times faster than that of a single workstation. Certain types of sophisticated mathematical calculation or the use of elaborate "expert system" software may require such specialized processors. Through the use of emerging "network operating systems software," in conjunction with a transparent communications network, the user need not be aware of where processing is actually being performed, either on the local workstation or by a remote specialized processor.

The key components expected in the 1990s IT architecture have been identified. In the next section the key capabilities, especially those enablers that facilitate increased connectivity, will be elaborated upon, and areas of concern that might act as inhibitors to attaining these full benefits will be discussed.

ENABLERS AND INHIBITORS

Through discussions with sponsor representatives and the associated MIT researchers, as well as through a review of the related literature, a consensus has emerged regarding key enablers and inhibitors expected to play a major role in the information technology environment of the 1990s. These key factors have been grouped into categories and summarized in Table 2-1.

General Advances in Computer Hardware and Software

As noted earlier, and to be elaborated upon later, the continuation of advances in both the reduction in cost and improvements in speed and function of computer hardware and software are expected to continue through the 1990s. This force, on its

Table 2-1. Overview of Enablers and Inhibitors

	Enablers	Inhibitors
General	Computer hardware/ software advances	
Communications networks	Powerful, transparent, internal networks External networks and standards (EDI)	Effective network management
Distributed database capability	Easy access to distributed databases	Effectiveness of software Data resource management policy Installed base Capability of dictionary/semantic resolvers
Workstations	Ubiquitous, networked, hierarchical workstations AI/expert systems to simplify system usage and access to network/ database resources	Interface with data/knowledge base resources Cognitive support/facilitations
IT architecture	Integrate existing operational systems	Application architecture for organizational flexibility
IT infrastructure/ usage	Improve group processes and performance IT-literate/IT-champion management	Effective IT standards General productivity (individual, group, firm) Support of management processes Systems investment rationale User attitude/readiness Quality of IT work force

own, will continue the trend of making IT a ubiquitous force throughout all areas of business endeavor and social life. Certain specific developments are expected to play a pivotal role in increasing the impact and importance of IT, if certain associated inhibitors can be overcome.

Communications Networks

We are seeing an ever-increasing ability to provide powerful transparent networks that bind together elements of corporations (internal networks) and the world at large (external networks). Although these endeavors can be quite expensive and time-consuming, often taking up to a decade to be fully established, most major corporations have such efforts well under way and moving rapidly toward completion.

Another important development is the emergence of standards for both the development of new networks and the interfacing of existing network protocols. The open systems interchange (OSI) effort, which has been progressing slowly, is expected to take on increasing importance in the 1990s.

In parallel with the development of the networks will be increasing applications making use of these networks to exchange information, both with internal divisions and with external customer and/or supplier relationships. Much of this activity is already evidenced through the increasing emergence of electronic data interchange (EDI) activities. In some industries up to 70 percent of all order-placing activities are being performed by direct EDI transactions between buyers and sellers. Because of the differences in structures among industries, the amount of EDI activity varies greatly. In all cases, it is expected that this activity will increase and become even more widely accepted as a basic way of performing business.

The technologies supporting the development of these communications networks and the standards that provide for interconnection between these networks and related parties, such as buyers and sellers, can greatly increase the efficiency of many activities throughout industry. But there are also concerns that must be addressed that otherwise will inhibit the full potential of these communications networks to serve our needs. There is a major concern regarding the ability to develop effective network management. We are currently contemplating networks significantly larger, more comprehensive, and more complex than any that have ever been established before.

Even within a strictly internal network, there are technical problems with effectively monitoring and understanding the activity on this network and management problems regarding the operation and growth of such networks. When one looks further into the difficulties of building interorganizational networks, both the technical problems caused by the diversity of network technologies and strategies that may be deployed and the lack of a central network management organizational structure pose serious challenges. There are various ways that these problems may be mitigated, such as through the emergence of various network coordinating bodies (such as CCITT regarding conventional public telephone networks) or de facto coordination by major network software or service providers (such as IBM with its Systems Network Architecture). Furthermore, advances in technology may help reduce the apparent complexities and difficulties of managing such networks.

Distributed Database Capability

A major driving force behind the emergence of such communications networks is the need to support and facilitate easy access to distributed databases. These databases may currently be distributed to various locations throughout the corporation, or may be centralized to a few locations, but with the need to be accessed from locations throughout the corporation. Furthermore, access and use of databases traditionally operated in isolation will be particularly important in increasing our effective connectivity in support of better-coordinated planning.

There have been significant advances in distributed database management systems software, including some currently announced products. Similar systems are expected from most of the major database management systems providers, including IBM, with widespread use accelerating from 1990 to 1995. With the proliferation of powerful communications networks supporting a distributed database capability, a user anywhere within the organization or within cooperating organizations would be able to access any authorized information transparent to its particular location.

Although prototype examples of such systems have already been demonstrated, there are major concerns that may act as serious inhibitors to the effective deployment of this technology. The first involves the rate at which this technology will evolve and the effectiveness of such distributed database systems. Most of the current implementations of such systems have many limitations, in terms of either their ability to provide complete transparency or their ability to provide adequate speed performance under all appropriate conditions. Increased experimentation and closer working relationships between the user community and the developers of such technology will be important in resolving these problems on a timely basis. If these function and speed problems are not overcome rapidly enough, effective distributed database management may be limited to that subset of circumstances that can be sufficiently addressed by available technology.

Several other major concerns, although identified as inhibitors to a distributed database capability, are, to a large extent, problems inherent in attempting to run large, complex organizations with increased coordination and cooperation. For example, a major concern involves the development of effective data resource management policies. In the past, each part of the organization or cooperating organization pursued both the functional definition and the IT implementation of its databases fairly autonomously. To gain increased effectiveness in sharing data, it becomes important to develop common data resource management policies. These policies are needed to address a wide array of issues. One example might be the standardization of part numbers throughout the corporation or throughout the industry, in much the same way as the Universal Product Code (UPC) represents a standardized part-numbering scheme for products purchased in grocery stores. Although there has been considerable interest in the issue of data resource management, there are widely differing views of how it might be best attained, considering the technical limitations of systems, the organizational realities, and the complexity of the problems being addressed.

Another major concern involves the legacy of the installed base of data systems. These installed systems represent a major asset for the corporation, since both their development cost and the cost of acquiring and accumulating the data they now contain can be enormously expensive. Furthermore, despite possible deficiencies, the use of these systems represents knowledge that has been gained by many individuals in the organization; therefore, considerable disruption and retraining costs could be incurred if such systems are changed significantly. Thus, one is often faced with a trade-off between a slow rate of change, which amortizes the value of the installed base over a longer period and minimizes the risks of technical or organizational disruptions, and the potential benefits of new systems that have been more effectively developed to support the need for increased connectivity and coordination. In almost every organization some form of evolutionary plan, possibly coupled with an overall data resource management policy, needs to be developed to deal with these opposing forces.

Our desire for an increasingly connected and coordinated organization, although having many potential benefits, does pose many challenges to our ability to manage such environments effectively. The old adage "Divide and conquer" in many ways represents the reality of how organizations and humans often function best. Limiting scope keeps the amount of information that one must process and comprehend within convenient limits. As we attempt to broaden this scope it becomes necessary to have capabilities to aid us in this process, particularly powerful global data dictionaries and semantic resolvers.

Global data dictionaries allow us to ascertain what information is in the system and how to request it. For example, we know that General Motors buys equipment from several of our divisions. How do we find out the total volume of business with GM? Which data systems, probably several, contain that information? What is it called? How is it accessed? The global data dictionary would assist us in this process.

Even more subtle issues involve the ability to perform semantic resolution. Within a specific part of an organization, or a specific culture, we make significant assumptions about our environment. For example, in the United States, if you were to ask a supplier the cost of a specific part and were told 16.45, it would be natural to assume that the price is expressed in U.S. dollars. When one starts to deal across parts of the organizations, or on a worldwide basis, traditional assumptions about the semantics or meaning of data need to be made more explicit and, often, transformed into compatible forms. For example, one supplier may express prices in terms of each individual part, whereas another supplier may express prices in terms of a dozen at a time. If one dealt with both suppliers on a continuing basis, these differences would be automatically assumed, but as we expand our scope we will start to develop new relationships where these assumptions have not been explicit. The capability of having semantic resolver software represents a major challenge for information technology. Without such a capability, we would be faced either with making erroneous decisions because of an incorrect interpretation of data that we have retrieved or with the need to resort to much less efficient and extensive human intervention to validate the accuracy of the information and to perform appropriate transformations before the data can be used.

Workstations

An important enabling force toward making IT usable throughout the organization is the emergence of the ubiquitous networked workstation. In much the same way that the desk telephone has become our access to the world of human communication through the telephone system, the workstation serves a similar role in accessing the new network of both humans and computer systems throughout these organizations.

An important enabling element is increased capabilities, especially through the deployment of artificial intelligence (AI) and expert systems (ES) technologies, that will allow these workstations to significantly simplify system usage and provide more transparent access to the network and database resources. This is an important area where the growing power of the workstation plays an important role. In a recent discussion with the developers of a sophisticated specialized information service, it was observed that the amount of software in the user's workstation to support an easy-to-use interface had increased from less than 50,000 bytes in earlier models to now more than 4,000,000 bytes. Thus, the advances in IT are serving as the fuel that makes possible significantly more powerful and easier-to-use interfaces in much the same way that the addition of automatic transmission technology has made an automobile easier to operate.

There is concern that the goal for the workstations of the 1990s to provide a significantly easy-to-use capability that makes the *complexities of the network and distribute data transparent* will not materialize as fast as desired and thus will be an inhibitor to rapid connectivity.

There is also considerable effort to use these powerful workstations, in conjunction with AI and ES technology, to support the user's *decision making and cognitive processing.* This type of support could significantly enhance individual productivity, and increasing connectivity throughout the organization will help to improve group productivity. Although these are reasonable goals to strive for, the capability of IT to be able to fully support and facilitate such cognitive activities is an area of significant concern and if not fully realized will be an inhibitor to their success.

IT Architecture

The IT architecture shown in Figure 2-4 provides an evolutionary way to integrate existing operational systems to provide the basis for new informations systems that can help the disparate parts of the organization and multiple organizations to work cooperatively. This type of architecture is the focus of considerable attention by many leading-edge organizations and needs to be pursued aggressively in order to provide truly connected and coordinated organizations.

As noted earlier, we must deal with a highly volatile environment. It is not only necessary to be able to integrate our operational systems as a one-time activity; we also need to provide an architecture that allows for considerable organizational flexibility. (Some suggestions for approaching this problem will be discussed later.) If we are not able to attain this goal, the inflexibility and slow adaptability of the information systems structure itself may act as an inhibitor to the rate of change necessary to survive in the highly volatile environment of the 1990s.

IT Infrastructure and Usage

Although the above sections stressed the technology aspects, there are many organizational concerns that can act as either enablers or inhibitors to the effective use of information technology.

Two important enablers have been identified in our discussions. The first involves the ability to significantly improve group processes and performance through the various technologies supporting connectivity and coordination throughout the organization. Second, the increase in the number of managers who are both comfortable and literate in IT will make it easier to identify and pursue these exciting opportunities, and the emergence of IT champions with the vision and leadership to move the corporation aggressively in these directions is expected to increase in the 1990s.

These positive directions in the IT infrastructure do not occur without significant obstacles that can significantly inhibit full attainment of our desired goals. Six specific concerns have been identified. The first involves the development of effective IT standards. The rapid development of new IT capabilities, including hardware, software, and applications, although providing tremendous positive opportunities, also give rise to diversities that can make connectivity and effective communication very difficult. The development of standards, or effective techniques for mapping between the alternatives, is a critical need.

The second factor involves our understanding of general productivity applied to individuals, groups, and organizations. One of the many clichés regarding IT is that it allows you to perform the wrong actions hundreds of times faster. In order to gain the improvements in productivity that we seek, it is necessary to rethink the processes that are currently being used and, in many cases, to transform the organization dramatically to gain the improvements in productivity that IT makes possible. Although this point has been raised by many researchers in the field, the identification of a general and widely accepted approach to attaining these transformations still remains a major challenge.

Although the preceding paragraph primarily alluded to the products and services of the corporation, a very similar argument can be made regarding the decision-making and general management processes of the organization. Their complexity has often made it difficult to identify ways to apply IT to improve these processes.

There is a need to reevaluate the systems investment rationale that has been traditionally applied to IT initiatives. Often IT investments are based on direct cost savings accomplished through personnel reduction. In the environment of the 1990s, where we are exploring new ways to perform business and coordinate activities among organizations, a direct connection to personnel reduction may not always be possible or fully reflect the benefits that are to be gained. Thus, we need new approaches to evaluate the information systems investment process in this environment.

There is also the duet of concerns regarding the quality of the IT work force and the user's attitude and readiness to accept and pursue the new options made available through advances in IT. We will look at these two factors separately. Unless sufficient progress is made on either effective software that can hide the complexities of such systems or the level of training and experience that will be generally available in the 1990s, there may be such a large mismatch as to inhibit the widespread deployment of new technologies. Furthermore, even if there is sufficient transparency of the complexity and a sufficiently well-trained work force, there is concern about how rapid a rate of change the users can endure, including both top management and middle management as well as the external partners to be interconnected and to work in a coordinated cooperative manner. Although the pressures to make such changes will be quite high, the organizational ramifications can be sufficiently onerous to act as major inhibitors to their adoption.

This section is intended to reflect the reality of the "good news/bad news" (or enablers and inhibitors) environment that will characterize the 1990s. To a large extent, the rate of progress and degree of success of the IT advances anticipated will influence the degree to which the enablers will be significant and, to a lesser extent, the degree to which the inhibitors can be mitigated. But many of the inhibitors represent management decisions and organizational changes that IT cannot completely minimize and will represent major challenges to the management of the 1990s.

Continuum of Proactive/Reactive Connectivity Environments

We have discussed the need to respond to the volatile environment of the 1990s by being able to support highly adaptable organizational structures. In looking at that volatility and the ways in which an organization can deal with it, we have identified two extremes which, although neither is realistic, do represent pedagogically interesting perspectives (see Figure 2-5).

The first category is referred to as proactive. As the extreme case under this environment, from the moment the organization is formed all future requirements for connectivity are anticipated and planned for in advance. For example, if a corporation initially operates in Massachusetts in the United States, appropriate modes of operation including definitions of part-numbering schemes, part-number codes, and financial reporting formats will be determined. As this organization expands geographically and over time, these procedures are carried forward in unison throughout the entire organization. Under such a proactive environment, if it becomes desirable to coordinate the activities of a plant outside the United States with its counterpart in Massachusetts, this organizational consistency would make the exchange of data and processes quite easy, assuming that technical decisions such as choice of programming languages, operating systems, and communications networks have also been proactively planned among the divisions of the corporation.

The other extreme is the reactive environment. In the purest form, each part of the organization proceeds independently of the rest of the organization. Only when a specific need arises to connect and coordinate activity will such a concern be addressed. At that time either one part of the organization will alter its data and procedures to match the other, or appropriate transformation capabilities will be developed to allow them to interchange information effectively.

Obviously, both of these extremes are unrealistic. In the first case, to be completely proactive would require a level of effort and detail that could be an enormous cost to the corporation, although advances in information technology can help to mitigate this cost. Furthermore, it requires a planning horizon and stability contradictory to the volatile environment that has been assumed. For example, even if every division of the corporation has been coordinated so as to have exactly the same procedures, part numbers, customer codes, and so forth, this carefully planned structure would be thrown into disarray by acquiring a division from another corporation (which would presumably have its own set of data and procedures) or by being acquired by a different corporation. Even if the intentions are to become rapidly restandardized, it is impossible for this task to be accomplished instantaneously; thus, one must endure a period of reactive behavior, at least temporarily. Furthermore, especially when considering the globalization of corporations, one finds that the disparate customs, environment, and legal differences within different countries would impose forces that may be at odds with the goal of corporate standardization.

Likewise, an environment of total reactivity would be extremely costly and inefficient, essentially resembling a Tower of Babel. Thus, certain types of activities, such as financial reporting to headquarters to enable corporatewide financial review and preparation of annual reports, would be a requirement of sufficient longevity and

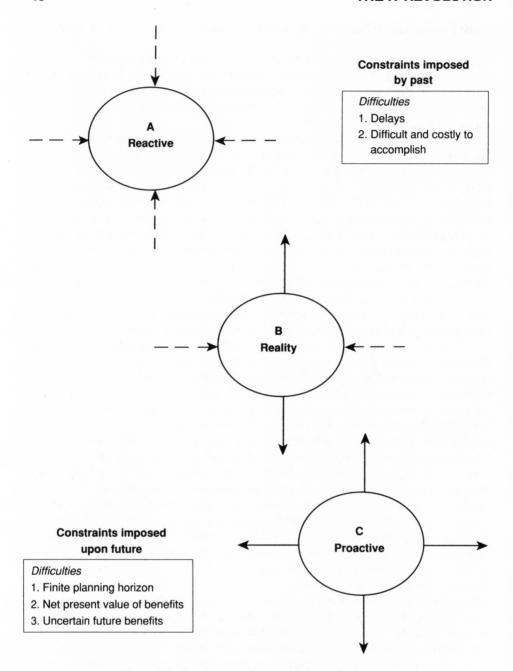

Figure 2-5. Continuum of connectivity environments.

value that procedures would likely be instituted in each of the divisions to make such reporting convenient and to minimize effort.

Although it would seem obvious from the descriptions provided here that neither extreme of proactive or reactive environment would be feasible or desirable, many organizations behave as if they are at these extremes. In reality, of course, we exist in the continuum between these extremes. For certain activities that are sufficiently critical and can be forecast with sufficient confidence, a proactive plan may be feasible and appropriate (such as setting up procedures for electronic data interchange between all plants and the major suppliers and/or customers). At the same time, it must be realized that situations will arise that are beyond the forecasting window or that are unexpected events, such as a unique opportunity to acquire a complementary business. Under those circumstances, it is necessary to be reactive in as efficient and effective a manner as possible.

In such a heterogeneous environment, one wishes to have information technology that can support both the proactive and the reactive strategies. In particular, as one colleague noted, in this uncertain world of the 1990s one wants to be able to "proactively plan to be reactive."

IT FOR BOTH PROACTIVE AND REACTIVE STRATEGIES

In studying the many information technology advances that have been identified as enablers in our research, it can be seen that they serve different roles and are of different levels of importance when seen in light of either proactive or reactive environments. We will use this differentiation to help organize the discussion in this section. Furthermore, another dimension has been found helpful in organizing this material: the distinction between physical connectivity and logical connectivity. In physical connectivity we are focusing on the communication technologies and networks that handle the transmission of the data without regard to the contents or meaning of the data. This may be viewed as analogous to the postal system which, through a complex and elaborate process, delivers the mail from sender to receiver without the need to open the envelope or understand the contents. Logical connectivity refers to understanding the content of the letter. Thus, if an order is sent from a buyer in Germany to a manufacturer in the United States, the postal system will be able to deliver it if the addressing information on the envelope is adequate. But when the plant in the United States receives the envelope and opens it, various difficulties may ensure. For example, if instructions need to be provided along with this order, either the sender in Germany will have needed to translate the instructions into English, or the plant in the United States would need to have an interpreter who understands German. Furthermore, if the part numbering of the two organizations differ, then either the sender will need to translate its requirements into the part numbers of the supplier, or the supplier will have to be knowledgeable about the part-numbering system of its buyer and be able to perform the translation itself. Although we have used analogies of a postal system and human buyers and sellers, we would like to have most of these activities performed through electronic technology. Thus, the problems of both physical connectivity and logical connectivity would need to be addressed.

Figure 2-6 provides a framework dividing the notion of connectivity into the categories of proactive versus reactive connectivity and physical versus logical connectivity. Exploiting that framework, we can now organize the many enabling information technologies or inhibiting factors that have been identified as part of this project into one of the four parts of this matrix as illustrated in Figure 2-7. With few exceptions, this framework has been found very effective in organizing the more than two dozen IT enablers and inhibitors that have been identified. Furthermore, this framework also has the benefit of being prescriptive by highlighting which ITs are most relevant to the particular form of connectivity being sought.

Proactive Physical Connectivity

We could start our discussion from any point in the framework of Figures 2-6 and 2-7. Arbitrarily, we will start by looking at physical connectivity in the environment of proactive connectivity, the upper lefthand box.

Given the complexity of the task, a homogeneous network management capability, whereby a consistent set of procedures and technologies for managing the network is employed throughout, is very important. Furthermore, by using standard protocols, the amount of diversity in the network can be minimized. There are many standardization efforts currently under way, such as the integrated services digital network (ISDN), which is primarily focused on the worldwide external network; the manufacturing automation protocol (MAP), which is focused on local-area networks for manufacturing factories; and Ethernet, which is primarily focused on general-purpose local area networks, such as in offices. Even though we may be able to minimize the number of different types of networks, there will be some variations because of the differences between the environment of a factory shop floor and the worldwide external network; thus, interconnectibility standards between these networks is important. These identified factors can be looked upon as enablers if the prospects for their advancement proceed as intended, or they may be inhibitors if we are unable to accomplish effective network management, develop standardized protocols, and resolve complexities and technical difficulties with efficient, convenient interconnectibility among the networks.

Furthermore, most external networks, often referred to as wide-area networks (WANs), are regulated by government bodies. The regulatory factors in such WANs may provide enabling or inhibiting forces. If the individual government bodies of each country adopt differing and incompatible regulations, then producing worldwide public external networks can be quite difficult, and, to a certain extent, these regulatory factors can impede worldwide corporate networks as well. On the other hand, if the various forces toward greater cooperation and standardization, both technical and regulatory, continue, many of the current difficulties will be significantly reduced.

Reactive Physical Connectivity

Although diversity and disparity are not explicitly sought-after goals, the rapid changes in perceptions, breakthroughs in technology, and differences in philosophy

	Physical (communications)	Logical (data)
Proactive		
Reactive		

- **PHYSICAL VERSUS LOGICAL**
  - Physical: communications and networks
    (for example, transmission of raw data)
  - Logical: semantics of data
    (for example, where is it? what does it mean?)

- **PROACTIVE VERSUS REACTIVE**
  - Proactive: systems are designed specifically to "fit together"
    (for example, standards, homogeneous networks and databases)
  - Reactive: requirement and planning to tie systems together occur after systems exist
    (for example, heterogeneous networks and databases, semantic resolvers, multivendor integration)

Figure 2-6. Connectivity framework: Definitions.

make it possible for reasonable people to come up with different approaches to solving their communication network needs. These alternatives range from differences in media, such as unshielded twisted pair versus shielded twisted pair versus optical fiber, and so on, to differences in low-level media access protocols, such as Ethernet versus Token Ring, to differences in higher-level protocols, such as IBM's System Network Architecture (SNA) versus Digital Equipment Corporation's DECNET.

Although these differences might be diminished through the forces of standardization described above, it is also likely that striving to use new and better media technologies and protocol discoveries will lead to increased diversity. In the reactive environment of the "loosely coupled" organization, we would expect the various parts of the organization to select the most appropriate network choices to meet their

	PHYSICAL (COMMUNICATIONS)	LOGICAL (DATA)
P R O A C T I V E	• Homogeneous network management • Standard protocols (ISDN, MAP, Ethernet, etc.) • Standards for network interconnect • Regulation of wide-area networks • Management of standards process	• Distributed homogeneous databases (transparent) • EDI (application-specific standards) • Internal data standards • Applications: group DSS, E-mail, computer conference • Standards for flexible application architecture and data architecture • Preplanned data resource management • Management of standards process
R E A C T I V E	• Media differences • Protocol differences • Gateways • Heterogeneous network management • More effective management of dispersed and disparate organizations	• Distributed heterogeneous databases (transparent) • Multivendor system integration • Distributed data dictionary • Data semantics • Data reconciliation • Postplanned data resource management • Organizational flexibility / integration • More effective management of dispersed and disparate organizations

Proactive involves management of standards process.
Reactive refers to more effective management of geographically dispersed organizations.

Figure 2-7. Connectivity framework: Enablers and inhibitors.

needs. Eventually, some of these groups will need to be connected. Thus, the ability to provide effective gateways that allow us to interconnect these networks will be quite important. Advances in information technology that make it possible to build general-purpose gateways that can interconnect multiple networks, as well as development support technologies that allow rapid production of new gateway facilities, will mitigate this problem. Finally, heterogeneous network management capabilities, though much more difficult to accomplish than homogeneous network management, will make it possible to monitor, control, and optimize these complex networks in much easier ways than are currently available.

Proactive Logical Connectivity

In the past the demands for logical connectivity have been fewer because of both the limitations of information technology and the lack of driving business needs. These situations are changing rapidly. Thus, organizations striving for increased logical connectivity are exploring new developments in IT. One of the most important technologies is transparent distributed homogeneous database management systems (DBMS). These systems allow one to treat data that are physically dispersed to multiple computers as if they were on a single system. The user interface and programming would appear similar to that of a traditional centralized site. By homogeneous we mean that the software is being supplied by a single vendor, or by software-compatible vendors, who designed the individual pieces to work cooperatively. There has been extensive research on this topic for several years which has led to the introduction of several commercial systems in recent times. It appears likely that most major vendors of DBMS software will be introducing offerings of this type by the early 1990s and that the technology will become well established by the mid-1990s.

Merely being able to access distributive information may not be sufficient unless there is agreement on data standards. These data standards may arise from two different sources. First, there are industrywide or application-specific efforts to establish electronic data interchange (EDI) data standards. Industry-specific examples include extensive activities in the railroad industry, and application-specific activities include EDI efforts in standardizing order entry applications data input across multiple industries. The advantages of these efforts are that they are focused on only that subset of data that needs to be interchanged between different organizations. There is still difficulty, of course, in the process of attaining agreement across an array of organizations and special interests.

The other activity involves internal data standards, whereby the organization attempts to coordinate all internal data, such as part-number standardization, so that information may be exchanged even in cases that have not been explicitly anticipated in advance. The positive aspect of this effort is that since it is within a single organization, there may be opportunities to set up organizational structures to facilitate this process, although even within a single organization there may be competing goals and special interests. Furthermore, the magnitude of detail that one might be attempting to coordinate could be enormous. In one study for a major corporation, more than 50,000 different tables were identified. If they averaged 50 columns to each table, then there would be approximately 2.5 million different data elements that might need to be coordinated (for example, the pay-grade codes used in the manufacturing plant in Hong Kong and the pay-grade codes used in the sales office in New York). A very promising approach, sometimes referred to as focused internal data standards, is where the critical needs of the corporation are identified, and only those data elements found to be vital to coordinating these activities are coordinated.

The value of having an environment supporting connectivity is most significant if there are ways to make use of this connectivity. Examples of connectivity applications include electronic mail encompassing the entire organization and its related parties, computer conferencing capabilities to allow collective agreement and activity to be reached, and group decision support systems (GDSS), by which people, aided by computer-supplied information and modeling, arrive at key decisions. Research has been progressing in all of these areas, with some coming to be widely accepted and others still at the emerging stages.

In addition to exchanging information, it is also important to be able to exchange the processing (i.e., the programs) being used. This would make it possible to take a transaction validation capability that previously had been performed at the corporate headquarters computer in New York and distribute it to the various branch operations to allow much faster and more effective feedback to the user. The development of standards for flexible application architecture represents an important area of attention in many organizations, especially those attempting to create a new proactive environment for the future.

Finally, we need to develop proactive data resource management that acts as a binding force for all of the other activities described above to ensure that the appropriate technologies are identified and evaluated to determine how they best serve important business needs and the organizational environment.

Reactive Logical Connectivity

In many ways, this is the most difficult environment to deal with, although it may also be the most important for many organizations. It is the area that has experienced rapid growth in importance and in which the previous information technologies have been most lacking. New developments in IT show significant promise for mitigating these problems.

Paralleling the discussion of proactive environment, an important development is that of transparent distributed heterogeneous database management systems. These systems would allow one to access data that are geographically dispersed throughout the organization and that are running under the control of differing DBMS software from multiple vendors, as if it were a single, centralized system. Although prototypes have provided such capability in certain experiments, significant effort is needed to extend the functionality, speed of operation, and comprehensiveness of these systems. For example, although these prototypes are fairly effective at retrieving data, they are usually unable to perform updates to distributed data. Although these developments will lag behind those of the distributed homogeneous DBMSs, they are likely to become more widely available by the mid-1990s.

Another area that has been gaining increasing attention is that of multivendor systems integration. Most organizations have, and will continue to have, equipment provided by multiple vendors. This provides both a need and a business opportunity for the systems integration industry, from traditional IT vendors that will support equipment from their competitors, as well as new business ventures that are strictly focused on the systems integration activity. The advances in this area will not only simplify much of the management of such a computer ensemble but also will significantly simplify and improve the performance of the distributed heterogeneous DBMSs.

As noted earlier, even though one may have the physical connection and DBMS software that would allow access to any information, there is still a need to know what data exist and what they are called (even if the distributed heterogeneous DBMS software makes its geographic distribution transparent). Advances in distributed data dictionaries provide the opportunity to address this problem. Through these facilites one would be able to inquire of the "data about the data." One would be able to ask questions such as what attributes are available regarding employees and what attributes are available regarding warehouse capacity. To a large extent, the advances in distributed data dictionaries represent a merging of the ongoing efforts at improving "traditional" data dictionary capabilities for centralized systems and the ability of the distributed DBMS software to make geographically distributed systems appear to be centralized. These capabilities will be particularly important when one needs to address connectivity requirements that have not previously been anticipated, as might be expected in a reactive connectivity environment.

Two additional important areas are data semantics and data reconciliation. Techniques in "data modeling" whereby the relationships between data elements are characterized and processed provide a starting point for data semantics efforts. More recent advances incorporate technologies of artificial intelligence and knowledge-based processing to further augment our ability to represent complex relationships among data. In the past, these efforts have primarily been focused on traditional centralized data systems. It is an even more complex and challenging problem to capture such meanings for distributed systems since that requires individuals throughout the organization to contribute knowledge about the meaning and interpretation of their information. Once one has captured the data semantics, the opportunity exists to be able to use this knowledge to resolve differences between data from multiple sources or restate information to meet the requirements of different individuals or parts of the organization.

Even though we have been assuming a reactive environment in this section, there is still need for data resource management. This need arises from two forces. First, we are never in a truly reactive environment, and thus we would wish to take the opportunity to be proactive and plan our data whenever possible. Second, in order to be as responsive as possible when new requirements occur, it is necessary to plan, develop, and maintain an appropriate infrastructure to support these activities, which might include procedures needed to continually update the distributed data dictionaries and the data semantics. This area has traditionally received much less attention than proactive data resource management activities, because the technologies have only recently emerged and the organizational problems that one would expect in an organization that is highly reactive can be very difficult.

Returning to the theme identified at the beginning of this section, we note that an important goal is organizational flexibility and integration. This goal is not the exclusive property of IT professionals but, in fact, represents the realities of the business environment of the 1990s. Thus, the interplay between the business forces and IT must be paramount, and the IT must be as responsive as possible in meeting these evolving needs. The technologies that have been identified provide important advances that can make these goals more attainable.

FLEXIBLE IT ARCHITECTURES

Given that we wish to support both proactive and reactive information technology strategies, certain IT architectures can provide considerable assistance. We want a flexible system architecture that can easily adapt to organizational changes, geographic shifts, and alternating forces of centralization and decentralization.

As part of our research, we have developed an example of such an architecture that consists of seven major functional components (see Figure 2-8). These components are separated into five layers. This architecture attempts to mediate the conflicts among the goals of autonomy, integration, and evolution. All the layers of this architecture, except for message control and data control, lend themselves to as much, or as little, autonomy as desired—and the balance can easily be changed.

Overview of Components

The components shown in Figure 2-8 are logical entities. Each may correspond to a separate computer, or all may coexist in a single computer. For purposes of an overview discussion, let us assume that each component is a physically separate computer. In this case, each group could acquire and manage its own resources, including (1) terminal/network gateways, (2) application processing computers and software, and (3) database computers and software. In the past these three decisions were often bundled together; with this architecture we can respond to the typical case where the highest degree of concern for autonomy involves the application processing, with a lesser concern for the database and often a minimal concern for the diverse external interface. This is because it is usually in the application processing that the key functionality of a group's activities is manifest. It is important that the group be able to adapt to changes in environments, goals, or products rapidly.

Whereas the application processing may be tightly coupled to the activities of the group, the database requirements are more variable. In many cases there are separate databases for each application. But it is expected that many of these will merge in response to the organization's need for integrated data access. The architecture of Figure 2-8 facilitates access to each of the databases and provides an evolutionary path for eventually integrating these databases, as the needs for integration intensify.

Integration and Evolution Aspects of the Architecture

The message control and data control components of the architecture address the issues of integration and evolution. They are the points at which all processing is coordinated. For example, in principle, any terminal can access any application (assuming appropriate permissions and authorizations). Similarly, any application subsystem can utilize the shared data resources to manage and maintain data that are common to more than one component.

Message control and data control are both conceptually *single* entities. The other components are *types* of processing functions. There may be many instances

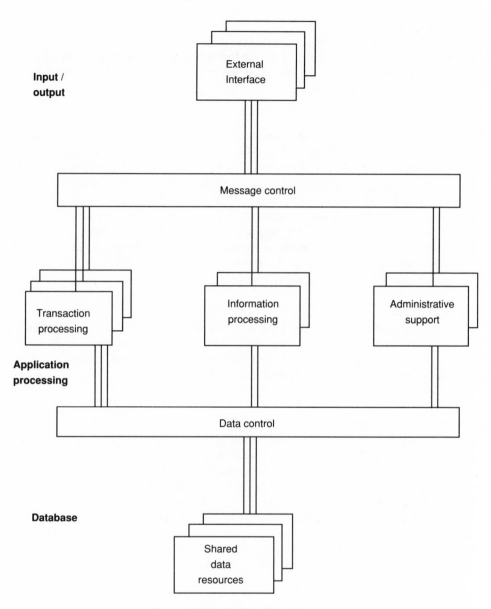

Figure 2-8. A flexible IT architecture.

of each type (multiple external interfaces, multiple transaction processing systems, and multiple shared data resources).

Components of the Architecture

It is important to reemphasize that the components of Figure 2-8 are *logically* separate. They can be mapped to physical hardware in various ways, some examples of which are provided later.

External Interface

The external interface provides the entry point to the system. In the case of banking systems, the external entities may fall into five categories: (1) payment networks, (2) communications networks, (3) customer terminals, (4) professional workstations, and (5) other intra- and/or interbank systems.

Message Control

Message control coordinates the passage of messages between processing components. This involves routing, translation, sequencing, and monitoring. *Routing* accepts a request for delivery of a message to a particular logical function and determines the currently appropriate physical address; thus, routing can accommodate changes in the availability and location of functions. *Translation* maps a limited number of protocols from one standard to another. *Sequencing* determines the order in which messages are delivered to recipients on the basis of priorities. *Monitoring* determines the state of the messages within the system at any given time; this includes ensuring the integrity of the message from the time it is presented by one component until it is accepted by another.

Data Control

Data control coordinates access, format, and passage of data between application processing functions and shared data resources. It routes queries and updates to the appropriate component of shared data resources, maintains concurrency control over the shared data, and returns responses to the requesting application processing function.

Shared Data Resources

Shared data resources holds the information for one or more applications. Although this activity is logically centralized in shared data resources, it may contain multiple separate components (for example, each storing different segments of the shared data of different organizations). Shared data resources performs two functions: information management and storage management. *Information management* determines what information must be accessed to satisfy the request, performs the data transformations necessary, and determines how the information is to be stored or retrieved. *Storage management* determines the physical location of data on the storage devices and controls the actual data movement.

Application Processing

The integrating application-independent layers (external interface, message control, data control, and shared data resources) surround the application processing components. These application processing components can be divided into three classes: transaction processing, information processing, and administrative processing.

Transaction processing refers to the applications that support specific operational activities, such as order entry in a manufacturing environment or account balances in a financial environment. This includes many application-specific subfunctions such as *validation,* which ensures that all information needed for processing is present and that the transaction does not violate limits, conditions, or policies that have been established; and *data update,* which records the impact of the transaction (e.g., update inventory balance) and initiates other transactions (e.g., billing) and manual instructions (e.g., a packing slip).

Information processing refers to all application processing subsystems that perform analysis, calculations, or restructuring of the data (e.g., producing a consolidated financial statement). Sample subfunctions include specialized user interaction (e.g., graphics), static reporting, ad hoc reporting, and coordination with external data resources.

Administrative processing provides facilities for the performance of office functions by administrative or managerial personnel. This activity is required to maintain organizational, procedural, or personal information. Sample facilities include electronic mail, word processing, correspondence files, and scheduling.

Sample Configuration

The hypothetical situation depicted in Figure 2-9 illustrates some of the various configurations possible using the above principles. The distributed system approach directly follows the "each component is a separate computer" route. These components could range from individual personal computers to individual minicomputers, or even to individual mainframe computers—depending on the performance requirements of each component. Appropriate communication facilities (depicted as vertical lines) interconnect the individual components, most likely a high-performance, possibly redundant, local area network.

The mainframe approach places all of the logical components on a single physical computer. There are explicit intracomputer communication procedures (depicted as vertical dotted lines) used to communicate among the components that parallel those used in the distributed system approach. Thus, in principle, identical or almost identical software modules can be used in both the distributed system and mainframe approaches. Although Figure 2-9 may imply that this approach would be most appropriate for large sites, it may, in fact, be used in very small sites where a single "small mainframe" (e.g., a minicomputer or powerful personal computer system) hosts all of the logical components.

Two other variations—minimal installation and partial installation—are also depicted in Figure 2-9. In the minimal installation only certain layers are present (such as external interface message control). Note that all of message control and data control components are connected (depicted as horizontal dark lines). Thus, any transaction entered from Hong Kong can be forwarded by its message control component to the appropriate site for processing that transaction, which could be either New York or London in Figure 2-9.

In the partial installation all layers are present, but not all components are. For example, the administrative support components may be present but not the transaction processing components. Thus, certain activities, such as word processing, may be completely processed locally, but other activities, such as order entry, will need to be forwarded to another site as in the minimal installation situation.

The minimal installation makes it possible to provide all of the company's information resources in a consistent, compatible manner to all locations, no matter how small. The partial installation makes it possible to customize a configuration to best meet the high-volume, high-performance requirements of a site yet still provide con-

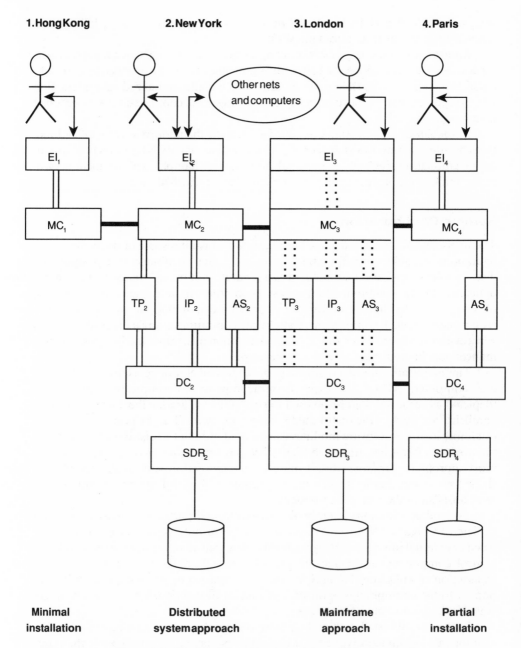

Figure 2-9. Flexible IT architecture: A hypothetical example.

sistent compatible access to other resources that may be of lower volume and are less critical. Furthermore, evolution from minimal to partial to full, or vice versa, can be accomplished in a smooth manner as the needs and structure of the organization change.

One more point is worth noting. Even the apparently full configurations, depicted as New York and London, may need to communicate with other sites for components that are not present locally. For example, if TP_2 and TP_3 support different types of transactions, New York will have to forward TP_3-type transactions to London.

To illustrate the cooperative nature of this architecture, consider a transaction of type TP_3 that needs to operate on data stored in shared data resource SDR_4 that is entered from a terminal connected to EI_1 in Hong Kong. The message control component MC_1 realizes that TP_3 is not local and forwards the request to its compatriot MC_3 in London for processing. TP_3 tells its data control component DC_3 that it needs certain information to process this transaction. DC_3 realizes that the data needed are stored on the shared data resource SDR_4, so it forwards the request to its colleague DC_4, who coordinates access to SDR_4. This path is then "rewound" as the data from SDR_4 are provided to TP_3, who processes it and in turn provides the appropriate response to the user in Hong Kong via EI_1. Although in reality we would expect most requests to be much simpler and only involve a single site, the situation could also be much more elaborate if the application required data from multiple shared data resources and/or it automatically generated one or more new transactions that circulated through the system to accomplish their functions.

The important thing to note about this architecture, and this simple example, is that it allows tremendous organizational flexibility and autonomy yet provides powerful capabilities for integration, cooperation, and coordination. Although this discussion has been somewhat abstract and idealized given current-day technical shortcomings, there are many organizations moving in this general direction already, such as Citibank's Foundation Software Architecture and the Internal Revenue Service's Vision 2000 Technical Architecture.

CONCLUSIONS

The key message of this section is that there is significant good news to look forward to from information technology. The advances that are forecast provide for significant improvement through dramatic reductions in cost and improvement in speed, performance, and functionality of such magnitude as to provide opportunities that cannot be fully identified at this time. This is similar to the way the advances in telephone technology made possible new ways to run organizations that were not foreseen at the time telephone technology was first introduced.

Some of the most revolutionary IT developments involve vastly improved and more convenient human interface to the systems, the ability to support the cognitive activities of the users, and the ability to access distributed information and use data semantics to gain a more compatible and comprehensive view across the entire organization.

It is important to realize that many of these benefits are not self-applying. Attention and action on the part of management are critical. An analogy I have found effective involves giving a power saw to a lumberjack. The lumberjack picks up this saw with a groan and attempts to move the saw back and forth in a cutting motion, complaining about how difficult it is because the power saw is so heavy and because the teeth on the chain keep moving. The problem is that nobody explained that there is an ON switch that would enable the power saw to perform the cutting motion itself. In a similar vein, merely "dumping" new IT into an organization does not necessarily mean that it will be used in a productive manner. This represents the major challenge for management of the 1990s.

CHAPTER 3

The Past and Present
as a Window on the Future

JOANNE YATES AND
ROBERT I. BENJAMIN

The focus of this chapter is shown in Figure 3-1. This chapter considers the MIT90s framework from a historical perspective, beginning with the development of the telegraph in the mid-1800s. By understanding changes accompanying information technology in the past we will be better able to understand its future possibilities as well as what is necessary to realize them. IT is revolutionary in many respects: the way it can be used to coordinate and control production processes; the way it has enabled unprecedented cost reductions of basic component prices (because of IT's generality of application, which has permitted massive market expansion); and the numerous ways the technology distances both blue- and white-collar workers from the physical elements of labor.

Over time IT has changed key business factors by orders of magnitude. For communicating limited amounts of important information, the telegraph reduced the effect of time and distance by two orders of magnitude and played a crucial role in enabling the establishment of the vertically integrated business organization, an organizational structure that emerged in the late 1800s and has been the dominant form for at least the last fifty years. For the last three decades IT components have been improving their cost performance at a rate of 30 percent or more per year and increasingly present an ever more favorable substitution for other forms of investment, thus encouraging new applications.

Historically, IT has been a vehicle of change in firms, both by itself and when coupled with other technologies. In all these instances IT has made possible better coordination of business enterprises. The improved coordination comes from three properties of IT: the ability to collapse time and distance effects, the ability to substitute generalized for highly specific tasks and processes, and the ability to capture and use organizational memory.

The historical record supports a fundamental lesson that has been learned from the program's case studies: that IT, to be successful, must be harmonized with its organizational context. An organization's choice of IT,

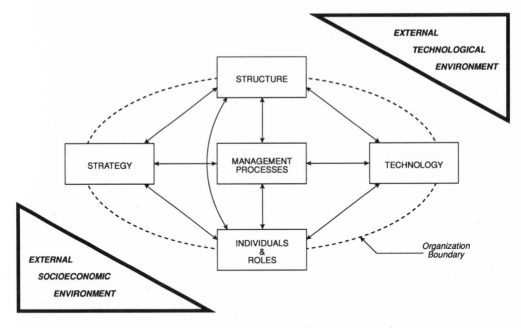

Figure 3-1. MIT90s framework—Chapter 3 emphasis.

and its implementation, must be consistent with its choices of strategy, organizational structure, management processes, and human resource policies and practices. Only then can its full potential be realized.

In the 1990s, organizations and managers must make important decisions about investments in and strategic uses of IT. Clearly these decisions should be predicated on the most complete understanding available to us of that technology and the changes it is likely to induce. This understanding requires that we look at IT from a broader perspective than is typically adopted. We might begin by asking whether the computer and other forms of information technology are essentially different from or similar to other technological innovations of today and yesterday. That is, to what extent can we expect to gain insight by studying changes related to other technologies?

Recently, several individuals have argued that the characteristics and uses of information make the role of information technology inherently different from that of other technologies. Beniger (1986), for example, argues that information is uniquely powerful because it can be used to control production processes. He positions today's IT as the latest phase of a control revolution that began in the nineteenth century in response to the speeding up of production technology. Malone (1988) defines IT's uniqueness and revolutionary nature in terms of its difference from production processes. He characterizes IT as the first *coordinating* technology, as contrasted with the production technologies that evolved from the Industrial Revolution.

Zuboff (1988) identifies another unique and revolutionary aspect of IT in her book *In the Age of the Smart Machine.* She states that IT does not simply *automate* information-handling processes; it also *informates,* or generates large quantities of information previously unavailable to the organization. She shows how this additional information can be used to improve the operation of the organization and identifies a crucial implementation issue: whether the increase in information will be used to further increase management's control over the work force or to empower the work force to make improvements in their responsibilities.

Jonscher (1988) notes two unique characteristics of information that shape its uses and consequently the role of IT in the economy. First, a very limited set of symbols can represent a virtually limitless variety of information on any subject. Thus, the market for IT is enormous, creating massive economies of scale. In addition, he points out, the value of information is independent of the physical form taken by the symbols expressing it. Thus, the physical resources (paper, magnetic tape, etc.) needed to represent information can be reduced without reducing the information's value. Together these two characteristics create unprecedented economic opportunities for IT.

Others have seen IT as revolutionary but not unique. Simon (1987), for example, compares the computer to the steam engine. The steam engine, he argues, triggered a revolution by its broad applicability: "No single-purpose device is going to bring about a revolution, however convenient or useful it may be. Revolutionary significance lies in generality" (p. 3). The computer has similar generality and a similar ability to be used for many different tasks. Just as the steam engine triggered the first Industrial Revolution, the computer seems to be triggering a second one.

Bolter (1984) also notes similarities in the revolutionary effects of the steam engine and of IT. He argues that IT is one of the defining technologies in our cultural history in that it, like the steam engine before it, has changed our perception of our relationship to nature. The steam engine opened up the potential for mass production, which led to the specialization of jobs one step removed from the task as a whole. The IT revolution has further distanced us from the physical task of production while in some uses enabling reduced specialization. For example, let us look at the various mental and physical steps associated with design and development: conceptualization, drawing, physical model building, and machine tool configuration. Now all the steps, including the model building and machine tool programming, are done on the computer screen. On the one hand, this change removes us further from our artisan roots (i.e., the physical fabrication of products); on the other, it allows a designer or design team to deal with the overall design and development, as in traditional craft industries, rather than fragmenting it among a series of specialists. Although the changes initiated by the steam engine and IT differ, both, he argues, have revolutionary implications.

The view that IT is revolutionary (whether or not it is unique) is in concert with the position taken in this section and throughout the 1990s program research: that business coordination is radically changed by IT and its applications. Later in this chapter we discuss characteristics of IT that enable increased business coordination. In developing our argument, we will take advantage of a set of comparisons not mentioned in any of the treatments of IT just described: historical comparisons to yesterday's information technologies. Because the recent revolution has been so rapid and extensive, we often consider IT wholly new, forgetting that it has a past. Yet its past was in many ways as revolutionary as its present. For example, the telegraph dramatically changed the nineteenth-century world by its shrinking of time and space. Understanding changes surrounding IT in the past can help us think more clearly about the opportunities and challenges of the future. The historical perspective provides us with long-term longitudinal data largely lacking in studies of current technology. Although historical comparisons are never perfect, they can be useful analytic tools in thinking about the future.

IT innovations have occurred throughout history, including such developments as writing itself and later the printing press. All of these had revolutionary implications for their times. In this chapter, however, we will focus on a single historical period that saw multiple IT innovations, the period from 1840 to 1950, as a basis for contrast with the modern period of IT innovation. Beginning with the telegraph, introduced to the United States in 1844, and including the typewriter, the telephone, and the Hollerith tabulating maching in the decades surrounding the turn of the century, a series of innovations in IT played a role in transforming the use of information in organizations. Both similarities and discontinuities between this period, which we will call the historical period, and the period of modern IT, beginning with the widespread adoption of the computer in the 1960s, can provide guidance in anticipating future changes.

We will begin by examining the nature of past and present ITs. Then a long-term view of the economics of IT will help us better understand the impact of recent changes. Next, we will discuss some key characteristics of IT: its compression of time and distance, its expansion and transformation of organizational knowledge, and its flexibility and adaptability to the needs of virtually any organization. From these characteristics come IT's ability to enable coordination between and within organizations, a dominant theme in the program research. Yet IT does not cause this coordination; it only presents opportunities. In the past and present, these opportunities have been realized only in the context of favorable developments in the key areas of the program's change paradigm: strategy, structure, control processes, and human resources. Based on that framework, we will discuss what is needed to exploit the opportunities offered by IT.

THE FUNCTIONS OF IT IN HISTORICAL PERSPECTIVE

Although *information technology* is a relatively new term, techniques for accomplishing the same tasks have been around for a long time. The similarities between past, present, and future technologies are clearest if we look at IT as having four different functions: conversion, storage, processing, and communications. These four functions are comparable to Jonscher's (1988) input-output, storage, processing, and transmission. Although this functional approach clarifies the continuities between past and present, it also reveals one key discontinuity. In the historical period and even into the early modern period, the four functions were handled more or less independently. Recently, however, the thrust has been toward increasing integration of these functions. This new trend has significant implications for the future of IT.

Let us begin by illustrating the four functions of IT, then look at their recent integration.

Conversion

Information can be converted from one form to another both when it is entered into an information device or system (input conversion or encoding) and when it leaves a device or system (output conversion or decoding). Input conversion transforms the information into a form appropriate to the device, whereas output conversion transforms the information back into a form convenient for the people who will be using it.

Today, input conversion for computers of all sizes occurs primarily via keyboard, a method that replaced the card punching predominant fifteen years ago. Document scanning is also playing an increasingly important role in input conversion. As artificial intelligence technology improves, through innovation and increased capacity, increasingly more complex modes of input conversion will be possible. In the future, for example, voice recognition technology should become more common. Input conversion is not a new process, however. In the nineteenth century, most telegraphs depended on the conversion of information into a series of Morse code taps on the telegraph key. At the end of the century, the Hollerith machine depended on punched cards (direct predecessors of the computer punch cards) that converted data into a form it could process.

Output conversion today can occur via a screen display, a printer, or a facsimile device, for example. Voice output is just beginning to join these other technologies as a method of converting information stored in machine language into a form understood by humans. In the nineteenth century, output could be converted to a form understandable to its users through a printing telegraph or an individual translating Morse code tapes. When used to transcribe handwriting or shorthand notes, the typewriter converted output to a form more readily understood by humans. Duplication, or the creation of multiple copies of an information output, may be viewed as a special case of output conversion. Carbon paper was an early version of this, and photocopying and printers provide more recent examples.

Storage

Information can be stored in a variety of forms (such as text or structured data) and media (such as paper or magnetic disks) for later output and/or processing. Storage must both preserve the information in as compact a form as possible and make it as readily accessible as possible.

Today, computer-readable information is stored on disks, tapes, and video disks (including CD-ROM). The information can be stored as alphanumeric data or text, as structured data (in a database or spread sheet), or as a bit-image representation of complex graphics, voice, or music. Because they require very large amounts of memory, bit-image representations are just becoming affordable. Depending on how it is coded and stored, information can be retrieved in different ways. For example, information in a database of customers might be accessible by company name, name of contact, date of last visit, order, and so on. Electronic mail messages can be retrieved by date, sender, and even key words in the subject line or message. Although voice mail users currently have fewer choices in how they retrieve voice messages, technological advances will surely widen their available choices in the future.

The familiar vertical files in every office today were viewed as a major innovation when they appeared at the end of the nineteenth century (Yates, 1982). Previously, copies of outgoing correspondence were stored in bound chronological volumes, separate from related incoming correspondence stored in pigeonholes or box files and from internal documents stored haphazardly, if at all. Vertical files were introduced as a storage system in which documents from any source could be combined and arranged by subject, region, or any other category.

Vertical files are still a major element of current office equipment, in spite of repeated predictions of the paperless office. They contain documents never converted to machine-readable form as well as paper backups of computerized text. It remains to be seen whether vertical files of paper will be drastically reduced in the future as developments in optical scanning and video disk storage technology, for example, make possible input and storage of enormous amounts of text and data in minimal space, at minimal cost, and in processable form.

Processing

Processing includes the manipulation of text or structured data, including arithmetic computation. Today, information can be processed at mind-boggling speeds in mainframes, minicomputers, and microcomputers. Applications range from the straightforward sorting and calculating of accounting systems to the more complex manipulations of expert systems. The growing processing speed and storage capacity, along with increasingly powerful computer languages, enable complex database manipulation, three-dimensional graphic design, expert systems, and other such applications.

The first serious attempts to speed up information processing in American business appeared in the late nineteenth and early twentieth centuries, as new methods of management came increasingly to depend on the compilation and analysis of quantitative information. First came manual methods of sorting cards with information encoded by means of punched holes or attached tabs. Mechanical adding machines, such as that patented by Burroughs, accelerated simple computations. Then electromechanical devices such as the Hollerith machine were developed to sort and compute the data encoded on punched cards. Originally developed to handle the massive amounts of data collected in the 1890 U.S. Census, this calculating technology soon found more general applications in the business world. These new methods of processing encoded information required input conversion and output conversion, an initial step toward the integration of IT functions.

Communications

As one of the functions of IT, communications is the transmission of information from one place to another. The distance spanned can be small (e.g., from a computer to a connected printer) or large (across the country or around the world). Today we can choose from a growing array of communications media. Information can be transmitted around the globe in audio, text, structured data, or visual forms, using technologies ranging from fiber optic cables to satellites. In the next ten years we can anticipate a move toward multimedia communications—combining audio (voice, music, etc.), text, full-motion graphics, and video—that will allow us more closely to simulate normal modes of face-to-face human interaction across enormous distances.

In the early nineteenth-century, the postal system, supplemented by various private mail services such as the Pony Express, handled the transmission of information as well as physical goods. Advances in the technology of transportation, from the improvements of roads for stagecoaches to the spread of the railroads, increased its speed. The mid-nineteenth century saw the introduction of electromagnetic communications in the form of two dramatic innovations: the telegraph and the telephone. Before the telegraph, information generally traveled no faster than humans or goods traveled; after it, information was separated from the limitations of the physical transportation infrastructure and could travel from one point to a far distant one in a matter of seconds and minutes. The telegraph transmitted alphanumeric text converted into Morse code rapidly from one point to another. The telephone, introduced a few decades later, transmitted the more complex human voice; this was the first increase in bandwidth of electromagnetic telecommunications. It supplemented rather than displaced the telegraph, since both had advantages: the telegraph left a record, whereas the telephone allowed real conversation. And neither replaced the mail. From the start, communications media have tended to be additive, always increasing our options rather than simply replacing one with another.

The communications network serves as an infrastructure of similar importance to the transportation infrastructure. Achieving common standards that allow easy intercommunication is critical to realizing the full advantage of a communications infrastructure. Market forces promoted the standardization of railroad gauges so that freight could travel across the country on different companies' rails but without being transferred to different cars. In the telegraph and telephone industries, competition, patent fights, and regulation led to the initial consolidation of monopolies in the United States. Even with the breakup of the Bell system, connectivity and consequently at least partial standardization are matters of U.S. government regulation. Internationally, standards in telegraph, telephone, radio broadcasting, and other communications technologies have emerged from cooperative efforts by international organizations (both governmental and nongovernmental) and/or from the political or economic power of some country or company to impose a standard on others. The economic value of interconnectivity of the infrastructure is so great (as Rotemberg and Saloner note in Chapter 4) that standards, such as ISDN, are likely to emerge to promote it.

INTEGRATING IT FUNCTIONS

As noted above, the functions underlying modern information technology as well as devices for facilitating them have existed for a long time. Many of the developments of the 1960s and 1970s simply made these functions faster and less expensive. But additionally, a new and important trend has emerged: the integration of the four separate functions into integrated information systems. Although certain earlier technologies might link two of the information functions (e.g., the Hollerith machine and punched cards linked storage with processing), the links were limited. Today, at a single microcomputer or workstation, one can type in data, manipulate them, store them in the computer (or print them out for storage in paper files), and send them to another location across a building or across a continent. The receiver of the data can do likewise.

The integration of all four functions, although still immature and still facing various compatibility problems, promises to generate enormous gains in the functionality of IT, and thus to create opportunities for new strategic uses of IT (see Chapter 2). One clear source of gain from such integration comes from reducing the number of times a piece of information must undergo input conversion. A buyer's order for a supplier's product used to require multiple reentries of the same data for various stages of storage and processing, first within the purchasing firm, then in communicating to the supplier, and finally within the supplier's firm. All of these input conversions took time and introduced many opportunities for error. IT integration within each of the firms, fairly common today, allows the order to be keyed in just once in the buyer's firm for storage, processing, and communication within it; then, after it is transferred to the supplier in paper form, the order is entered just once for all its uses within that firm.

Moreover, with integration across firm boundaries, just beginning to emerge as electronic data interchange standards emerge, the supplier can receive the order electronically rather than on paper, eliminating the need for that firm to enter the data at all. Thus, although outputs are possible at any stage, only one input conversion is needed. The elimination of multiple conversions is particularly valuable since, as Jonscher's analysis of IT cost drops has shown, the cost of input/output technology has declined less than that of storage, processing, and communication technology.

Additional gains may be realized as IT integration is used to collapse more steps in existing processes. The elimination of steps reduces the number of intermediaries in the process, with potential reductions in direct labor cost, inventory cost, and process time. A number of writers have noted the importance of eliminating intermediaries. This new integration of the IT functions clearly has enormous implications for firm strategy and structure, which will be discussed later in this chapter. It also demonstrates both the value and limitations of historical analogy. To use knowledge of past IT in studying present and future IT, we must keep in mind both the continuity of IT functions and the discontinuity of their integration.

THE ECONOMICS OF IT

As the preceding discussion illustrates, the four IT functions have long been with us, though their integration is quite recent. This integration is one source of IT's remarkable dynamism in our economy today. Another, perhaps more basic source resides in its economics. In this section we explore what might be termed the economic imperative of IT, examining its causes and implications.

Rapidly falling costs alone have been a powerful factor in the evolution and applications of information technology in recent decades. Beginning in 1960 with the mass production of the transistor, however, several basic components of IT (electronic memories, logic devices, and random access storage) have shown cost performance improvements in the range of 30 to 40 percent per year (Jonscher, 1988; Benjamin, 1982). This rate of change adds up to more than an order-of-magnitude improvement in cost performance per decade. The major research labs in the IT industry expect this trend to continue for at least twenty to thirty years.

Certainly this cost performance exceeds that of ITs of the historical period. With technologies such as the telegraph, the typewriter, and the adding machine, the innovations generated lowered costs for the functions when they were introduced but did not continue to generate such savings over time. A ten-word telegram sent from New York to Chicago declined in price only 50 percent in the entire century from 1850 to 1950 (0.7 percent per year), for example, whereas Jonscher estimates that the cost of data transmission has fallen at approximately 15 to 20 percent per year for the last two decades. IT appears to have fallen in price at no greater rate than other technologies up until 1960, but since then its cost performance has been exceptional.

Jonscher attributes this rapid drop not to the characteristics of microelectronic technology but primarily to enormous demand generated by the growth of information management as a component of the economy and by the wide applicability of the technology. A huge market for IT drives rapid progress down the learning curve, lowering cost and consequently further expanding demand. His explanation does not account for why this downward spiral only began in the 1960s, rather than earlier with the introduction of the typewriter, adding machine, and telegraph. We note, however, that both the level of scientific and technical knowledge attained (in particular, the development of the transistor) and the vast resources the military invested in IT during and after World War II may acount for the starting point. Certainly the demand for such flexible and generalizable technologies explains its continuance since then.

The mass market from expanded use of IT enabled mass production and consequent learning curve effects. These in turn translate into rapidly falling cost, newly affordable applications, and further enlargement of the mass market. For example, there were about 5.8 million workstations (personal computers and on-line terminals) in American offices in 1981. At that time, Benjamin predicted that by 1990 workstations would be as common as the telephone in the office. Current statistics as well as predictions suggest that workstation ubiquity is fast approaching. By 1986 the figure for total workstations had risen to 27 million, and the Institute for the Future (1988) predicts that by 1995 there will be 60 million workstations. At that point, according to the forecast, nearly 90 percent of the white-collar work force will have workstations. This growth in the number of workstations will, of course, bring further learning curve effects and new affordable applications. Moreover, the IT now being adopted for consumer products such as watches, cameras, copiers, and cars will also feed the spiral.

Although the falling cost and growing use of IT is instructive, its relationship to other factors such as the cost of labor in the United States further highlights its power in transforming the workplace. Given the rapid drop in cost of IT, the ratio of technology to labor cost has changed much more rapidly than the corresponding ratio for other technologies we have observed. Over the three decades from 1950 to 1980 the ratio of general technology cost (for a composite of such technologies as automobiles and cameras) to the cost of labor in the United States showed a very modest improvement of about 1.5 times for each decade (Benjamin and Scott Morton, 1988). For the same period, given the decrease of IT's cost by about 30 percent per

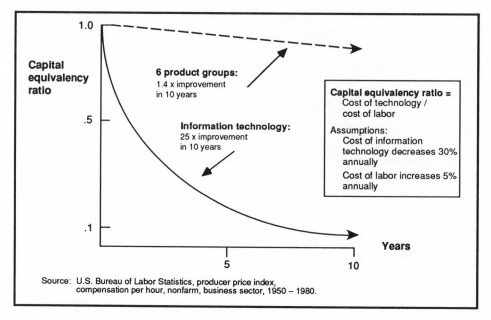

Figure 3-2. Capital equivalency ratio: Information technology vs. six product groups.

year, along with an increase of labor cost of 5 percent per year, we get an improvement in the capital-to-labor ratio of twenty-five times per decade (see Figure 3-2). Thus, IT capital is uniquely leveraged with respect to labor cost, making investment in IT highly attractive. This rapidly changing ratio also means that the cost of the IT necessary to support a person or process has become such a small percentage of the cost of that person or process that the emphasis is shifting from optimizing the IT system to optimizing the process or the person's efforts. With this shifting emphasis, human resource issues become increasingly central to the implementation process.

IT's cost imperative shows itself in several ways: pure cost reduction, increased functionality, and combinations of both. Switzerland's loss of the watch market to Japan (Landes, 1984) is an example of pure cost reduction. Within ten years the Japanese, riding the cost curve of IT, were able to reduce the cost of the digital watch to about 3 percent of the cost of its competitors, and to sell more reliable timepieces. The Swiss watch market was decimated. Only when the Swiss began competing on other dimensions (such as fashion) could they reclaim any of the lost market.

Increased functionality has been more important than reduced cost in the personal computer market. The microcomputers of 1980 and 1988 cost about the same, but the functionality of the 1988 workstation is enormous compared to that of the 1980 workstation. In Chapter 2 of this book, Madnick predicts similar gains in functionality and thus in applications by 1995. Although the 1980 mass-market personal computer offered basic word processing, today's more powerful machines offer sophisticated desktop publishing. The next generation of personal computers will have the power to offer a number of high-performance and artificial intelligence aids (e.g., hypertext, page layout advisors, etc.) for the reader or writer of documents, as well as for other applications.

Developments in the large computer show both cost reduction and increased functionality. The same computing power would cost the equivalent of one year's clerical labor of 2,000 people in 1970, of 200 people in 1980, and of fewer than 10 people in 1990 (Benjamin, 1982). In addition, the newer mainframes include such features as much more sophisticated operating systems and massive virtual memory.

The case of facsimile transfer makes an interesting illustration of the dynamics by which lowering costs and improving functionality have brought a richer communication medium within reach. The first facsimile system for rapid transmission of images was a telegraphic technology created in the mid-1840s. It used a needle that scanned an image written on metal in nonconducting wax, transferring a reverse image to paper on the other end of the telegraph wires. This technology was slow and expensive; moreover, documents at that time rarely contained pictures or graphic displays. Thus, the system never became commercially viable. By the first half of the twentieth century, technical capabilities had improved considerably, promoting, for example, extensive use of wire photo services by newspapers throughout the world. After World War II, facsimile had been sufficiently developed for a wide range of applications to be considered and tried (Jones, 1949).

With the advent of the transistor and its ability to miniaturize and reduce costs, this technology was poised for growth. Yet in the 1970s, it penetrated the United States and Western European business markets only very slowly. Transmission time (about four to six minutes per page) and cost were still high and image quality low relative to the obvious applications. Japanese companies, however, saw that fax had extra value to them in transmitting their image-based language, for which Morse code could not be used (Katakana, a set of about fifty phonetic symbols used primarily for words adopted from other languages, makes some encoding possible, but it is severely limited in what it can express compared to the normal Japanese mix of Chinese and other characters.) Moreover, when a Japanese company wanted to communicate via telegram or telex with a Japanese employee or customer in another country, the message had to be translated into English, encoded into Morse code for transmission, then retranslated into Japanese. Facsimile technology could bypass these extra steps and their opportunities for error. Thus, Japanese companies invested rapidly in the development of facsimile technology, driving down the cost curve and rapidly expanding the market in Japan. (See also Chapter 4.)

By 1988, these advances had brought the cost down and speed and quality up sufficiently to make it affordable and desirable as a replacement for one-day express delivery services for many Western applications, as evidenced by the rapid market expansion in the United States and Europe. Further improvements in quality and speed at a given price should continue to expand its market.

The dramatic lowering of IT costs, along with the changing relationships between IT costs and labor costs, helps explain IT's enormous influence and rapid adoption. But focusing on cost alone ignores other factors. IT's power is equally rooted in its ability to compress time and space, to expand organizational knowledge, and to increase flexibility.

COMPRESSION OF TIME AND SPACE

The communications component of IT has radically compressed time and space over the last one and a half centuries. The telegraph's effect was perhaps the most dramatic. It reduced the transit time of information across the United States from weeks and even months to minutes. Communications technologies introduced since then— such as the telephone, radio and television, computer data communications, and fax—have focused on increasing the bandwidth of information that can be transmitted in an instant, thus continuing the compression. Recently, in analyzing coverage of superpower summits, Marvin Kalb noted that "the new sophistication of cameras and satellites has obliterated time and space. There is now no story, anywhere in the world, that cannot be covered live" (*New York Times,* June 7, 1988).

One way to gain perspective on the compression of time and space is to examine the relationship between those two factors as well as cost in communications technologies. In Table 3-1, we can see the gains in transmitting a page of text from Chicago to New York in the historical and modern periods. As this table shows, the biggest gain in speed occurred during the historical period. The telegraph speeded up communication by three orders of magnitude, with only one order of magnitude gained since. If we take cost into account as well, we see a more complete story. The railroad and the telegraph raised the speed per dollar by two orders of magnitude within less than two decades. The increases in bandwidth in the modern period have realized another three orders of magnitude improvement. The telegraph's effect on speed was profound, but its cost was still high enough to limit its uses. The falling cost, along with increasing speed, of recent advances in telecommunications has greatly increased its feasible applications.

Effects of Increased Speed

The changes wrought by improvements in the communications infrastructure were profound. By changing people's perceptions of time and space, they dramatically reduced inertia to expansion. For example, the telegraph, along with the railroad that

Table 3-1. Distance/Time/Cost Ratios (Transmitting One Page of Text From New York to Chicago, Approximately 850 Miles)

	Pre–railroad 1840s	Railroad 1850s	Telegraph 1850s	Data Communication 1988
Time (hours)	252	48	.083	.0019
Speed (mi/hr)	3.37	17.7	10,240	447,000
Cost (dollars)*	0.25	0.03	7.50	0.31
Mi/hr/$	13.5	590	1,370	1,440,000

*For pre–railroad and railroad, cost is the U.S. mail rate for a letter. For telegraph, the page of text is assumed to be reduced to 50 billable words by means of the compression and codes typically used then. Transmission time of five minutes includes conversion at both ends. For data communication, the cost is based on a one-minute phone connection at daytime rates. Time is assumed to be seven seconds. All costs are expressed in actual (not constant) dollars. The effects of inflation between the 1850s and 1988 would increase the miles/hour/$ further, making the contrast even more dramatic.

was spanning the continent at the same time, profoundly reduced the importance of distance in market interactions. Before its advent, markets were, with a few exceptions such as cotton, generally small and regional. Firms or individuals too far away from a given market center were at too great a disadvantage to want to compete in most markets. The new, high-speed mode of communication enabled regional stock and commodity markets, for example, to consolidate into national markets in the United States. The New York Stock Exchange became the node for a national stock market, and the Chicago commodities market became the node for an emerging national market of commodities futures made feasible by telegraph. The transoceanic cables of subsequent decades allowed interactions among the markets of different nations to develop as well.

The telegraph's ability to compress time and space was important in the expansion of firms as well as the growth of markets. Companies such as the British East India Company had shown that far-flung organizations were possible without instantaneous communication, but they sacrificed either responsiveness to changing conditions or central coordination and control, or both. They were inherently more risky, and most firm owners were not prepared to accept that risk. The telegraph gave firms a less risky opportunity to broaden market reach, enabling them to respond quickly to market demands while still retaining some central control. It thus may have helped them overcome their inertia with regard to geographical expansion. In the decade following the telegraph's march westward across the continent, many companies that had agents only along the well-traveled corridor from Philadelphia up to Boston, with its one- to two-day mail service, added agents in Chicago and other western cities. Because the telegraph was relatively expensive on a per-word basis, most firms used it primarily for urgent communication concerning specific transactions, though a few used telegraphic communications as part of rudimentary control systems.

Effects of Increased Bandwidth and IT Integration

More recent advances in IT have further compressed time and space, not by increasing speed but by increasing affordable bandwidth and by integrating communication with conversion, processing, and storage. Early in the modern period, international direct dialing made telephone communication with much of the world convenient and more affordable. Modern technologies such as fiber optic cable and satellite transmission speed ever-increasing amounts of data around the globe. This high-bandwidth communication makes more elaborate internal control systems feasible and affordable for geographically dispersed companies. For example, Rockart and DeLong (1988) describe Xerox's use of a worldwide document management network to coordinate business planning and executive decision making. Greater bandwidth can also be used to increase the richness of the communications medium. For example, image-based technologies, such as facsimile transmission, go beyond simple alphanumeric data to transmit visual images such as pictures, graphics, and signatures. We have seen that the cost of fax has fallen to the point that most businesses can afford to have them onsite. Video conferencing, an even richer medium, is still too expensive for most businesses to have at their own sites, and going to a regional conferencing center is both expensive and inconvenient. Tomorrow, falling prices of high-bandwidth communication should also bring this medium down a cost curve that makes it widely affordable.

Another way in which recent advances in IT have compressed time and space is by integrating communication with the other IT functions: conversion, storage, and processing. Telegraphic communication was converted into Morse code for transmission, then out of code into written form at the receiving end. It was storable in this written form but not ready for processing. The telephone, introduced in the 1870s, was a richer communications medium but left no record. With the emergence of telephone answering machines in the twentieth century, telephone messages could be stored, but storage was primitive and chronological (much like the early document storage in bound chronological volumes), requiring extensive searching to locate a given message or piece of information. Moreover, the stored messages could not be processed.

Modern IT increasingly combines functions to eliminate many conversion steps. Data transmission, for example, transmits data in a machine-readable and structured form that can be processed directly, as well as converted into understandable output. Such an integrated information system further compresses space. For example, the telegraph enabled a national stock market to emerge by making communication rapid, but actual trades still took place between individuals on the floor of the exchange. Today NASDAQ, the National Association of Securities Dealers' Automatic Quotation System, provides a fully electronic marketplace for the stocks of companies listed with it. Trading takes place not in any specific physical location but within the computer network. Similarly, although the Toronto Stock Exchange has a trading floor, relatively little activity takes place on it; instead, much of the activity takes place through its computer-assisted trading system (CATS) terminals.

Another example of the effects of integration has occurred in the news industry. In the mid-nineteenth century, the telegraph spawned wire services such as Reuters, AP, and UPI, which collected news from reporters stationed around the world. Photographic facsimile transmission enabled them to send news photos routinely by the early decades of the twentieth century. More recently, integration of IT functions coupled with high-bandwidth transmission have enabled national newspapers such as *USA Today* and the *Wall Street Journal* to compose text and pictures at a central location but electronically distribute the finished product to the printing facilities of local newspapers (which always had excess capacity) for daily production.

Opportunities for further IT integration are still plentiful. For example, voice messaging systems have integrated communication, conversion, and storage and have improved on the storage and retrieval capabilities of telephone answering machines. The systems still cannot be linked to processing, however. As voice recognition technology improves, we may anticipate that computers will be able to convert this voice signal directly into machine-readable form, thus also integrating it with word processing capabilities. Similarly, fax transmits images over telephone lines quickly and inexpensively, but usually not in a form that can be stored, retrieved, and processed. As the quality of document processing improves, the bandwidth of transmission increases, and the IT economic imperative drives down cost, we can expect further integration and thus compression of time and space.

Both the increases in bandwidth and the improvement of integration can be used to make IT processes across a distance more like those that occur naturally in a single location. ISDN, now in its initial stages, allows both voice and data communication over the newly implemented version of the telephone network. Eventually, it may be used to provide multimedia applications such as a combination of video conferencing, mutual access to a database for storage and processing, and shared document processing that would allow joint work on a report in real time, in a form approximating that of two people working in the same room. These forms of cooperative work via computer technology are receiving considerable attention in business and academic publications. As such capabilities emerge, they further reduce the constraints imposed by space and time.

EXPANSION AND TRANSFORMATION OF STORED KNOWLEDGE

As communications technology has compressed time and space, storage technology has expanded the amount and changed the nature of stored knowledge readily accessible to organizations. Before the mid-nineteenth century, most organizational knowledge was maintained in the minds and bodies of individuals and passed on by word of mouth and apprenticeship, if at all. Recorded information was scanty and inaccessible. Vertical filing and the Hollerith machine were among the first of many innovations in the historical and modern periods that have permitted an explosive growth in accessible organizational knowledge. Information became accessible through increasingly sophisticated means of retrieval. Although earlier forms of stored knowledge could only be retrieved by categories designated at the time of storage, for example, computerized texts can now be retrieved by searches for word combinations. As the cost performance of computer technology continues to improve, such retrieval methods are now on the verge of more widespread use.

The forms and uses of stored knowledge have evolved and expanded as the quantity and accessibility have increased. Vertical files stored and provided access to information in text form, and the Hollerith machine stored and processed structured data on punched cards. Today we can also store knowledge as procedures and even expertise to be evoked and used in conjunction with other types of data. Moreover, recent IT allows compact integration of storage and processing. For example, structured data stored in a database can be retrieved directly for use in programmed procedures, then stored again, with no intervening conversion. All of these factors—the increasing amount of knowledge we are accumulating, the increasingly sophisticated methods for accessing the particular kernel of information we need, the ability to store knowledge in a variety of forms, and the increasingly easy integration of stored knowledge with processing—contribute to the revolutionary power of modern IT. Let us examine these issues as we look at the four forms of organizational knowledge noted above: text, structured data, procedures, and expertise.

Vertical files stored information as text, whether it consisted of descriptions of procedures or records of operating data. To use operating information embedded in text, clerks had to locate the relevant documents, extract the needed data, perform comparisons or calculations as needed, and produce further documents with the results of the analysis. Vertical filing facilitated this process by allowing documents to be stored and retrieved more efficiently, according to any desired predesignated categories. The importance of this development to organizations of the time is demonstrated by statements such as this one: "It will already have become evident that it is impossible to sever the problem of finding a good practicable filing system from the whole problem of business organization" (Cope, 1913, p. 14). We could replace "filing system" with "information access system" and make the same statement today.

Today we can store many times more information in electronic text form and do much more with it. Text must undergo an initial conversion process (usually by keying it in) to be stored in electronic form, but conversion shows promise of becoming easier with improved optical scanning technology. Once in computer-readable form, text is much more accessible than before: it can be electronically indexed under a variety of preset designations or searched by word combinations. And although the storage itself may be centralized, modern networking enables access to a text from virtually anywhere in even the most widely dispersed organization. In fact, access has improved so much that the technical aspects of access are now secondary to political ones. As Zuboff (1988) points out, "Defining access rules to information de facto describes how the organization works." Moreover, although the text is not structured in a standardized form as data files are, we can "process" that text extensively, combining it with other texts, transforming it, and otherwise manipulating it.

All of these elements are contained in a system to support the legal staff at Xerox. Information is entered into the system either by scanning of documents or by direct input by the legal staff as they do their case work. Case information is then available to all legal staff internationally, through a centralized filing system and a network. Searches can be made for any desired logical combination of word patterns. Moreover, outside knowledge such as the Westlaw Legal knowledge base is also accessible through the system. Finally, the network allows the transmission of textual knowledge from one lawyer to another, in an example of an electronically linked cooperating work group. These innovative applications are still relatively rare but should increase with the emergence of generalized document management products such as that produced by Filenet.

Storage of structured, rather than textual, data has already had a great effect on the amount and nature of knowledge retained and used by organizations. At the end of the nineteenth century, at about the same time that vertical files were adopted, punch cards for manual, mechanical, and electromechanical storage and retrieval of standardized and structured data were introduced. These systems stored and provided rapid access to large quantities of predominantly quantitative data. The manual systems helped locate the desired cards but still required that a clerk extract the data, then convert them (by writing them down or entering them into an adding machine) before doing any processing. With the electromechanical Hollerith machine came the first partial integration of storage and processing of data. When punched cards were dropped through the preset machine, it not only "retrieved" the relevant data but also summed them. This advance greatly increased the organization's ability to manage and process large amounts of data. At the same time, it introduced a level of abstraction to management. Processes once managed and evaluated by personal oversight could now be judged by abstract standardized data.

The Hollerith machine, though advanced for its time, was, of course, quite primitive compared to current capabilities for storing and processing structured data. Modern computers and databases have increased the amount of standardized information that is available in organizations by several orders of magnitude per decade. These data can be plugged directly into processing without intermediate conversion. Moreover, as networks proliferate, the data become accessible from virtually anywhere.

The enormous growth in data would have outstripped methods of handling them if not for a further development in the storage of organizational knowledge during the modern period: the capturing of procedural knowledge in computer programs. Applications software automates a processing procedure to be applied to structured data, thus combining the two forms of stored knowledge. It is hard to overestimate the impact of this powerful combination on organizations. From accounting to planning and control, such applications have transformed the way organizations function. In addition, as Zuboff (1988) has pointed out, each time such a process is automated, a very large information by-product is created, increasing organizational knowledge even more.

Increasingly, such combinations of procedural and structured data have been built into products and services of strategic importance. For example, Otis Elevator has developed a "smart" elevator that monitors its own operation and lets the service force know it needs repairs before it becomes inoperable. In many cases, large databases and procedures for using them are offered as service products. The *New York Times* database is an example of such a product.

A final and recent development in organizational knowledge is the capturing not just of algorithmic procedures but of expert rules and decision criteria. Such knowledge can be used in situations that are much less structured than those appropriate to applications of procedural knowledge. We are now in the early stages of expert systems. These systems can be developed within a firm to capture and apply the knowledge of its own experts. For example, Digital's XCON helps determine the correct configuration for installing the computer systems it ships out, and American Express's credit advisor helps authorize charge purchases. Expert knowledge can also be embodied in a product that delivers this knowledge to organizations that do not have it in-house.

The increased quantity and the expanded range of organizational knowledge offered by modern IT promise advantages to organizations that know how to use that knowledge. There are, however, several implementation problems that must be solved. One class of issues that must be managed concerns the locus and use of captured organizational knowledge. Will this information be used to empower or to control individuals within the organization? Another set of issues surrounds the abstraction of data from physical reality. Ignoring the differences between physical experience and structured data can be counterproductive. These issues are discussed in Chapters 8 and 9 of this book and developed in considerable detail in Zuboff.

FLEXIBILITY

Information technology's power and its attractiveness in the marketplace reflect its flexibility, as well as its ability to compress time and space and to expand organizational knowledge. Its ready adaptability to many different types of information and tasks increases its range of applications, thus reducing its cost and increasing the tempo of adoption. Moreover, the combination of IT flexibility and human adaptability and innovation is a powerful creative force.

In the historical period of IT innovation, devices such as the typewriter, the telephone, vertical files, and the Hollerith machine all were adaptable to many different types of organizations and tasks. Many other information-handling devices with narrower ranges of application—such as ledger-posting equipment designed especially for use in a particular type of bound ledger, and pneumatic tube systems designed to deliver paperwork from one area of a facility to another—were also introduced. Because wide adoption of these general-purpose devices promoted further improvements to the technology as well as falling prices, the more flexible devices tended to dominate and often to drive out the more specialized ones.

Today's personal computers are even more flexible than the earlier ITs, integrating into a single system the role of the typewriter, the Hollerith machine, and even, via modems or local area networks, the telegraph. The stand-alone PC helps the individual perform many varied office tasks. When data communication is added, the PC becomes part of an even more flexible information system that transcends location. The microchip itself is perhaps the most flexible of all ITs, performing its generic information processing functions in everything from computers to manufacturing machinery to consumer products.

Early IT tended to be adopted with specialized operators—typists, file clerks, and Hollerith keypunch operators—as intermediaries. As the flexibility of the technology has further increased with the integration of IT functions, however, the trend toward specialized intermediaries has been reversed. The ability of word processing software to allow quick and easy corrections has reduced the need for expert typists, and the integration of word or number processing with communication has increased the incentive for managers and professionals to give up intermediaries in these tasks. Similarly, technologies such as bar code readers and portable computers that can be carried on the factory or warehouse floor reduce the need for specialized data entry clerks.

The increasing flexibility offered by IT is also being used to increase flexibility of manufacturing arrangements. Highly specialized mass-production assembly lines are beginning to give way to more flexible setups that can be changed quickly and easily. These provide a number of advantages to manufacturers, allowing them to reduce response time for meeting new market demands, to control just-in-time manufacturing for critical components, and to provide greater product variety to the customer. A final manufacturing goal available with the assistance of IT is mass customization. Early examples of this already have appeared. For example, Benjamin Moore Paint Company outlets now have intelligent paint blenders that analyze paint chips brought in by a customer and calculate the proper mix proportions to match it. Another example of mass customization is the new ability of telecommunications companies to configure their basic network into a number of virtual private-line networks to satisfy individual large customers. In both cases the technology also reduces specialized intermediaries. With the advent of the more powerful computing technologies of the next generation, we can clearly anticipate more and different forms of mass customization.

IT AND BUSINESS COORDINATION

We have now seen both the economic imperative driving information technology and its ability to compress time and space, expand organizational knowledge, and increase flexibility. Now let us focus more specifically on what may be defined as IT's key contribution in organizations: the role of information technology in coordinating business tasks, both within and between firms (e.g., Malone, 1988). IT can be used to achieve geographical coordination of a single stage in the value-added chain or to coordinate successive stages of the chain, such as the production of a product and its procurement as an input into another production process. ITs can be used by themselves or in tandem with other technologies to achieve coordination of business functions.

Coordination via IT

Advances in any one of the four functions, but especially in the communication function, have traditionally allowed and promoted improved coordination. The telegraph, for example, played a very important role in coordinating the efforts of multiple firms in market structures, thus promoting the growth of markets in the second half of the nineteenth century. Similarly today, growing networks of high-bandwidth data communication allow the stock markets of various nations to interact with each other in ways that make them more and more closely linked. They could, in theory, be linked to create one stock market for the whole world. At this point, the differing technical standards and public policies of different nations block complete coordination. If and when market pressures come to exceed political ones, however, we can expect the adoption of compatible standards and policies and the emergence of a single worldwide market.

   Communications technology can also be used as a mechanism for coordination within a firm. In America, since early telegraph wires usually ran along the railroad right-of-way, railroads were given extensive free or very inexpensive use of the wires as part of their contracts with the telegraph companies. Initially, most of them used the telegraph solely for urgent but incidental communication such as requesting that extra empty cars be sent to a station that had a batch of grain to be transported. The trains themselves were still moved, safely but inefficiently, on the basis of elaborate published rules and specific written orders. The discovery that the telegraph could be used to coordinate the flow of trains along the tracks was made almost accidentally by a superintendent of the New York and Erie Railroad in the early 1850s. In a few years, the Erie had developed an elaborate system of telegraphic dispatching to control train movement for better safety and efficiency. In subsequent decades, when growth had brought diseconomies of scale, the routine telegraphic reports of train locations came to be seen as a source of data to be recorded, stored, and analyzed to improve efficiency further. In Zuboff's terms, the railroad discovered and took advantage of the potential of this primitive and predominantly manual information system to "informate." Operations throughout the growing railroads could thus be coordinated for maximum efficiency.

   More recently, when the telephone network providers installed electronic switching centers to replace their old electromechanical relay systems, they had available both a high-volume transmission system for data and telephonic transmission and a control signal path between the electronic switching centers. As the utility of the control path slowly became apparent, AT&T discovered that it could use that control line to optimize its flow of traffic along the network. Again, the "informating" potential of an IT was realized.

The integrated IT systems that have evolved in the modern period can also be used to assist in coordinating business within and between firms. For example, multinational firms increasingly use computers and high-bandwidth data communications for coordinating operations within their far-flung operations. Moreover, the combination of great computing power with ready communication of large amounts of data allows increased coordination with less cost. Conversion time and costs can be minimized by initially converting the information to a machine-readable form, then processing, communicating, and reprocessing it all in the same form.

Large computerized databases often serve as a link between various functions, either within a company or between two companies. The same database can be used by engineering in design work and by production to guide production work, for example. Or, as firms such as American Hospital Supply (now Baxter Health Care) have shown, a single database can serve as the seller's order entry system and as a buyer's purchasing system, connected by terminals and data communications links. When industry standards become widely accepted, such databases can also serve as the center for electronic markets helping to match buyers and sellers (Malone, Yates, and Benjamin, 1987).

Coordination via IT Integrated with Other Technologies

Information technology can also be used in conjunction with other technologies to improve internal or external coordination. In the late nineteenth century, meatpackers such as Armour and Swift used the combination of telegraphic communication with mass slaughterhouse technology, rail transportation, and refrigerated cars to vertically integrate the meatpacking industry (Chandler, 1977). Western cattle had previously been shipped east on the hoof and sold to local slaughterhouses for each eastern metropolitan market. Both the transportation of the whole cow and the small-scale local slaughtering were expensive. Armour and Swift discovered that they could slaughter the cattle in large quantities and with economies of scale in the Midwest, if they could get the meat to market without spoiling. Refrigerated railroad cars, a recent innovation, made that possible, but communications technology was necessary to make this system profitable. By setting up a network of regional distribution houses along the East Coast and establishing a steady flow of telegraphic communication between these and the centralized slaughterhouses, the flow of perishable meat could be matched to the demand in such a way as to keep spoilage to a minimum. Thus, the telegraph helped promote vertical integration in this industry.

Today computers and telecommunications can be used in conjunction with production and transportation technology to match supply and demand of products in ways that reduce inventory expense. Just-in-time manufacturing systems allow a buyer and supplier (whether part of the same corporation or different ones) to coordinate production and shipment of an input to another production process, reducing the buyer's inventory of supplies to almost nothing. As the cost of electronic coordination has gone down and inventory costs have not, such close coordination has become economic even in industries with nonperishable products. Moreover, if the buyer has adopted flexible manufacturing technology, the ability to keep supplies very closely matched to needs on a weekly and even daily basis can be even more important in allowing it the full benefit from manufacturing flexibility.

Modern electronic coordination such as that used to achieve just-in-time manufacturing often spans the boundaries between firms, creating what we might call virtual vertical integration. Traditionally, transactions between firms have required more communication than those within firms (Malone, Yates, and Benjamin, 1987). Modern, high-bandwidth IT reduces the burden of transaction costs considerably. Moreover, integration across firm boundaries via IT eliminates some of the data entry and conversion steps previously required in the transaction. Both these advantages have the effect of encouraging more creative organizational options.

REALIZING THE OPPORTUNITIES OFFERED BY IT

In all of these examples, information technologies have been used to forward closer coordination both within and among firms. Yet IT only presents opportunities; other elements must be present to take full advantage of those opportunities.

IT and Strategy

In both the historical and modern periods, IT has made more efficient the implementation of existing firm strategies. By lowering costs and speeding processes, IT improves firms' profitability and competitiveness. More significantly, though perhaps less commonly, especially in the historical period, IT has also been used to support and even to drive new strategies. As Venkatraman demonstrates in Chapter 5, only when firms go beyond the efficiency-motivated uses to more creative, strategic uses of IT do they stand to gain its full potential benefits. Thus, strategic vision is often necessary to take full advantage of IT.

In some cases, the critical strategic insight involves recognizing that IT enables a firm to extend its business scope by changing the nature of its product. Certainly Armour and Swift benefited from their recognition that they could sell butchered meat rather than live cattle as their product. American Hospital Supply recognized that it could enhance its products with the ancillary services (e.g., purchase history files) offered through its order entry system. When the telephone network adopted electronic switching centers with a control signal path, network providers discovered that they could use the control network to differentiate special products such as 800 numbers. Finally, with the advent of integrated services digital networks (ISDN), telephone companies could further expand their product line by allowing the customers themselves to reconfigure the amount of line capacity they want on particular parts of their system and the way that capacity should split up (among voice, data, video, etc.), thus managing their own virtual private-line networks within the larger network.

Innovations in IT can also create opportunities for whole new businesses or product lines. For example, the telegraph opened the way for futures trading, to supplement or replace consignment trading. It also enabled firms such as the Bradstreet Agency (later to combine with R. G. Dun as Dun & Bradstreet) to establish regional and national credit-reporting services with frequently updated information. There are many current examples of new businesses evolving with the aid of IT, especially in the financial services sector. Merrill Lynch's Case Management Account, for example, started a shift that brought financial services companies into direct competition with banks. Each of these new businesses was built on an insight into new strategies made feasible by IT.

In other cases, the key strategic insight in a new and innovative use of IT is a reconfiguration of the value-added chain within or between firms. We have noted several changes in firm and market coordination of transactions in our discussion on IT and business coordination, and we will discuss structural issues in more detail below; nevertheless, it is worth emphasizing the potential importance of seeing the opportunities IT provides for such reconfigurations. The meatpackers, for example, had to see the potential for vertical integration offered by telegraphic coordination combined with refrigerated railroad cars. Such examples were rare then but more common now. For example, both American Airlines and United Airlines had the vision to extend their reservations systems, originally built for their own agents, into systems that included flights of other airlines, thus locking in large numbers of travel agents and benefiting from the revenues obtainable from making electronic markets.

Other strategic opportunities offered by IT involve ways to gain at least temporary competitive advantage. In the historical period, for example, newspapers saw the telegraph as offering the opportunity to gain an advantage over their competitors. They supported reporters in distant locations who could feed them stories via telegraph. In this case, as in some recent ones, the competitive advantage was only temporary; many newspapers took advantage of the telegraph to gain such news. Soon the cost of supporting reporters around the world became onerous, while the resulting news had become a competitive necessity rather than an advantage. The banding together of several newspapers to form a cooperative wire service, the Associated Press, provided a long-term solution. In the recent case of the airline reservations services, what started out as a way for American and United to gain competitive advantages over rivals rapidly created an opportunity for a new, revenue-generating business as an electronic market providing access to many airlines. We can anticipate many more cases in which uses of technology for competitive advantage are temporary, and in which the erosion of competitive advantage requires a shift of strategy.

As more individuals and firms become attuned to the strategic potential of IT, timing will become increasingly important to the success of such shifts. In Chapter 4, Rotemberg and Saloner note that the first mover has advantages in many realms. For example, the early moves by American and United to include other airlines on their systems gave them enormous advantages in that new market for reservations systems. A similar situation may exist in the hospital supply business. Baxter Health Care has recently begun to include other complementary and competing products on its previously mentioned order entry system (Malone, Yates, and Benjamin, 1989). Thus, Baxter has apparently concluded that it could gain an advantage as an early market maker, as well as a supplier, in that market.

One of the key issues in many areas of IT is what Rotember and Soloner call strategic interrelatedness. Standardization has important benefits for interconnected networks and for products demanding compatibility of components or of human skills. In cases where network connectivity benefits users, as we noted earlier, standards have typically emerged, whether through competitive forces, regulation, or the cooperative efforts of many. Similar forces are likely to operate in the case of data communications networks. Comparable mechanisms and outcomes have also emerged in other cases where standardization is not demanded by network connectivity but is highly desirable for other reasons. For example, as Rotemberg and Saloner note, the QWERTY typewriter keyboard (so-called after its top row of letters) was not the sole or even the most efficient arrangement for typewriter keys. In fact, the order was devised to minimize key jams in early models, not to make typing more efficient. Yet touch-typing skills were learned for a specific key arrangement, and skilled operators who could use any machine were clearly highly desirable. Thus, in ensuing competition, the keyboard with an early and large "installed base" won out and became standard. The inefficient but ubiquitous QWERTY keyboard still maintains its hold over all keyboard technologies.

Although the same dynamic operates in many realms today, the more rapid pace of innovation often makes the standards short-lived and consequently may make cooperation more desirable. The CPM operating system touted as standard on 8-bit personal computers at the beginning of the 1980s is now forgotten, and forms of DOS dominate on today's 16-bit systems. If 32-bit machines become the dominant form of personal computer in the 1990s, a different operating system will surely become standard. This speeding up of technological change makes rapid emergence of standards via cooperative action more desirable than ever. Long and expensive battles to establish standards may yield competitive advantage for periods too short to be worth it. Thus, the most valuable strategic vision may increasingly take cooperative rather than competitive forms, as we can see in some cases today. At this stage, for example, we see gradual cooperative movement toward an open UNIX operating system, even though competitive behavior is still in evidence as well.

Taking full advantage of IT clearly requires strategic vision. Of course, a strategy alone is not enough. Often, as we have already noted, the strategy requires initiating structural change as well.

IT AND ORGANIZATIONAL STRUCTURE

Information technology has repeatedly played a role in the evolution of organizational structure. In both the historical and modern periods, innovations in IT have made feasible new organizational forms, and vice versa. In the early nineteenth century, the typical manufacturing firm was a small operation, producing a narrow range of related products for local and sometimes regional markets. Typically, those firms concentrated on a single business function—production—and contracted out sales and sometimes purchasing to independent agents. In the mid-nineteenth century, the telegraph and railroad helped expand markets, and new mass-production technology created potential economies of scale. Chandler has explained that vertically integrated, multifunctional firms and later multidivisional firms emerged in the nineteenth and early twentieth centuries as organizational pioneers increasingly internalized within-firm coordination once handled by markets in order to exploit the new mass-production technology efficiently. That coordination was facilitated by new forms of IT, including the telegraph for communication across distance and the typewriter for rapid production of the paperwork needed to manage internal coordination. For example, Armour and Swift used the telegraph as the crucial link in the administrative coordination system that allowed them to take over all functions, from purchasing live cattle to marketing it all along the East Coast, thus capturing the benefits of scale economies in slaughterhouse technology via vertical integration. In the early twentieth century, with even more innovations in IT in place to facilitate internal coordination, firms such as Du Pont and Standard Oil adopted a multidivisional form with product-oriented or geographical divisions, each of which had its own functional departments.

Williamson (1979, 1981) has explained these and other forms of business organization (including markets as well as firm structures) as resulting from a balance between transaction costs and production costs. In general, market coordination tends to yield lower production costs at the expense of higher transaction costs, and internal coordination lowers transaction costs while often yielding higher production costs. Of course, specific attributes of the product or market may modify this tradeoff. As the cost of IT has fallen in recent years, the unit cost of transactions, whether internal or external, has dropped dramatically. The result of IT's economic imperative should be unit transaction costs approaching zero. This change, like earlier advances in IT, enables new organizational forms to evolve, as noted in Chapters 4 and 5 of this book. We see emerging evidence of two basic categories of changes: linkages between firms and restructuring within firms (see Malone, Yates, and Benjamin, 1987).

Linkages with other companies can take two basic forms: one-to-one linkages and market linkages. Just-in-time inventory systems are based on a close buyer-supplier link that allows the two firms to operate as a virtual organization. A tire manufacturer, for example, is part of the virtual organization of the automobile manufacturer to which it has a just-in-time link; in some cases, that tire manufacturer, in turn, may be linked in a second virtual organization with a supplier to its retail outlets (Benjamin, DeLong, and Scott Morton, 1988). One-to-one linkages can also center on a design database shared by the buyer and the supplier of a large and complex product, the design of which requires protracted exchanges between the two companies. In the historical period, such one-to-one relationships were often stepping stones to actual vertical integration, since transaction costs between two firms were greater than those within a firm. Now, as transaction costs approach zero, firms may prefer to remain in or move to such virtual organizations in order to capture advantages in production costs or other areas.

In many other cases, interfirm linkage will take the form of what we may call an electronic market. When the product being purchased is standardized and easy to designate, an electronically coordinated market can help the buyer minimize price by shopping around among potential suppliers. Even in the historical period, the telegraph enabled, for the first time, nationwide market transactions for standard and simply designated items with a very large market, such as stocks and commodities. Now, large databases and affordable high-bandwidth data communication make economic electronic markets that allow the coordination necessary for easy and inex-

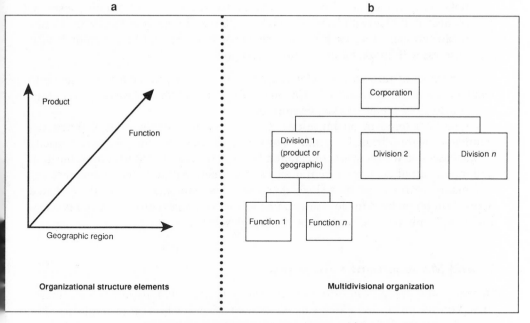

Figure 3-3. Multidimensional organizations.

pensive market comparisons of slightly more complex products and services, such as airline reservations. Similarly, an electronic market for spare airline parts allows airlines to reduce their inventories of parts and to locate the closest and cheapest spare part when one is needed quickly.

In yet other cases, firms are being internally reconfigured. To understand these changes most clearly, let us visualize company organizational structure as a three-dimensional problem balancing requirements of function, market, and product (see Figure 3-3a). The traditional family firms were limited on all dimensions, with their narrow product lines, limited market scopes, and single-function emphases. Beginning in the late nineteenth century, firms began developing along the three dimensions, as follows:

One-dimensional. The vertically integrated, multifunctional organization satisfies the requirements of multiple functions but retains a very limited product line in a single (albeit perhaps larger) market.

Two-dimensional. In the multidivisional forms of the organization (see Figure 3-3b), function and one other dimension are satisfied at any one time. In the early twentieth century, the multidivisional organizations evolved, according to Chandler (1962), to have functional units within product divisions (Du Pont and General Motors) or within geographical divisions (Standard Oil, Sears, and many railroads).

Three-dimensional. As radically cheaper IT reduces transaction costs, organizational forms that attempt to satisfy all three dimensions have begun to take hold. The earliest such form was based on the strategic business unit construct, pioneered at General Electric in the late 1960s and refined in the 1970s. In this organizational form, each product sector or business unit is a multidivisional business with market and functional components.

A number of authors have referred to these three-dimensional forms as network, team, or matrix organizations. In Chapter 7, Rockart and Short develop this concept in more detail as the networked organization.

One final trend in organizational structure is the reconfiguring of functional boundaries within firms. In certain companies, for example, the increased capacity of databases and the increased integration between these and various communication and input/output devices make it desirable for functional units such as engineering and manufacturing to share a single database. This joint database, like those shared across firm boundaries in close one-to-one linkages, reduces conversion and processing steps, facilitating redesign of the product development process.

IT and Management Processes

In some cases, applying information technology to a new task requires new management control processes, which can be thought of as intellectual technologies. For example, the railroads had to come up with ways of charting the locations of trains at every point in time in order to implement telegraphic dispatching. When they realized that the data sent in for dispatching could also be analyzed to improve efficiency—that is, when they realized the system's capacity for "informating"—they had to devise consistent methods for recording and storing the data. Then they had to develop mathematical and graphical modes of analysis to make use of the statistics. Similarly, during and after World War I, Donaldson Brown, working first in Du Pont and then in General Motors, developed return on investment as a criterion for investment decisions between competing divisions and implemented control systems based on it. At Du Pont, a mechanical chart room was devised in the early 1920s as a decision support aid for the senior executives in reviewing operations and investment decisions in their operational divisions, certainly a harbinger of the executive support systems currently emerging.

A more recent example of the adoption of innovative new control processes in conjunction with IT ocurred in the airline industry. The airlines had always been plagued with no-shows which reduced their overall seat utilization. Bumping passengers because of overbooking created very bad publicity, so the airlines tended to be conservative in their overbooking. However, when experiments indicated that customers would sell back tickets to the airline for various combinations of free flights and cash, the airlines adopted sophisticated computer modeling to play the probabilities on flight capacity much more boldly, significantly increasing flight yield. Another recent example is the new control process adopted by Otis Elevator as part of its implementation of a service program centered on IT. This system has a central national repair phone bank hooked to a large database. When an elevator breaks down, a call to a single, nationwide number results in the rapid dispatch of a local service person with full information to repair the equipment. The management control system that made this application particularly successful took advantage of the system's informating capacity to highlight repetitive problems for rapid attention by senior management.

Today's control systems—generally divided into operational, decision, and strategic control—were designed for traditional management hierarchies. It is not at all clear that the requirements of the interdependent firms will be satisfied by the traditional hierarchical controls. In general, as Rockart and Short note in Chapter 7, these new organizational forms will require management control systems that operate across as well as up and down the organization.

IT and Human Resources

In a climate of accelerating IT-induced organizational change, the importance of human resources in realizing the potential of new IT has become the subject of considerable attention. As researchers have studied successes and failures in the adoption and implementation of IT, the importance and complexity of human resource issues have become increasingly salient. Although once the focus was solely on IT's impact on people in the organization, now attention has also focused on the effect of organizational culture and human resources on IT. Recent research has made clear how important firm norms and labor policies are in what ITs are chosen, how they are implemented, and how successful they are in meeting organizational goals. In fact, organizational implementation may be the constraining factor for developing strategic applications. The historical record highlights these issues as well.

As Osterman notes in Chapter 8 of this book, much of the discussion of the effects of IT on jobs has focused on two issues: how IT affects the level of employment and how it affects the nature of specific jobs. In the historical period, the labor-saving aspects of new ITs were virtually always accompanied by rapid growth of the type of work they were designed to facilitate. Thus, although the technologies may have reduced the amount of labor needed to accomplish a specific task, firms and their information-handling needs were growing so fast that the labor saved resulted in only slightly less employment growth than might otherwise have occurred.

The typewriter, for example, was more than three times as fast as handwriting. Its adoption in large numbers in the period from the late 1870s to 1900, however, coincided with enormous growth (in actual and proportional terms) in all types of clerical and secretarial positions (Rotella, 1981), as a result of business growth and changes in management methods that led to much greater dependence on written documents (Yates, 1989). The increase in clerical labor continued in the first three decades of the twentieth century—as vertical filing, calculating machines, and other new office technologies were adopted. Jonscher indicates that this is part of a larger trend of the need for information workers and demonstrates that this increase is proportional to the growth in the productivity of the economy. In fact, we could argue that without such innovation, the even greater need for clerical and secretarial labor could have constrained either the business growth or (more likely) the increasing use of written documents. That dynamic has continued in some areas, such as the substitution of electromechanical switching for operators in the telephone system in the mid-twentieth century. The new technology was necessitated by the insatiable demand for operators that, according to some stories then circulating, would soon have employed all the women of working age in the nation.

Some more recent cases have had mixed effects, however, as Osterman shows in his discussion of studies of the impact of computers on clerical employment (Chapter 8). In some cases, certain types of employment have actually decreased with the advent of computer technology, whereas in other cases employment has shifted. Nevertheless, a view that sees IT as gradually eliminating most human employment is clearly extreme. As new forms of IT continue to spread in the future, issues of retraining for shifts in the nature of employment will surely be more important than issues of massive unemployment.

Let us look now at the impact of IT on the nature rather than the number of jobs. One of the major debates in the popular and scholarly literature has centered on whether IT *deskills* jobs, narrowing their scope, or *upgrades* jobs, making them broader and more fulfilling. In Chapter 9, McKersie and Walton argue a more balanced view that applications aimed at reducing cost also reduce job specification scope, whereas applications aimed at increasing effectiveness tend to increase job scope. Here the historical perspective initially seems to support the deskilling view, though this is an area where the differences between historical and contemporary IT seem to be creating a change in direction.

In general, earlier IT innovations, which emphasized cost reduction, tended to create new, more limited job categories of operators. Telegraph operators, stenographer-typists, and file clerks were all more narrowly defined than the general clerks who preceded them. These new operators mediated between the new technologies and the ultimate users, the managers. The positions were substantially deskilled compared to the jobs of the earlier general clerks who were in training to rise in the company. This pattern seems to emerge from one ideological and one technological factor. The ideological factor was the spread of the systematic management philosophy, which sought efficiency through tightened control over workers and managers alike. Efficiency was often viewed as inherent in specialization and subdivision of jobs. The technological factor was the relatively unsophisticated nature of the technologies at that point. The typewriter and adding machine carried out simple, repetitive tasks. Although a clerk or manager with broader responsibilities might carry out these tasks as part of his or her work, the advantages of doing these tasks were not great enough to outweigh the economies attained by subdivision of the tasks.

The historical record seems to provide more support for the deskilling than for the upgrading hypothesis. Countering this pessimistic and deterministic view of technology, however, are two changes in the nature of IT today. Today's IT is much more sophisticated than that of the earlier period, and it is, as we noted earlier, often integrated across IT functions in ways that allow it to span job, departmental, and even organizational boundaries. Rather than simply replacing repetitive and mechanical tasks, it often serves as a sophisticated decision-support tool that is most valuable in the hands of a sophisticated user with broad responsibilities. The expert systems that draw on developments in the artificial intelligence field perhaps exemplify this trend most vividly. Moreover, the integration of IT functions and business tasks also seems to encourage use within a broader context. Thus, IT's impact on the nature of work is more mixed now than in the earlier period. Depending on how it is used, it may enhance or deskill occupations. Piore and Sabel (1984) provide evidence for movement to a new job shop/generalist work environment which they assert may be the predominant form for future production work rather than the deskilled specialized worker model.

The impact of IT on the number and nature of jobs, then, is likely to be mixed, depending on the context and the technology. This contingent view suggests the crucial change in perspective we mentioned above. The key question now becomes how the organization and its employees shape IT. In general, as McKersie and Walton have argued in Chapter 9 of this book, the full potential of IT can only be realized when business purpose, use of IT, and organizational/human resource policies are all aligned. Frequently, new uses of information and of IT have been initiated to improve efficiency, with no attention to their impact on the people involved. Then the organization finds itself reacting to unexpected consequences.

We see such a case in the late nineteenth century, when American managers adopted systematic management. Based on this philosophy and its emphasis on systematic collection and analysis of data, individuals at all organizational levels were required to submit data in the form of standardized periodic reports. These reports, sometimes via telegraph and sometimes simply typed onto forms, were used to compare and evaluate the performance of individuals and of segments of the business. This new statistical control was itself a form of IT that was adopted in the interests of increased control and efficiency.

The direct and indirect responses to this new IT when executives attempted to impose it were predictably negative. Workers reacted to the depersonalization of the workplace with reduced loyalty and increased incidences of labor strife. The early years of the twentieth century were rife with strikes and other forms of labor problems. Although exogenous factors such as European labor movements also played a major role in these problems, the impersonal IT of systematic management reduced the loyalty often present under more paternalistic managements, leaving workers more susceptible to the other pressures. Managers also resented the imposition of this new IT that was used to evaluate and control them. Their resistance took more subtle but often quite effective forms, such as insisting that the cost of collecting a certain set of requested data was too great to be justified. Stonewalling often held up the implementation of such systems.

The companies that were most successful in adopting systematic information flows managed the implementation process (rather than reacting to consequences), working to gain the trust and involvement of middle management and workers from the start. When Du Pont bought up dozens of dynamite plants in the early twentieth century and wanted to consolidate them into a single, systematically managed department with a statistical control system for maximum efficiency, department management used frequent plant superintendents' meetings as a way of easing the implementation of the system (Yates, 1989). These meetings, initially at monthly intervals but eventually subsiding to yearly intervals, served as a channel of communication between the superintendents and the departmental management. They allowed the two groups to work together to deal with implementation issues as they arose, and they created an atmosphere of relative trust and openness. The superintendents frequently set up similar meetings within their plants, carrying the cooperative approach down the organizational hierarchy. The result was a rapid and relatively smooth implementation of the system that yielded enormous gains in efficiency in a short period of time. Du Pont's success was demonstrated by its incredible expansion of output during World War I, only a decade after the plants were initially purchased.

The broad lessons of the adoption of systematic management techniques clearly apply to more recent attempts to adopt IT designed to improved efficiency and control. Systems adopted with little regard to human resource policies typically run into much greater problems than those in which human factors were considered. The studies of the auto industry described in Chapters 8 and 9, for example, have found that improved efficiency in plants is more closely correlated with the adoption of new human resource policies than with the simple adoption of new technology. Plants that have bought large amounts of new IT without reconsidering their organizational strategy have been faced with many unanticipated problems that have thwarted the ultimate aim of the technology—to increase efficiency. On the other hand, firms that take into account human issues as they adopt technology, especially by encouraging high involvement at multiple levels, have been more successful.

Based on experiences of the past and present, we can safely predict that human and organizational issues will continue to be keys to successful implementation of IT in the future. In fact, given the ever-increasing growth in applications that transform organizations and people's roles within them, it may be the constraining factor. Companies adopting IT in hopes of realizing efficiency gains ignore these issues at their peril. Their efforts can too readily be derailed.

In general, then, the relationship between organizational and human resource issues, on the one hand, and IT, on the other, has long been critical in the adoption of IT. Both sides of that equation—the impact of IT on human resources and the impact of human resource norms and policies on IT—must be considered to make the most effective use of IT.

CONCLUSION

This view of IT and its applications in the historical and modern period has provided a useful perspective for thinking about future use of IT. We believe that many of the trends we have identified will carry over into the 1990s. The economic imperative that drives these trends will continue at least through the decade. Moreover, the changes resulting from these trends will occur at an increasingly rapid rate. Thus, it will be increasingly important for individuals and organizations to develop effective modes of implementation and adoption.

Specifically, the following key trends will continue to provide opportunities for new forms of business coordination:

Compression of time and space. Our business world will continue to shrink as high-performance networks arise throughout the world and as the necessary standards emerge to provide interconnection. The increasing bandwidth of such networks coupled with richer communication media will enable new compressions of time and space.

Expansion and transformation of stored knowledge. The quantity of stored textual and structured data in organizations is enormous and still growing. To enable organizations to make optimal use of this knowledge, we will need to continue improving methods of access to information and improving our understanding of how to use procedural and especially expert knowledge in taking advantage of the vast quantities of data at our disposal.

Increase in flexibility. IT's flexibility, combined with increased power, will continue to expand the range and flexibility of IT applications.

All of these trends will fuel changes in business coordination that will shift relationships among businesses, their customers, and their suppliers. To benefit from these shifts, companies must learn one key lesson from the past and present: IT cannot be divorced from its organizational context. It must be seen as part of a system that balances several forces: strategy, structure, management control processes, and human resource policy. Consequently, the key to achieving the benefits of IT is the management of organizational implementation in a way that continually restores the equilibrium of these forces.

REFERENCES

Beniger, J. R. 1986. *The Control Revolution: Technological and Economic Origins of the Information Society.* Cambridge: Harvard University Press.

Benjamin, R. I. 1982. "Information Technology in the 1990's: A Long Range Planning Scenario." *MIS Quarterly* 6 (June): 11–31.

Benjamin, R. I., and M. Scott Morton. 1988. "Information Technology, Integration, and Organizational Change." *Interfaces* 18 (May–June): 86–98.

Bolter, J. D. 1984. *Turing's Man.* Chapel Hill: University of North Carolina Press.

Chandler, A. D., Jr. 1962. *Strategy and Structure: Chapters in the History of the American Industrial Enterprise.* Cambridge: MIT Press.

———. 1977. *The Visible Hand: The Managerial Revolution in American Business.* Cambridge: Harvard University Press.

Cope, E. A. 1913. *Filing Systems: Their Principles and Their Application to Modern Office Requirements.* London: Sir Isaac Pitman and Sons.

Institute for the Future. 1988. *1988 Ten-Year Forecast.* Menlo Park, Calif.: Institute for the Future.

Jones, C. R. 1949. *Facsimile.* New York: Murray Hill Books.

Jonscher, C. 1988. "An Economic Study of the Information Technology Revolution." Management in the 1990s Working Paper 88-053.

Landes, D. 1984. "Time Runs Out for the Swiss." *Across the Board* 21 (January): 46–55.

Malone, T. W. 1988. "What Is Coordination Theory?" Paper presented at the National Science Foundation Coordination Theory Workshop, MIT, February 19.

Malone, T. W., J. Yates, and R. I. Benjamin. 1987. "Electronic Markets and Electronic Hierarchies: Effects of New Information Technologies on Market Structures and Corporate Strategies." *Communications of the ACM* 30 (June): 484–97.

———. 1989. "The Logic of Electronic Markets." *Harvard Business Review* 67 (May–June): 166–72.

Piore, M. J., and C. F. Sabel. 1984. *The Second Industrial Divide: Possibilities for Prosperity.* New York: Basic Books.

Rockart, J. F., and D. W. DeLong. 1988. *Executive Support Systems: The Emergence of Top Management Computer Use.* Homewood, Ill.: Dow Jones–Irwin.

Rotella, E. J. 1981. "The Transformation of the American Office: Changes in Employment and Technology." *Journal of Economic History* 41 (March): 51–57.

Simon, H. 1987. "The Steam Engine and the Computer: What Makes Technology Revolutionary." *Educom Bulletin* 22 (Spring): 2–5.

Williamson, O. E. 1979. "Transaction Cost Economics: The Governance of Contractual Relations." *Journal of Law and Economics* 22, 233–61.

Williamson, O. E. 1981. "The Economics of Organization: The Transaction Cost Approach." *American Journal of Sociology* 87, 548–75.

Yates, J. 1989. *Control through Communication: The Rise of System in American Management.* Baltimore: Johns Hopkins University Press.

Yates, J. 1982. "From Press Book and Pigeonhole to Vertical Filing: A Revolution in Storage and Access Systems." *Journal of Business Communication* 19 (Summer): 5–26.

Zuboff, S. 1988. *In the Age of the Smart Machine: The Future of Work and Power.* New York: Basic Books.

PART II

STRATEGIC OPTIONS

CHAPTER 4

Interfirm Competition and Collaboration

JULIO J. ROTEMBERG AND GARTH SALONER

In terms of the 1990s model, this chapter focuses attention on the high-lighted "forces" in Figure 4-1. This section discusses these changing patterns of competition and collaboration from both the industry- and firm-level viewpoints. Information technology has a unique characteristic that has the power to alter an industry's competitiveness and the nature of interfirm rivalry. This characteristic is IT's ability to create "interrelatedness" among firms, markets, and products. The drivers and consequences of interrelatedness are discussed here.

This introduction of interrelatedness creates new market opportunities and new openings for gaining first-mover advantage. Under some conditions it changes the route to success from competition to collaboration.

This chapter lays out a map, or framework, that can be used to understand these changes and their implications for corporate strategy. The framework is developed starting with the concept of interrelatedness. The first of two sources of interrelatedness is networks. There are two key attributes of electronic networks: they become more valuable as they grow in size, and they can be shared by both competitors and collaborators. The second source of interrelatedness is compatibility in one of three forms: through interconnectivity, common human skills, and complementary products and/or services.

To interrelatedness is added the traditional industry analysis viewpoint, and a framework is constructed that relates the ability of a firm to exploit market or product strengths ("exploitability") with the degree of interrelatedness that exists. The framework is used to identify the characteristics of firms that occupy each cell as well as potential "migration paths" within the matrix.

This framework provides a way of understanding where each business is positioned and the forces that are at work. This has major implications for the strategic options open to the organization, a subject addressed in Chapter 5.

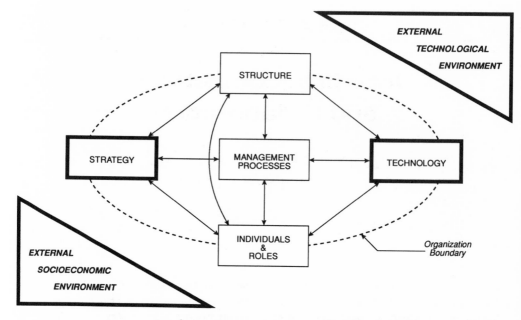

Figure 4-1. MIT90s framework—Chapter 4 emphasis.

The information technology revolution is having profound effects on the nature of interfirm competition and collaboration. In the IT era, the products and services that firms provide are *interrelated* in a way that their predecessors were not. Consider, for example, services that are offered over joint networks such as networks of automated teller machines (ATMs), or the importance of offering computer equipment or software that is compatible with the offerings of one's rivals. In situations where there is a high degree of strategic interrelatedness, two effects play a central role. First, the advantages of being the first to recognize a market opportunity may be magnified. Second, profitability may be gained by working together with rivals rather than against them: competitive advantage may give way to cooperative advantage.

In this chapter, we describe the major determinants of the firm's strategic setting and the implications for overall firm strategy. The degree to which a firm's product or service is interrelated with that of its rivals is the novel aspect of the analysis IT provides. At the same time, traditional determinants of industry profitability continue to be important. Combining these traditional factors with the degree of interrelatedness yields a framework for strategy formulation in the 1990s.

INTERRELATEDNESS

In conventional markets, a firm's products and services stand alone. Of course, they are judged by comparison with rivals' offerings, and the extent to which they are better, or just different, may determine market shares. But one firm's gain may be another's loss, and battles for market share consist of rivalries to gain a competitive edge—to be the first to come out with an innovation.

How does this view change when considering information or information technology? Does IT bring special considerations to bear? Our finding is that markets involving IT are highly atypical. Moreover, the effect of the unique IT characteristics is subtle: although in some circumstances they act to exacerbate existing competition and can turn a traditional rivalry into a winner-takes-all battle, in other circumstances they soften existing competition, even occasionally turning rivalries into cooperative ventures.

The key distinguishing characteristic of IT is its degree of interrelatedness. The most important sources of interrelatedness are networks and a concern for compatibility.

Networks

By a network we mean a collection of separate locations that create value by virtue of the fact that they are interconnected so that transactions can take place between them. Examples of networks of this kind are the airline computer reservation systems (CRSs), networks of banks' automated teller machines (ATMs), or the network of outlets that perform public money transfer for Western Union.

Networks are, of course, not new to the IT era. Railroads, airlines, and the telephone network are important conventional examples. What is new to the IT era, however, is the degree to which networks will arise and the extent to which the firms who are the consumers of their services will participate in their provision. Networks will arise more often because advances in telecommunications and computer technology make electronic communication of voice and data more economical than in the past. Firms will participate more in the provision of the networks that they use because, as we shall discuss below, control of networks may be a source of competitive advantage.

Two characteristics of networks are the keys to their importance as sources of interrelatedness: (1) the value of a network is often greater the more extensive the network is, and (2) networks can be shared: they are nonrivalrous in usage so that separate enterprises can use the same network.

An example where the value of the network is greatly enhanced by its size is Western Union's network of public money transfer outlets. To see how networks create value in a case like that, consider the following simple example. Suppose that by providing outlets in two locations the firm generates $1 of business between them. That is, the outlets in locations A and B are used to generate business traffic between A and B that is valued at $1 by the firm. Now consider adding a third outlet, C. Since $1 of business can now be transacted between A and C and B and C, the revenue of the network is trebled with a 50-percent increase in its size. By extending this argument, a network of ten outlets produces revenue of $45. Even if the tenth outlet costs as much to establish as the first, the value of the network grows disproportionately to the number of outlets.[1]

There are two main ways in which the possibility of sharing networks can enhance their value. The first is to obtain the benefits of network size by combining two small networks into one large one. Thus, for example, CIRRUS and other national ATM networks increase the value of each of the member networks by linking them together. The second is by increasing the quality of the network by providing the services of different firms on the same network or by providing separate outlets or firms with access to a common database. Computer reservation systems, discussed in more detail below, are an example of this.

Where there are benefits to sharing a network, it is obvious that common interests are created. Where network size is the issue, however, the implications for interrelatedness are more subtle: the implications depend on the number of networks that can profitably coexist in the market under consideration.

One extreme is where the benefits of a large network are so strong that only one network can exist. This may be true of the public money transfer market, for example. On the other hand, there are instances in which many networks can coexist. Consider, for example, a city in which there are several banks of comparable size. If each offers a network of ATMs even if some networks are smaller than others, customers of the bank with the smallest network are unlikely to bear the costs of changing banks unless there is a large difference in the size of the networks.

The implications are radically different depending on whether many or few networks can coexist. When only a few can coexist, control of the networks becomes a source of possible competitive advantage. The network creates a high degree of interrelatedness, but one that can be turned to the advantage of the firm that gains control of the network. If membership of a network is critical in order to be able to compete effectively in the industry, a situation in which many firms competed on an even footing can be transformed into an industry in which a relatively few firms dominate the market. In some cases the introduction of ATM networks have had this effect on local banking.[2]

In the case where many networks can coexist, firms can benefit by combining and sharing networks. Self-interest is replaced by common interest, and the drive for competitive advantage gives way to the need for cooperative advantage.

A large number of factors determine how many networks can survive. One factor is the degree to which different networks can differentiate the services they offer. When network are able to do this successfully, the specific tastes of consumers for the characteristics that serve to differentiate the networks may overwhelm the economies of scale that come from larger networks. A second factor is the capital costs of setting up a network. Third, in the case where the network consists of a network of outlets, the number of networks may be limited by the number of suitable locations for such outlets. Finally, the size distribution of firms is important. If one firm is dominant in the market before the introduction of the network, its participation in the network may be crucial to the success of the network.

Compatibility

Firms' interests are also interrelated when they care about the decisions made by other firms about the equipment or products they produce. This can arise even if the products will not be linked in a network or used to share information. Rather, the interrelatedness arises here because of the way different firms' products are interrelated in their use by customers. These fall into three main categories:

Interconnectivity. It is often the case that buyers want to be able to to purchase equipment from independent manufacturers that is compatible in the sense that it can be interconnected. The desire for such interconnectivity underlies the attempt by General Motors, through its manufacturing automation protocols (MAP) initiative, to provide standard interface protocols that would enable "robots" manufactured by independent companies to be interlinked so that they can operate in concert. Similarly, Digital Equipment Corporation's DECNET system provides the capability to network computers from various vendors together. GTE currently uses TCP/IP protocols to link Sun Microsystems computers with Apollo CAD work stations.

Human skills. Compatibility raises concerns for the efficient use of human resources as well. Just as equipment is configured in ways that either does or does not allow it to work interchangeably with other equipment, the training of individuals may enable them to work on a particular set of equipment but not another, if the equipment is "incompatible" in this way. Thus, the value of programmers trained in the FORTRAN language depends on the ubiquity of that language across firm boundaries, and the near universal adoption of the QWERTY typewriter keyboard is a result of the benefits of standardization and not the intrinsic efficiency of that keyboard layout.

Complementary products. Another important source of interrelatedness arises where it is desirable to add peripherals or other complementary products to existing equipment. Computer software, terminals, or disk drives are examples.

Questions of compatibility arise naturally and frequently in the IT context. The importance of compatibility has implications for the strategic behavior of manufacturers. Interconnectivity of equipment is much like the ability to connect to a network. The greater the number of other manufacturers with whom a manufacturer's equipment is compatible, the larger the market for their own equipment. At the same time, for a manufacturer that succeeds in achieving a dominant position, the ability to prevent interconnection may be a possible source of competitive advantage. For example, it was recently reported that Ashton-Tate has attempted to prevent the adoption of its Dbase language as an industry standard. The firm's chairman stated: "The Dbase language belongs to Ashton-Tate and Ashton-Tate intends to vigorously protect it."[3] Thus, when interrelatedness arises from compatibility it can, as with networks and depending on the particular circumstances, be a source of either competitive or cooperative advantage.

Furthermore, once a firm gets a head start on its rivals and has an installed base of equipment in the marketplace, it may be difficult to dislodge as the market leader. This is because each individual firm's technology adoption decision is likely to depend on the prior adoption decisions of others. A firm's usual inclination to look for production methods that are slightly better than its rivals, even if different from them, is mitigated by the concern to remain compatible with the existing installed technological base. A first mover in the technology adoption game faces the risk that it will not be followed and instead be stranded with a new technology. Even if the firm would prefer that technology if it were adopted by other firms, it may find itself worse off if its move to the new technology is not followed. In short, the desire to break away from the pack is diminished by the desire to do what others do. Accordingly, a firm that has a strong market position in the technology of choice may be able to parlay that position into even greater profitability later.

Compatibility issues help to explain the evolution of standards for computer operating systems. The desire of rival hardware manufacturers to maintain compatibility among software written for their various systems underlies attempts to achieve acceptance of a common operating system. Yet, at the same time, none of the firms is keen to adopt a system for which a rival has proprietary rights, for fear that that rival will be able to appropriate a disproportionate share of industry profits.

DEGREE OF INTERRELATEDNESS

The degree of interrelatedness of firms' products or services depends on the desire of the purchasers of those products to use them in conjunction with one another.[4]

Some interrelatedness exists with virtually any technology one can think of. For example, any firm that utilizes nuts and bolts as part of its production processes benefits if other firms use nuts and bolts with the same specifications, such as bolt size and the angle of the thread.[5] In other cases interrelatedness looms much larger, as, for example, in the case of telecommunications networks.

Thus, interrelatedness is all a matter of degree. However, with the growth of networks, greater possibilities for shared information, the necessity of compatibility in the IT era, and the fact that the increased pace of technological change means that networks and interfaces change over time, interrelatedness will arise more frequently and with increasing importance.

The following are importantly correlated with a high degree of interrelatedness.

High Human Capital Specificity
Coupled with High Labor Mobility

In this context, human capital specificity arises when the skills of the work force are specific to the IT under consideration. High Labor mobility exists if the workers who have acquired these specific skills can move from one organization to another without significant retraining.

The combination of these conditions exists, for example, in the case of a computer programmer trained in the computer language FORTRAN. These skills are highly specific to computer programming, and yet a skilled programmer can move fairly easily from one organization to another. The set of skilled programmer, therefore, forms a common resource for the firms requiring their services.

By contrast, consider the case of a computer systems designer who have invested years in establishing a "one-of-a-kind" computer system. Although the knowledge associated with that project is highly specific to that IT application, since to a large degree it is not transferable, it is associated with low interrelatedness.

High Frequency of Interactions
across Firm Boundaries

This measures the degree to which a firm's own decisions and efficiency regarding a particular IT application depend in an ongoing way on what other firms do. As an example, suppose that a number of industry participants have implemented automated procurement systems of the kind offered by American Hospital Supply. Such a system is used frequently by the hospitals, and the interactions under consideration take place, at least in part, across firm boundaries. A high degree of interrelatedness results.

At the other extreme are intraorganizational mail systems or LANs. When these do not involve transactions across firm boundaries, issues of interrelatedness do not arise. Once individuals in different organizations require inter-LAN communication, however, the degree of interrelatedness rises dramatically.

More generally, as discussed above, whenever separate firms are physically linked in a network, interrelatedness is likely to be high. In the case of CRSs, for example, a travel agent uses the same CRS to make reservations on a number of different airlines.

Important Use of Compatible Complementary Products

A product is said to be complementary to another if it must be used in conjunction with it. The most important example from our perspective is computer software—a product that is complementary to computer and computerized manufacturing hardware. Even if the hardware itself does not exhibit high interrelatedness, the overall system may if the software does.

As an example, consider microcomputers. For the most part these are not linked across organizational boundaries. Indeed, many are not even linked within the organization. Thus, it may seem that they do not involve a greater degree of interrelatedness than, say, pens and pencils. Yet, even when they are used as "stand-alone" pieces, they are intrinsically linked by the fact that the software that drives them is common and that the same software is used across firm boundaries. Thus, the ubiquity of word processors and LOTUS spreadsheet programs turns the microcomputer into an interrelated resource. Alternatively, if the skills associated with using a particular piece of software are idiosyncratic and labor mobility is high, the software again leads to a high degree of interrelatedness.

A Low Degree of Customization

In some cases, IT developed outside the firm can be implemented lock, stock, and barrel. In other cases, it must be customized to fit the idiosyncratic needs of the particular organization. In still other cases, it must be essentially built from scratch. Where the application is of the off-the-shelf variety, interrelatedness is likely to be high. Again, the example of word processing packages comes readily to mind. On the other hand, the greater the degree of modification that must take place in-house, the lower the degree of interrelatedness.

To illustrate how this framework can be used to classify the degree of interrelatedness, let us consider some examples. ATMs, credit cards, and point-of-sale debit cards involve physical networks and, therefore, high interrelatedness. "Designer chips" involve a low frequency of transactions and a high degree of customization and hence low interrelatedness. Similarly, software tailored to a company's specific needs, such as a customized inventory system, involves low interrelatedness. Finally, given the presence of a standardized Universal Product Code, bar code information readers do not involve transactions across firm boundaries but are stand-alone systems and hence involve low interrelatedness. But the product code itself is most valuable if it is used by all and so has high interrelatedness.

CONVENTIONAL DETERMINANTS OF INDUSTRY PROFITABILITY

Although interrelatedness will grow in importance as the IT era unfolds, the nature of the firm's strategic environment will continue to be influenced by more conventional factors: those that determine the firm's strategic environment in conventional (non-IT) environments. Broadly speaking, the two factors that determine a firm's profitability in a particular market are the potential profitability of the market as a whole and the ability of the firm to capture a large share of potential profits.

Market Profitability

The profit potential of the market as a whole depends on the strength of demand relative to costs of production. Although numerous factors affect the strength of demand in the economy as a whole, perhaps the major determinant of demand for a given product relative to others is whether or not these are good substitutes for it. In particular, the extent to which customers perceive the products of different manufacturers to be different from one another is an important determinant of profitability. Where product differentiation is high, customers will be prepared to pay a premium for the features of the product they care about most, and prices will be higher. Within a given market, a high degree of product differentiation insulates a firm from competition because customers are reluctant to substitute the products of other firms for the product they most desire. Many consumer items have this characteristic.

However, product differentiation alone will not lead to high profitability. If it is easy to enter the market with products that are close substitutes to successful ones, entry will occur and, as discussed in more detail below, drive profits down. Thus, although restaurants exhibit a fair degree of differentiation, entry keeps average profitability low. Such imitative entry will be difficult if development and promotional costs are high, or if it is important that the existing brand has developed a reputation for product quality. Black and Decker has had great success in building up a profitable set of hand machine tools based on its earlier reputation, and Sears is a clear example of the brand name guaranteeing a high degree of consumer acceptance. Similarly, if the product is protected by a patent, imitation is impeded and substitution more difficult.

Substitution may be difficult for reasons other than that customers value different brands differently. For example, it may be costly for a customer to switch from an existing supplier to another. This can occur, for example, when the customer is a manufacturing firm that has configured its production process to the characteristics fo the input of its supplier. In that case, customers are somewhat captive, and prices can be raised without a dramatic loss in sales. Automobile parts provide a classic

example. For many such parts the original equipment manufacturer is the only supplier and is able to charge very high prices. Thus, purchasing a car in parts is many
times more expensive than buying it assembled (although this is partly a result of
differences in handling and storage costs).

The Ability to Exploit Potential Profitability

Demand substitutability is a major determinant of potential industry profitability.
But what determines whether the firms that are providing a given product will be
able to exploit the product's profit potential if it is high? The first factor here is the
number of efficient rivals each firm faces. When there are many rivals, each typically
has a relatively small market share. When a firm cuts its price, therefore, although it
earns less on those customers to whom it is already selling, they are few in number
compared to those it can potentially attract by the price cut. The temptation to cut
price is high, therefore, and so price competition is strong and profit margins low, as
is the case, for example, for nonspecialty textiles.

When there are few firms, however, price competition will tend to be blunted
for several reasons. The first is the converse of the one just given for why competition
is cutthroat when there are many rivals: the cost of a price decrease in terms of the
discount to the firm's customers in any case looms large relative to the potential gains
from luring away the rival's customers. The second reason is that it is easier for rivals
to reach and police "implicit understandings" that prices should be maintained at
high levels when there is small number of rivals. The U.S. automobile manufacturing
industry in the 1950s and 1960s and the bulk chemical industry are examples of cases
where relatively small numbers of large firms set prices consciously aware of their
mutual price interdependence.

For such implicit understandings to be maintained, the firms must be able to
"agree" (without explicitly communicating) on what the price should be. Moreover,
they need to monitor one another's behavior to ensure that there is no secret "cheating" on the implicit understanding, and they need to respond swiftly when cheating
is detected. Such behavior requires unconcerted coordination, "leadership," and
"industrial statesmanship."

Perhaps the most striking example of "industrial statesmanship" was the role
played by U.S. Steel as the recognized price setter for the industry until the 1060s.
In the early part of the century, Judge Gary, chairman of U.S. Steel's board of directors, augmented market price setting with social dinners that he hosted for his rivals.
As Gary explained, these dinners generated such "respect and affectionate regard"
that the industry leaders all felt a stong obligation to cooperate.

Similarly, after the breakup of the Tobacco Trust in 1911, the cigarette industry
developed a pattern of price leadership in the 1920s and 1930s where prices were
changed infrequently and the rivals moved rapidly to match price changes, both
upward and downward. The industry leaders obtained much higher profit margins
after the introduction of this pricing than they were able to before. Delicate and subtle behavior becomes difficult, however, when many firms are involved, when change
is rapid, or when the products the firms are offering are not homogeneous.

So what gives rise to a small number of actual and potential rivals? Many factors
are involved. First, the extent of economies of scale in production is an important

factor. The number of plants that can profitably survive in an industry is low if the minimum efficient scale of operation is high relative to industry demand, as, for example, in the automobile industry or the steel industry prior to the advent of the minimill.

A second important factor is the presence or absence of differences in production technologies. Where some firms have proprietary production know-how or patented processes, the few low-cost producers will achieve a position of market dominance. Similarly, firms that accumulate production experience resulting in lower costs will have an advantage over late arrivals. Thus, the extent to which established manufactureres of memory chips have "moved down the learning curve" puts new entrants at a substantial disadvantage. Similarly, the proprietary know-how possessed by the leading manufacturers of disposable diapers gives them a significant edge on potential rivals.

A third factor that is sometimes important is the degree to which start-up costs are also sunk, that is, the degree to which it is impossible to retrieve the expenses incurred in entering an industry when deciding to exit. Where sunk costs are high, firms may be more reluctant to attempt to enter a new market because of the high degree of commitment involved. This is important whenever technology is required that is specific to the particular market being entered or when a significant amount of introductory promotional expenditure is required.

In what follows, we summarize the industry characteristics that lead to high firm profitability according to the type of conventional industry analysis sketched here as "exploitability." Exploitability can be high because the firm faces a small number of actual rivals as a result of the presence of economies of scale or economies of scope, or because it possesses special know-how. Exploitability can also be achieved by virtue of the perception of customers that good substitutes for the firm's product do not exist. In order to continue to enjoy those profits, however, it is necessary that entry by firms offering close substitutes be impossible.

THE INTERACTION OF INTERRELATEDNESS AND EXPLOITABILITY

In this section we combine the conventional analysis of market structure with questions arising from issues of interrelatedness. Because IT is dynamic and, relative to conventional technologies, still in its infancy, it is important to distinguish between conditions that are likely to pertain early on and those that will pertain as the industry and technology mature. Accordingly, we will comment on the likely evolution of each of the categories we consider.

We distinguish broadly between high and low interrelatedness and exploitability. This allows us to identify four broad categories, as shown in Figure 4-2.

High Exploitability and High Interrelatedness: Preemptive Penetration

The combination of high exploitabiblity and high interrelatedness is a volatile mixture. High interrelatedness ensures that all the industry participants have an interest

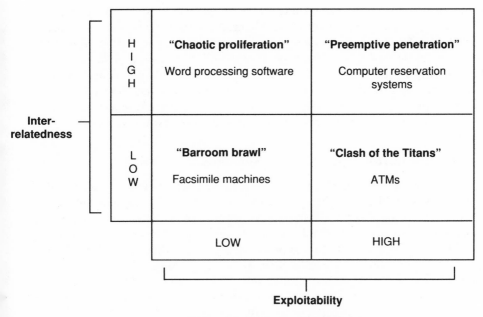

Figure 4-2. Industry characteristics.

in the outcome of the rivalry: every industry member is a participant in the contest. High exploitability implies that the winners will win at the expense of the losers: contests are likely to have winner-takes-all features.

In such markets there tend to be strong first-mover advantages. The firm or firms that get a jump on their rivals may have the possibility of building an insurmountable lead over them: the markets tend to be characterized by "preemptive penetration."

Firms that are quick to spot these market opportunities and who are well positioned to take advantage of them may be able to gain early and decisive market leadership positions. By contrast, if there exist few dominant firms who are thereby in the best position to take advantage of the new opportunities, smaller rivals may find advantage by banding together to ensure that they are not preempted by their larger rivals.

The shifting alliances among hardware manufacturers in the quest for open network architectures provide an example of firms seeking cooperative advantage. The major European computer manufacturers—including Bull, ICL, Nixdorf, Olivetti, Philips, and Siemens—formed the X/OPEN Group in early 1985. Their hope was to establish open standards around the UNIX operating system to provide an alternative standard to the dominant proprietary IBM operating system. The high interrelatedness created by the desire to use applications software from many suppliers creates the possibility that a firm that is able to gain acceptance of its own operating system would be able to obtain market dominance. Clearly this fear gave rise to the X/OPEN initiative. Interestingly a major tenet of the X/OPEN Group's founding agreement was that they would not promote any one of the proprietary operating systems of the member firms themselves. As the UNIX system (over which AT&T

has some proprietary rights) gained increasing acceptance, however, the fear that AT&T would gain preemptive control has changed the strategic alliance. This fear was fueled by AT&T's announcement that it would form a partnership with Sun Microsystems to develop a standard version of UNIX. In response, Bull, Siemens, Digital, and others of the X/OPEN Group have formed a new alliance with IBM (the Open Software Foundation) to develop their own open environment for software.

An example of an IT innovation in which preemptive advantage has been obtained by a small number of firms is that of computer reservations systems.[6]

Example: Computer Reservation Systems

Prior to the introduction of CRSs, travel agents made bookings telephonically with each airline, using published flight schedules as their guide to flight availability. The airlines themselves, however, used automated reservation systems to keep track of bookings and to provide updated information to their own reservation agents. The modern CRS systems grew out of these proprietary systems when the major airlines offered travel agents direct access to their automated systems. The CRSs were expanded beyond single-airline listings and now offer listings of flights on many different airlines. Using a CRS, the travel agent can view up-to-the-minute schedules and seat availability information on virtually any route and make the booking directly on the terminal.

For example, American Airlines' Sabre system has 50,000 terminals in 12,000 travel agency offices around the world.[7] The system lists 17.5 million route fares on 650 airlines. Of these, 40,000 are updated each day. Moreover, a travel agent can directly book a flight on more than 300 of the carriers listed on the system.

The effect of this innovation has been dramatic. The vast majority of bookings are now made in this manner. More than 60 percent of airline bookings are made by travel agenst, and by 1983, 90 percent of those bookings were made on CRSs. In 1985 there were six CRSs. Their market shares of travel agency booking revenue in 1983 and 1985 are presented in Table 4-1.

Importantly, two airlines—United and American, with their Apollo and Sabre systems, respectively—have captured the lion's share of CRS business. These two CRSs accounted for 74 percent of domestic revenue booked by travel agents in 1985 (46 percent for Sabre and 28 percent for Apollo). These statistics understate the dominance of these two systems because they are based on national figures. On a regional basis, one or the other of these systems has achieved an even more dominant position. To see this, one can examine the thirty-seven metropolitan areas that were

Table 4-1. CRS Market Shares

CRS	1983	1985
Apollo (United)	31%	28%
Datas II (Delta)	2%	6%
Mars Plus	2%	1%
Pars (TWA)	12%	10%
Sabre (American)	49%	46%
Soda (Eastern)	5%	10%

responsible for the most revenue booked. (These accounted for 75 percent of total booking revenue.) In seventeen of these areas the Sabre system accounted for more than 40 percent of the bookings, whereas in ten Apollo had a market share of that magnitude. In Cincinnati, Dallas–Ft. Worth, and Anchorage, the Sabre system had a market share in excess of 80 percent.

Interrelatedness

There are two reasons why interrelatedness of interests among airlines is high. First, CRSs constitute a physical network. Second, and more importantly, an airline benefits from having its flights listed on CRS systems even when these are operated by rival airlines. Since most travel agents consider the CRSs offered by different vendors to be substitutes and so purchase only one of them, it is important for each airline's flights to be offered on every CRS. This view was succinctly stated in a U.S. Department of Justice report: "Even a major national airline would find it very costly *not* to be listed in any CRS that is used exclusively by a sizeable portion of the travel agents in a city that the airline serves." CRSs are therefore an essential component of airline operation. If a CRS is in the hands of a rival, an airline's ability to compete depends on the quality of a service provided by its rival.

The fact that CRSs are used for booking is not the only source of commonality, however. Rather, the CRS can be used to compile data on the percentage of bookings each travel agent makes on each airline that serves a particular segment. This information, which is valuable to all airlines, can be used to pinpoint travel agents where marketing effort would likely have the highest payoff.

More importantly, the CRS can generate information that indicates the responsiveness of demand to changes in relative fares. Most CRS vendors regularly generate market information from their systems. Since this information is potentially valuable to all airlines, issues of information sharing arise. Indeed, the Sabre system gives American direct access to the internal databases of thirteen airlines, including British Airways, KLM, and Air France.

Exploitability

Several factors combined to make entry into the CRS market difficult. One possible strategy would have been to enter as a second system for a travel agent who was already using either Sabre or Apollo. However, both of those systems required contracts that essentially involved an exclusive arrangement between the travel agent and the CRS vendor. For example, United required that an Apollo subscriber use Apollo for at least 95 percent of its bookings that include at least one United segment. Entry was therefore only possible by inducing travel agents to switch from their current system to that of the entrant. However, switching requires installation of new equipment, which is estimated to cost between $5,000 and $20,000 per agency. Moreover, switching would also involve some disruption while employees learned the new system. Finally, both American and United succeeded in signing long-term contracts with many of their travel agents who would naturally be reluctant to break their contracts.

Furthermore, the large carriers are at a natural advantage. Agents prefer to have complete and current information. By using the Sabre system they get particularly accurate information on American Airlines. For example, "last seat availability" data are only available on the carrier's own CRS. Thus, in a city where the majority of flights are offered by United, a local travel agent would prefer to have the Apollo system.

These factors in combination amount to a large barrier to entry. The Department of Justice has estimated that entry would involve expenditures of $100 million and take between six months and two years. It is estimated that American and United each spent more than $500 million over ten years on their systems.[9]

The Effect of High Exploitability and Interrelatedness

If entry into the market were easy and could be accomplished on a small scale, we would expect to see travel agents using several CRS systems. Although booking would have been more efficient since agents would have up-to-date information and be able to make bookings electronically, this would not involve a large change in the nature of competition. Moreover, there would be substantial scope for cooperative advantage: carriers could combine systems to economize on costs and facilitate information sharing.

The present of entry barriers, however, means that relatively few systems can coexist. Moreover, the natural advantages of the large carriers means that it is particularly difficult for the small carriers to compete in this market. Yet because of the high degree of interrelatedness, control of the CRSs is a direct source of competitive advantage to the "winning" airlines, American and United.

There is, in fact, substantial evidence that these airlines were able to transform their dominance in CRSs into competitive advantage in the air travel market itself. Perhaps the most important means of achieving this arises from the ability of the CRS vendor to "bias" the sytem in its own favor. When a travel agent requests information on a particular route, the system must incorporate a rule that decides how to display the plethora of available flights on the screen. In an analysis that it conducted to travel agent behavior, American discovered that 53.5 percent of sales were made from the first line of the first screen of flights that were put up on the terminal when the travel agent made his or her request. Moreover, more than 90 percent of sales were made from flights listed on the first screen (each screen lists about six flights). Clearly there is an advantage to having one's own flights displayed first. In 1983 both American and United used selection procedures that gave prominence to their own flights. For example, in a 1981 internal memorandum, an American vice president concludes: "When you get through the date, the conclusion is clear—sales deteriorate screen to screen and line to line. We must achieve first screen, first line in every competitive situation. A lot of testing is under way to improve our position by modifying the display build rules."

In addition, the bias could be used in a more directed way to target specific rivals. Thus, prior to 1981 United had two classes of arrangements by which it would allow Apollo to list flights: as a "cohost" or "noncohost." A "cohost" was charged a per-booking fee in return for which it was given an improved display position. In the case of Frontier Airlines, however, which was a rival to United in many markets and which also (like United) had a hub in Denver, United refused to allow Frontier cohost status.

An additional source of competitive advantage is the ability to raise the costs that rivals face by imposing a booking fee each time a rival's flight is booked on a

CRS. Prior to 1983 American and United typically charged less than 50 cents to carriers providing flights that fed into their own flights, but higher fees (of $3.50 or more) to direct competitors. Such price discrimination was later banned by the CAB, and uniform fees fell to $1.75 to $1.85.

In addition to these direct exercises of market power, there were also several other ways in which rivals were placed at a disadvantage. For example, in one case American deliberately suppressed a "supersaver" fare offered by Continental Airlines. There were also suggestions that CRS information was used to "switch passengers from competing flights to United flights."

The conclusion that CRSs provided a source of considerable market power is one shared by American: "With the establishement of such a large and sophisticated industry distribution network American has been able to increase its influence over the flow of passengers through the air transportation network in a manner most beneficial to American." In a 1980 report to its board of directors, American concluded that 1980 profits would have been $78.5 million lower if American had not had Sabre.

Because of the profound first-mover advantages that arise, preemptive penetration may be critical. First movers have bandwagon-starting power. This differentiates the situation from others in which first-mover advantages are important, such as when a firm makes a product innovation. The task of playing catch-up is substantially more difficult for a late mover in the case of networks. Because of the enormous benefits to large networks, catch-up may be impossible once the leaders have a sufficient head start.

Low Exploitability and High Commonality: Chaotic Proliferation

The low degree of exploitability differentiates this category from the previous one. Because of the lack of exploitability, successful innovation will be either independently duplicated or imitated. As a result, slightly differentiated variants of the same basic product will proliferate as each seeks profitability in its own market niche.

We are, of course, used to seeing proliferation of this kind. Indeed, the ability of the free enterprise system to supply products that closely match the needs of consumers—whether they are firms or individuals—is often extolled as one of the great virtues of that system.

Yet, because of the high degree of interrelatedness, this niche-seeking behavior is different in many respects from that in traditional differentiated products markets. First, because interrelatedness is high, consumers might well favor fewer offerings and a more coherent market. Indeed, the product proliferation will appear chaotic. Second, those products that are successful in building up an installed base of users become increasingly attractive to future buyers who benefit from the interrelatedness among the installed base. Thus, there is a bandwagon effect as the leaders continue to build their leads at the expense of those with small market shares. Third, firms are somewhat insulated from small innovations made by their rivals since switching costs tends to help maintain the loyalty of current users until the innovation can be imitated.

Because of these features, the dynamics of a typical product in this class is as follows. First, numerous entrants jump into the market, hoping to gain market share. By a combination of superior product and pure luck, some first will begin to emerge as the market leaders. This will precipitate a bandwagon that will hasten the shake-out until only a small number of "winners" survive.

In the end, there will be many similarities between these products and those that begin with high interrelatedness and high exploitability. The winners will be protected by the presence of the installed base and interrelatedness from new entrants. Their high market shares will also yield high profits. The major difference is that here the high exploitability must be created, whereas in the other case it is an inherent feature of the market. Thus, the few winners will look profitable ex post, but average profitability will be low as vast resources are expended on the battle to emerge as a winner.

Once the industry has matured, there may also be gains from cooperation among the rivals. In contrast to the case of high exploitability, in this case the purpose is not to gain preemptive penetration but for survivors to increase market coherence and profitability for all by ironing out product incompatibilities and achieving product standardization.

Example: Microcomputer Word Processing Programs

Interrelatedness

From the user's point of view, a word processing package is a simple extension of the conventional typewriter keyboard. In addition to representing the alphanumeric keyboard on the screen (and eventually in the document), special keys or combinations of keys provide a formatting capability and the ability to produce additional fonts.

The benefits that would arise from a common word processing standard therefore include those that are gained from the existence of the standardized keyboard that has the letters QWERTY on the top row. Even though typewriter keyboards are not physically interlinked, they are linked in the sense that typists who learn to type on one such keyboard can easily transfer their skills to another of the same kind. Two keyboards are compatible if they can both be used interchangeably by the same typist.

Such compatibility concerns makes the use of a standardized keyboard valuable to all typewriter users. It makes typists mobile within and between organizations and thereby enhances efficiency. This in turn increases the value to the individual of learning to type.

In addition, however, there are advantages that would accrue from standardization of word processing that are not present in conventional typing. For example, standardized interfaces with printers could be established, eliminating time-consuming adaptation of particular packages to different systems. As a result, word processing packages exhibit a high degree of interrelatedness.

Exploitability

The creation and production word processing software is not an activity in which economies of scale are important. An extremely labor-intensive operation, it requires very little in the way of capital investment. Moreover, the rapid growth of the market

Table 4-2. Sales of Word Processing
Packages

	Sales Growth
1981	119,000
1982	265,000
1983	754,000
1984	1,504,000
1985	1,906,000

provided an environment ripe for new entry. Table 4-2 shows the growth in sales of word processing packages between 1981 and 1985.

In this respect, word processing is the classic low-cost, easy start-up operation spawned by the high-tech era. A viable operation can be started in a "garage" by a handful of programmers with a microcomputer. Indeed, this is how most word processing packages were developed.

For example, Multimate started as a project for Connecticut Mutual Life Insurance. William H. Jones and some fellow programmers developed the program to mimic Wang's word processing system. Jones then marketed it as a general-purpose word processing package.[10]

The Effect of High Interrelatedness but Low Exploitability

The result has been a proliferation of word processing packages. In a recent issue, *PC Week* lists forty-two vendors who produce word processing packages that run on the PC-DOS or MS-DOS operating system. (*Consumer Reports* also lists twenty-six spreadsheet programs, thirty-one personal finance packages, and thirty-nine database programs.) Some of the best-selling packages in 1987 are listed in Table 4-3.

The reasons for the proliferation are not hard to find. Because of the low-entry barriers, any entrepreneur with a "better mousetrap" or a product that serves a spe-

Table 4-3. Best-Selling Word Processing
Packages, 1987

	Units
WordPerfect	640,000
MicroSoft Word	630,000
Wordstar	303,000
pfs:Write	250,000
MacWrite	210,000
Displaywrite	175,000
Multimate	133,000
MicroPro EZ	105,000
Easyword	96,000
Volkswriter	55,000
Peachtext	50,000
Samma Word	40,000

cialized niche is able to enter the market. Early on, the first entrants, particularly Wordstar, benefited from the high degree of interrelatedness. Many adopters were willing to sue that package merely because it had developed a large installed base. However, because of the rapid pace of innovation, it was not long before a new processing packages were introduced that were sufficiently superior that new adopters were willing to forgo the benefits of being compatible with the installed base.

Once this proliferation was set in motion, it was self-perpetuating. The more dispersed the usage of word processing packages, the more difficult it is for any particular package to achieve dominance. The result, at least in the beginning, was chaotic proliferation.

Eventually, however, it seems likely that bandwagons will develop on a relatively small number of programs which will ultimately achieve market dominance. As the microcomputer market matures, the importance of installed base will grow relative to new sales, and it will become extremely difficult for new products to enter. The ultimate winners will be profitable, but the battle for market share is likely to be expensive.

There is some evidence that the shake-out has already begun. For example, MicroSoft Word, which sold a mere 64,000 units in 1984, sold 630,000 units in 1987. WordPerfect's sales have increased even more rapidly, from 57,000 to 640,000 units in the same period. Over the same time period, several others have not only lost market share but have suffered decreases in unit sales. For example, Volkswriter's sales fell from 79,000 to 55,000 units over that time period.

Low Exploitability and Low Interrelatedness: Barroom Brawl

Under the condition of low interrelatedness, suppliers are able to concentrate on satisfying the individualized needs of their customer firms without regard to the interests of the broader community. That is to say, coordination is not an issue, and clearly articulated needs can be precisely fulfilled. In the presence of low exploitability, each potential supplier possesses the advantage of being able to operate on a small scale and the disadvantage that, as a result, easy entry leads to very competitive behavior.

The outcome here depends somewhat on the degree to which the preferences of the customers (individuals or firms) for the product differ from one another. In the case where the desired product is fairly homogeneous, competition will drive prices close to the production costs of the most efficient firms. Profitability will tend to be low, only efficient firms will survive, and competition will take the form of striving to make slight improvements in any area where such improvement is possible.

Where the needs and desires of different customers differ, firms will attempt to satisfy the idiosyncratic desires of niche markets. Each variant of the product or service may be supplied by a single firm that has a monopoly over that product or service. However, since there is so much competition from substitute products, the market is nonetheless very competitive. Overall, then, the market is "monopolistically competitive."

In the cases of both homogeneous and differentiated products, the "barroom brawl" is an appropriate characterization. Competition resembles a scrap among many rivals using whatever source of competitive advantage they can find. Small differences in strength determine the outcome of each fight, and there is virtually no chance for anyone to dominate. In the end, the participants will all have received their lumps, and those that emerge with the fewest consider themselves to be the victors.

Example: Facsimile Machines

The first business facsimile machine was introduced in 1965 by Magnafax, a joint venture between Xerox and Magnavox. Adoption of the technology has been most rapid in Japan, where its ability to transmit Japanese characters is a great advantage. By the end of 1985 there was an installed base of 850,000 machines in that country. The comparable figures for the United States and Europe are 550,000 and 120,000, respectively.

Interrelatedness

Two issues arise with respect to interrelatedness. The first is that the value to a consumer of owning a facsimile machine, like a telephone, depends on the number of other users who also do. There is therefore a network effect. The second issue is that the relevant network is the network of compatible machines, that is, the number of machines that can interpret the message sent by one's own machine.

Early on, a de facto standard was established by Magnafax, adherence to which would enable communication between the fax machines of all manufacturers. Some new entrants attempted to build up independent installed bases by introducing their own incompatible technologies. Recognizing the importance of compatibility, the Japanese government acted early and established universal protocols that were embodied in international standards.

Once a standardized interface had been established with the telephone company's "local loop," the producers of the facsimile machines themselves had a very low degree of interrelatedness. A fax machine now exhibits no greater degree of interrelatedness than does a photocopier.

Exploitability

As Table 4-4 shows, the fax market is booming.[11] Entry barriers are low. The technology combines a photocopying capability with a transmitting technology. Since the latter is nonproprietary, any firm with experience in the former can easily enter the market. This, combined with the rapid growth of the market, has drawn many new entrants into the market. Although only five producers were active in 1982, that figure has increased about thirty.

Table 4-4. Fax Sales

	Unit Sales
1983	50,000
1984	90,000
1985	135,000
1986	190,000
1987	295,000 (estimate)

The Effect of Low Interrelatedness and Low Exploitability

Table 4-5 provides estimates of market shares for U.S. vendors from 1982 to 1986. For the most part, U.S. vendors sell machines produced in Japan. Table 4-6 lists the manufacturers of the products sold by some of the major vendors. From these two tables it is apparent that even accounting for the fact that in some instances more than one U.S. vendor sells the products of the same manufacturer, no firm has a sizeable share of the U.S. market. Moreover, as predicted by the framework we are using, there has been substantial new entry. Although there has also been some exit, more firms are now active, and the market share of the four largest vendors dwindled from 74 percent to 48 percent in just four years. Moreover, according to *Business Week*, "increased competition has driven list prices down by 15 percent a year."[12]

Low Interrelatedness and High Exploitability: Clash of the Titans

High exploitability guarantees that the equilibrium industry structure will be highly concentrated. Yet the low degree of interrelatedness means that there is not the additional propulsion toward monopoly: the winner-take-all aspect of competition is absent. Nonetheless, the market power that a paucity of rivals confers on the fortunate few implies that the driver toward product differentiation and the satisfaction

Table 4-5. Estimates of Market Shares (Percent) for U.S. Vendors, 1982–1986

	1982	1983	1984	1985	1986
AT&T	—	—	—	4	3
Burroughs	12	8	8	8	—
Canon	2	1	1	7	8
Eastman Kodak	2	3	—	2	—
Exxon	13	6	1	1	1
Fax	—	—	—	1	—
General Instruments	—	—	—	—	2
IBM	3	4	—	2	—
ITT	—	—	—	—	1
3M	16	18	5	12	12
Minolta	—	—	—	1	—
NEC	2	1	2	3	9
Omnifax	—	—	—	2	—
Panafax	6	8	n/a	6	5
Panasonic	—	—	—	2	—
Pitney Bowes	—	—	1	6	4
Qwip	—	—	—	2	—
Ricoh	—	—	7	7	9
Savin	—	—	1	1	—
Sharp	—	—	—	2	1
Teleautograph	2	1	3	1	2
Valutek	—	—	—	—	1
Xerox	33	39	41	20	18

Table 4-6. U.S. Vendors and Japanese
Manufacturers of Fax Machines

U.S. Vendor	OEM
AT&T	Ricoh Corp.
Burroughs	Fujitsu
Canon USA	Canon Corp.
3M	Oki
NEC	Nippon Electric Co.
Panafax	Matsushita
Pitney Bowes	Matsushita/Toshiba
Ricoh	Ricoh Corp.
Sanyo	Sanyo Electric Co.
Sharp	Sharp Co.
Teleautograph	Hitachi/Matsushita/Toshiba
Xerox	Fuji Xerox

of transient customer preferences will be dulled. Large-scale production emerges, leaving no room for the small.

The picture that emerges, then, is typical of an industry with high barriers to entry and high minimum efficient scale. The dominant firms here will be the U.S. Steel and General Motors of the information era. Success will be predicted on the same factors as in traditional concentrated industries. The result is a rivalry among a few giant firms—a "clash of the Titans."

Example: Automatic Teller Machines (ATMs)

The first producer of ATMs was the Money Machine, which was selling cash dispenser machines in 1967. By 1976, however, the total installed base of machines in the United States was a mere 6,000 and fewer than 5,000 in Europe. By 1982 the number in the United States was 25,000, and by the end of 1985 it had climbed to 50,000. The respective numbers for Europe are 10,000 and 25,000. By the end of 1985, there were 40,000 machines in Japan.

Interrelatedness

Despite the fact that ATMs are used in networks, two features result in their exhibiting a low degree of interrelatedness. First, the bank cards used in the machines use the same standardized magnetic strips as credit cards. Second, the machines are all connected to mainframes. That interconnectivity is simply a matter of adapting the interface software.

Exploitability

As Figure 4-3 shows, the ATM market exhibited rapid growth until 1983. Since then, however, demand has flattened out.

Three main areas of expertise are useful to ATM producers. First, the machines have attributes of safes, and experience with security products is useful. ATMs must be protected from vandalism, theft, and fire. Second, the machines embody some computer hardware and software, and therefore knowledge of computer technology

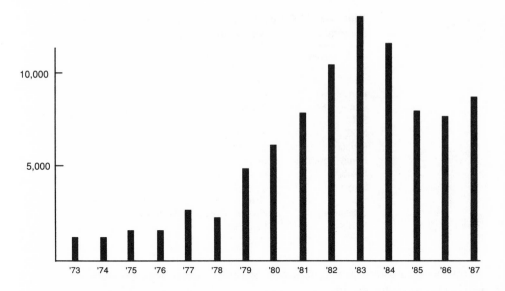

ATM industry sales in units. (Source: *American Banker,* (December 1, 1987)

Figure 4-3. ATM industry sales in units. (From *American Banker,* December 1, 1987.)

is useful. Finally, and perhaps most importantly, the ATMs must be integrated with the bank's accounting system, and experience with those systems is useful.

The limited number of firms with expertise in these areas limits the amount of potential entry. Moreover, although it grew rapidly prior to 1983, the market has remained relatively small: fewer than 10,000 machines are sold each year, at an average price of between $25,000 and $30,000. As a result, it is to be expected that the industry would be somewhat concentrated.

The Effect of High Exploitability and Low Interrelatedness

Lane reports that twenty firms had entered the industry by 1986.[13] However, there has been a substantial industry shake-out. Since 1984 three firms in the United States—Diebold, IBM, and NCR—have commanded a 70-percent market share. Similarly, in Europe the lead is taken by IBM and NCR (followed by Dassault, Docutel, Transac, and Chubb).[14]

INDUSTRY COMPETITIVE DEVELOPMENT

In the previous section we examined the effect of interrelatedness and exploitability in a static framework. In practice, however, both the degree of interrelatedness and the exploitability can change over time, as can their effects on interfirm rivalry. In this section we explore the most important possible transitions from one quadrant of the Figure 4-2 matrix to another. These dynamics are discussed further in Chapter 5.

Preemptive Titans

The most important strategic possibilities are opened up when information technology creates interrelatedness among firms in the lower righthand corner of the matrix (the "Titans"). As with CRSs and ATMs, the firms that are able to become the "gate-keepers" of the IT innovation can use that position to leverage themselves into dominant market positions. Because exploitability is high there, the profits that the firms earn are unlikely to be whittled away through entry of new rivals.

A possible, but uncommon, outcome for the "Titans" is that the barriers to new entry erode, reducing exploitability and reducing the firms to "barroom brawlers." It is arguable that the advent of minimills had this effect on the U.S. steel industry.

Victorious or Standardized Proliferators

One of two outcomes is most likely for firms in the "chaotic proliferation" quadrant of the matrix in the long run. One frequent outcome is that one (or a relatively small number) of the chaotic proliferators eventually wins a dominant market share. Because customers favor fewer offerings, once a bandwagon starts to grow around one of the offerings, that success feeds on itself. The outcome then starts to resemble that of the top righthand corner ("preemptive penetrators") since entry barriers are high and the profits of the winners are high. It is important to note, however, that since there is vigorous competition to emerge as the victor in the first place, average profitability is nonetheless low. The high profits of the victors after the shake-out are balanced by the losses of the losers.

An alternative mechanism that also has the effect of shifting proliferators into the high-exploitability/high-interrelatedness quadrant is the formation of strategic alliances and other cooperative ventures. If a few proliferators are able to combine forces by offering compatible products or a larger network, they may be able to gain an edge on the competition. Thus, small banks often benefit by combining their ATM networks.

Another outcome that is often observed is that compatibility (or interface) standards among the competing products are established. This may occur (1) through the auspices of a voluntary standards committee, (2) through the provision of converters (or adapters) that make otherwise incompatible products compatible, (3) through changes in product design by the vendors themselves that result in greater compatibility, or (4) because one vendor's product becomes a de facto standard but, because exploitability is low, that vendor is unable to prevent imitation. The standardization of FM stereo is an example of (1), and the case of IBM-compatible clones is an example of (4). When this occurs the chaotic proliferation is reduced to a traditional barroom brawl.

The Future of Barroom Brawlers

There appear to be many IT products for which competition resembles the barroom brawl, with many relatively small firms competing tooth and nail.[15] It is important to point out, however, that proliferation of firms is typical in new industries. As industries mature, small innovations, particularly process innovations, lead relatively few firms to thrive while others disappear. Also, these innovations lead over time to the creation of barriers to entry. As a result, the industries in this category come to resemble those with low interrelatedness but high exploitability.

If IT leads to higher interrelatedness, however, the barroom brawlers, in attempting to satisfy customer needs (often through differentiation), will precipitate chaotic proliferation. As discussed above, this may eventually lead to higher market shares for the winners, or redescend to the barroom brawl if there is standardization.

The Decline of Preemptive Penetrators

Although preemptive penetrators are usually insulated from competition, in some cases a change in technology may not only reduce the degree of interrelatedness but concurrently destroy exploitability. This occurs when compatibility standards are introduced that enable customers to switch easily from the products of one manufacturer to those of another. When that happens, it may be possible for new firms to enter the industry since the products they offer will now be compatible with those of the dominant producers. Accordingly, the market shares of the dominant firms erode, and competition increases.

This is the fear of many computer industry observers with respect to the advent of "open systems." Open systems will consist of a set of interface standards that will allow software and hardware designed for any given computer to also operate on computers manufactured by other vendors. As a result, customers would no longer be "locked in" to the proprietary systems of particular vendors. A concern expressed by stock analysts for the major computer companies is that this will lead to increased competition in the industry and, therefore, lower profitability.[16]

CONCLUSIONS: IMPLICATIONS FOR MANAGEMENT IN THE 1990s

Where interrelatedness is low, the situation is "conventional." There, apart from the speed of technological change and some special considerations that it implies, opportunities for competitive advantage have been extensively studied. Accordingly, we concentrate here on cases in which interrelatedness is high.

High Interrelatedness and High Exploitability

In this situation it is most important that the firm correctly diagnose the character of the situation early on. As in the case of networks of ATMs or CRSs, the effect of interrelatedness can be to completely alter the industry structure and the nature of interfirm rivalry.

Since the networks themselves exhibit great economies of scale, an industry in which many firms could survive on an equal footing can easily be replaced by one in which a relatively small number of firms have a large degree of market power and dominance.

Because of the benefits of joining an existing installed base, the early movers are also those that are likely to achieve this dominant position. Later entry will be extremely difficult, and firms that miss the boat will have to accept membership of the existing networks on terms dictated by their rivals.

At the same time, the average rewards to the early movers will be large because they will be insulated from later competition. The implication of these factors is obviously to be alert to these possibilities and to act early to capitalize on them. Although average rewards are likely to be high, in some instances only one of several early movers will emerge as the winner, in which case the losers will end up with very small market shares, and buyers who have been unfortunate enough to adopt early may find themselves stranded with an unpopular technology or network.

Firms that are too small to successfully innovate on their own may be able to enter into strategic alliances for this purpose. An example is the X/OPEN Group's initiative.

As the market matures, however, there may be rewards from cooperative, rather than competitive, advantage. Firms that succeed in establishing a viable network may be able to further enhance the attractiveness of that network by combining their networks with other successful early entrants. In this way the economies of network size can be reaped in a way that is mutually advantageous to all. This pattern has been followed in the credit card market and the market for ATM networks.

High Interrelatedness and Low Exploitability

This case can be viewed from both sides of the mirror. On the one hand are the firms who are producing the products under consideration, those that are responsible for the chaotic proliferation. On the other are the users of the products.

From the point of view of the producing firms, the considerations are those that usually apply to monopolistically competitive markets. Competitive advantage is attained by finding a niche and satisfying it.

Yet there are other considerations that arise because of the high degree of interrelatedness. Even though entry is easy and it is easy to provide similar products that are competitors to existing brands, it is quite possible for a small number of winners to emerge. If a bandwagon starts rolling on one particular product, the benefits of joining a large installed base may make that product much more attractive than competing brands even if there are small intrinsic differences between them.

A firm may be able to use penetration pricing early on to get some momentum going. A more important factor, however, is often the ability of a product to gain the acceptance of a major purchaser. Such acceptance may be sufficient to endow the product with the status of de facto standard, and with it the spoils of the contest. There are numerous occasions where this has occurred. For example, Delco (supplier of car radios to GM) adopted the Motorola FM stereo technology, and HBO created a de facto standard in its adoption of satellite scrambling. Thus, acceptance by a major adopter is a major source of competitive advantage.

Finally, where dominant buyers do not dictate standards and "the market" does not automatically generate coordination, one should not conclude that industry groups are doomed to live with chaos. Indeed, the market's response to coordination problems of this kind has been one of the most striking institutional responses of the century. In order to meet this growing need for coordination, a large collection of interrelated standardization organizations have emerged. This community is large and growing rapidly and consists of both national and international organizations. Particularly striking is the fact that, for the most part, this community is privately organized and constituted.

An alternative to the voluntary standards route is for small numbers of firms to band together in strategic alliances. In this way they may be able to gain a market share for a compatible set of products sufficient to set a bandwagon in motion on their chosen "standard." The recent formation of a coalition of PC-clone manufacturers to champion a rival standard to IBM's Micro Channel Architecture is an example of an attempt to do this.

The more interesting considerations arise when viewed from the other side of the mirror: the position of the users of the technology. What is a firm to do when a product it requires as an input is subject to chaotic proliferation? Here the firm's options are more limited. However, there are several useful courses of action.

First, users are typically entitled to participate in voluntary standards negotiations. Where users are small, however, it will often not be worth their while to bear the costs of participating in those proceedings.

Second, firms can at least ensure that their internal equipment is compatible. To insulate itself against the chaos in the marketplace, the firm can adopt a coherent set of requisites for its own procurement decisions.

Third, a large firm should recognize that it may have the ability to reduce the chaos by its own adoption decisions. The U.S. Department of Defense has long recognized its power to do this in its own procurement decisions, and Safeway Supermarkets is credited with ensuring the adoption of the Universal Product Code by its decision to require suppliers to adhere to that standard.

Finally, a large firm that does not have the power to impose its will on suppliers may be able to enter into strategic alliances toward that end. The most spectacular examples along these lines are the MAP and TOP protocols championed by General Motors and Boeing, respectively. The road for MAP has been a rocky one, and only 9 percent of Fortune 1000 companies believe they have been able to influence its progress.[17] Moreover, the attempt to reach consensus has been plagued by vendors trying to use the process to their own advantage. Yet, because users are finally taking a concerted and tough line, a large step may finally have been taken. The MAP/TOP users group has declared that MAP Version 3.0 will undergo no major revisions during the next six years. This provides a stable environment in which users can plan with some degree of confidence. Similarly, vendors have said they expect the announcement to "cause future sales to escalate."[18]

NOTES

1. Notice that the economics of networks differs in important ways from that of chains of outlets that are not intrinsically connected. As an example, contrast the qualitative difference between the existence of a McDonald's restaurant in Chicago with that of a local telephone exchange there. In the former case the absence of the Chicago restaurant does have an effect on other McDonald's restaurants as travelers from Chicago to other cities will be less aware of the chain's reputation and so less inclined, perhaps, to patronize McDonald's on their travels. By contrast, the absence of a local telephone exchange affects all telephone subscribers since those who live outside the Chicago area are deprived of the ability to speak to Chicagoans.

2. In some markets the market power of the "network gatekeeper" is so strong that government regulation will inevitably be brought to bear. Thus, access to telecommunications networks is tightly regulated both in the United States and abroad.

3. For additional discussion of this point, see S. M. Besen, and G. Saloner, "Compatibility Standards and the Market for Telecommunications Services." Management in the 1990s Working Paper 88-049, May 1988.

4. This can arise, for example, from an individual customer wishing to combine the products of two different manufacturers (as in the case of a firm creating a computer system from the components of diverse suppliers); from two customers wishing to use related equipment (as in the case of firms desiring standardized software); from two customers wanting to be connected to the same network (as in the case of airlines who all wish to be listed on a common CRS); or from a single customer valuing access to a large network of outlets providing the desired service (as in the case of ATMs).

5. The greater the degree of standardization of these inputs, the easier it is for them to be mass produced and the lower the costs to all users. However, interrelatedness of this kind is usually not of great importance. Many manufacturing organizations are of sufficient size that they could exploit essentially all the scale economies that are to be had by producing only for their own consumption, and for many others nuts and bolts are an insignificant input into the manufacturing process.

6. This example draws heavily on two reports by the U.S. Department of Justice on the CRS industry.

7. The data in this paragraph are from the *Wall Street Journal,* November 21, 1986.

8. Ibid.

9. Ibid.

10. R. W. King, "A Texas Yankee's Software Sensation," *Business Week* May 27, 1985, p. 110.

11. *Business Week,* August 3, 1987.

12. "Will There Be a Fax in Every Foyer?" *Business Week,* August 3, 1987, p. 82.

13. S. Lane, "Entry and Competition in the ATM Manufacturers' Market," working paper, Economics Dept., Stanford University, May 1988.

14. These statistics are from T. Forester, *High-Tech Society* (Cambridge: MIT Press, 1987).

15. Consider, for example, the cases of manufacturers of PC clones, add-on boards for IBM personal computers, and CAD workstations.

16. This issue is discussed in much greater detail in G. Saloner, "Economic Issues in Computer Interface Standardization," mimeo, MIT.

17. *Computerworld,* April 1987.

18. *Computerworld,* September 1987.

CHAPTER 5

IT-Induced Business Reconfiguration

N. VENKATRAMAN

This chapter explores the structural and process changes required of a firm given the competitive threats and opportunities discussed in Chapter 4 (see Figure 5-1). In terms of the 1990s model, this chapter focuses more on the internal "forces," as shown below. Chapter 4 developed a framework that allows any given business to understand the new competitive threats and opportunities presented by the new information technology. Having understood this, management is then faced with the reality of making business investments to keep competitively strong and move toward its objectives. IT represents one major area in which the organization can make such investments. The 1990s program research has identified five levels of business reconfiguration associated with increasing investment in IT.

The starting point for such consideration is the role of general management. As was pointed out in Chapter 3, IT is not just a simple set of tools but one that can alter the way work is done and can shrink the effects of both time and space. IT can be thought of as a new engine for the organization. Such a fundamentally powerful tool, as IT will become in the 1990s, is best deployed by those with enough vision to see what it can realistically mean to the organization. In short, general management, and preferably senior general management, should be in direct control of the pace and direction of its use. This need for commitment of senior general management stems from two factors. The first is that we appear to be at a point when all organizations are beginning to apply IT. Therefore, options and opportunities are appearing rapidly and must be seized quickly—and carefully—if organizations are to remain competitive through the 1990s. Secondly, an organization cannot just choose to implement, without any planning, a particular piece of technology. Research has shown that it must do so in context, that it must consciously align its business strategy and its organization with its technology.

Strategy has traditionally been thought of at three levels: corporate, business (or strategic business unit), and function. Historically, IT has been considered one of the support functions. This is still the case in many companies today. As a support function IT has usually been considered an administrative expense rather than a business investment.

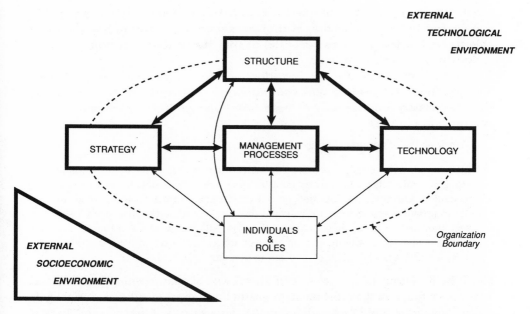

Figure 5-1. MIT90s framework—Chapter 5 emphasis.

Thus, senior general management has two important tasks if IT is to have any strategic impact. First, it must align the three levels of strategy; second, it must reposition IT from its historical support function to where it can play a critical role in strategy formulation and implementation. IT-enabled business reconfiguration is an evolutionary process and can be thought of as consisting of five stages.

Stage 1 is characterized by localized exploitation. In this stage IT is exploited within existing, isolated business activities, normally within one function.

Stage 2 can be thought of as building the internal electronic infrastructure, or platform, that permits the integration of tasks, processes, and functions. Stage 2 is a necessary condition if the investments in stage 1 are ever to be fully exploited.

The combination of stages 1 and 2 is the springboard for the remaining three stages. Without this base there is no evidence that an organization has the necessary foundation for the future. Stages 3, 4, and 5 are not sequential. Given that stages 1 and 2 have been accomplished, organizations have the option of deciding among the remaining three options.

Stage 3, business process redesign, results from a fundamental rethinking of the most effective way to conduct business.

Stage 4 is business network redesign. This is the use of IT by the organization to include suppliers, customers, or anyone else who can contribute to the firm's effectiveness. In a sense one is moving from the traditional formal organization to a "virtual" or "networked" organization that works together to accomplish a particular purpose. The 1990s program research has identified four transition steps.

In Stage 5, business scope redefinition, an organization decides to break out and exploit the new technology in the marketplace or in products. The contention in this section is that no single organization has yet been able to exploit the ultimate potential of this stage, and that many organizations have not even started.

A major challenge for organizations in the 1990s clearly lies in implementing these stages in a way that supports the degree of organizational transformation required to maintain effectiveness in the turbulent 1990s and beyond.

Consider the following quote:

> Information technology . . . is becoming increasingly the key to national economic well being, affecting virtually every industry and service. One would be hard pressed to name a business that does not depend on the effective use of information: to design products and services, to track and respond to market demands, or to make well-informed decisions. Information technology will change the world more permanently and more profoundly than any technology so far seen in history and will bring about a transformation of civilization to match. (Diebold, 1984)

This is by no means unique, as several quotes with similar meanings and implications can be found in the evolving literature on this topic. Nevertheless, it highlights the emerging impact of IT capabilities on the various facets of the economy. Even if we do not subscribe to such views in their entirety, it is clear that at the level of the individual firm, managers have to seriously evaluate the emerging role and implications of IT for strategic management in the next decade.

Peter Keen, writing at the beginning of the 1980s, remarked: "As yet there is no field entitled 'telecommunications and business policy (strategic management).' Discussions on the impact of communications technology usually focus on hardware, public policy, and regulation, or on specific applications such as office automation, teleconferencing, and electronic banking" (Keen, 1981). We certainly have not yet reached the point of clearly articulating the nature of interconnection between strategic management and IT—with a finite set of concepts, analytical framework, and normative prescriptions—but we are clearly observing the emergence of fundamental linkages between strategic management and IT.

This chapter is predicated on a fundamental logic that IT is to be increasingly viewed from a general management (or strategic management) perspective in addition to the traditional perspective of the information systems (IS) function. This reflects a logic that effective exploitation of the power and capabilities offered by IT could involve significant changes in organizational strategy, management structure, systems, and processes that cannot be accomplished from a functional perspective. It is that dynamic coalignment between the organization's strategic context and its IT infrastructure that contributes to increased efficiency and effectiveness. This chapter provides an overview of the emerging role of IT in strategic management, identifies a set of themes reflecting IT-induced business reconfigurations, illustrates their importance through research results from the Management in the 1990s Research Program, and develops implications for both theory and practice of strategic management in the next decade.

Our premise is that—within strategic management—if the decade of the 1970s is best known for formalized, analytical approaches to strategic planning, and the decade of the 1980s for its pronounced emphasis on competitor analysis and the search for competitive advantage, the dominant strategy theme of the 1990s will be the recognition and exploitation of IT capabilities for fundamental strategic choices of business scope, governance mechanisms, organizational reconfiguration, and competitive actions in the marketplace.

THE SHIFTING ROLE OF IT IN ORGANIZATIONS

The Traditional Supportive Role

Within strategic management, there is widespread agreement on a three-level categorization of the strategy concept in terms of corporate, business, and functional strategies, where the levels are formally linked through strategic planning processes and systems. Thus, corporate-level strategy develops the overall vision and sets the agenda and guidelines for business-level strategies, which in turn direct functional strategies. In this perspective, the IS function has been typically viewed as a support activity concerned with the efficient utilization of its resources for providing the required level of information support for management; and IT is its technological core or architecture. IT is thus viewed as the supporting infrastructure for the implementation and administration of "higher-level" strategies, and the allocation of resources for the IS function reflects this view of IT as a utility. The level of resources is based on "administrative expenses" considerations rather than as business investments that could potentially reshape the organization's strategic thrusts.

The Emerging Strategic Role

However, in recent years, we have observed a significant transformation in the role definitions for IS and IT within management. Astute managers have recognized that IT offers the capability to redefine the boundaries of markets and structural characteristics, alter the fundamental rules and basis of competition, redefine business scope, and provide a new set of competitive weapons. The evolving literature in this area is replete with (1) anecdotes of innovative uses of IT to gain, albeit short-term, competitive benefits, and (2) descriptive and normative frameworks that are intended to enable managers to identify and evaluate potential IT-based applications. It has become fashionable to refer to IT as offering attractive sources of strategic advantage—although the fundamental causal forces for creating and sustaining them is still unclear. What is clear, however, is that the traditional role definition needs to be changed to reflect a more central, strategic role for IT within management.

The emerging redefinition in the role for IT within organizations can be best understood as the result of convergence of two concurrent (and perhaps equally powerful) forces—referred to here as *technology push* and *competitive pull*—as shown in Figure 5-2.

The general characteristic of the first force is perhaps well known even to the casual observer, but two issues deserve special mention. One is the significant improvements in the price-performance ratio of IT. As discussed in Chapters 2 and 3, rapid advances in the various components of information technologies have resulted in continuous improvements in the sophistication and price-performance ratio of information technologies in the last decades, and this trend is expected to continue at least as rapidly in the future. Thus, it is now possible for firms to design and deploy IT-based applications as competitive weapons at a fraction of the cost

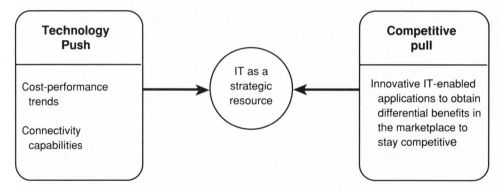

Figure 5-2. The emergence of a strategic role for IT in organizations.

that prevailed just a few years ago. The second issue is the increased connectivity capabilities over time. It is now possible to develop sophisticated forms of connectivity involving multiple types of hardware, software, and communication systems. These have significant implications for enhancing productivity at different levels: (1) individuals (e.g., better informational and decision support for structured and unstructured tasks); (2) task groups (e.g., increased coordination and group support); (3) across organizations (i.e., electronic integration enabled by the acceleration of electronic data interchange, EDI, and the consequent changes in business processes).

The nature and importance of the second force, competitive pull, can be understood by focusing on the level of competitive intensity in various markets. It is perhaps a truism that markets are becoming highly competitive and that the traditional sources of competitive advantages are diminishing as competitors strive to attain parity with one another. Hence, managers are constantly looking for new and innovative mechanisms to obtain differential advantages, and IT offers the best potential to provide new and powerful sources of obtaining distinctive advantages in the marketplace. The increasing array of innovative uses of IT seen in the marketplace is a reflection of the potential that IT offers for creatively exploiting these capabilities to obtain differential competitive benefits. Thus, the key issue for competitive pull is not the mere deployment of new systems and applications but leveraging them to obtain firm-specific differential benefits in the marketplace. This specific issue is the theme for discussion in the following paragraphs.

THE CHALLENGE FOR STRATEGISTS

Our fundamental premise is that it is no longer a question of whether IT has a strategic role but how to exploit IT in strategic management or, more precisely, how to develop strategy-IT alignment. For strategists—who have long treated IT as belonging to the technical and/or the administrative core of their business—the new challenge is how best to reconceptualize the role of IT in business, how to identify the applications relevant to their particular strategic context, and how to reconfigure the

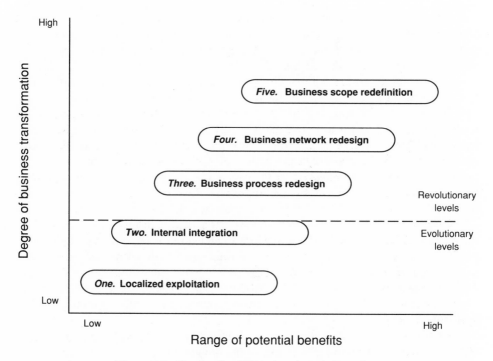

Figure 5-3. Five levels of IT-induced reconfiguration.

business to not only fully exploit the available IT capabilities but also to differentiate their operations from this competitors.

Based on our research, we classify the emerging challenge for the strategists in terms of a hierarchy of five levels of business reconfigurations. These levels are not conceptualized as a stages-of-evolution model but as distinct levels of business reconfigurations with an explicit focus on the role of IT. Figure 5-3 is a schematic representation of these five levels, along two basic dimensions—the degree of business transformation and the range of potential benefits from IT.

Level one is *localized exploitation,* concerned with the exploitation of IT within business functions such as manufacturing or marketing or even isolated business activities within the functions. This involves the deployment of IT applications that improve task efficiency of operations. Thus, applications achieve some function-specific goals (i.e., localized) without necessarily influencing related areas of operations.

Level two is *internal integration,* which is a logical extension of the first in the sense that IT capabilities are exploited in all the possible activities within the business process. Two types of integration are critical here: technical integration, namely the integration of the different systems and applications using a common IT platform; and the organizational integration of different roles and responsibilities that exploits the technical integration capabilities. In other words, the deployment of a common IT platform serves to integrate the organization's business processes, potentially enhancing efficiency and effectiveness.

These two levels are viewed as evolutionary, requiring relatively incremental changes in the existing organizational processes. In contrast, the other three levels are conceptualized as revolutionary, requiring fundamental changes in the nature of business processes, as discussed below.

Level three is *business process redesign,* involving the reconfiguration of the business using IT as a central lever. Instead of treating the existing business processes as a constraint in the design of an optimum IT infrastructure, the business process itself is redesigned to maximally exploit the available IT capabilities. This reflects conscious efforts to create an alignment between the IT infrastructure and the business process, rather than simply superimpose the technology platform on the existing business processes. If we believe that the capabilities of IT signal a major departure from the capabilities offered by the Industrial Revolution, then the distinction between levels two and three can be better understood.

Level four is *business network redesign,* concerned with the reconfiguration of the scope and tasks of the business network involved in the creation and delivery of products and services. This includes the business tasks both within and outside the formal boundaries of a focal organization and the consequent redesign of this "virtual business network" through IT capabilities. Thus, electronic integration across key partners in the changed business network becomes the dominant strategic management challenge.

Finally, level five is *business scope redefinition,* concerned with the *raison d'être* of a corporation, pertaining to the possibilities of enlarging the business mission and scope (through related products and services) as well as shifting the business scope (through the substitution of traditional capabilities with IT-enabled skills).

Level One: Localized Exploitation

This is the most basic level at which IT capabilities can be exploited within a business. At the outset, it is useful to distinguish between the exploitation of IT within a business activity or task and the role of IT in decision making. For example, while the deployment of a computerized order entry system has implications for both the decision-making process and changes in the tasks and activities, our focus is on the latter.

A Schematic Representation

Figure 5-4 is a schematic representation of a business process in terms of input, operations, and output—each consisting of two (illustrative) stages. The business tasks/ activities are separated from the management and administration to better delineate the specific areas of exploitation of IT capabilities. It represents the process at two points in time: before, depicting the process prior to the exploitation of IT; and after, depicting the state after the exploitation of IT (alternatively, readers can substitute the terms *without* for *before* and *with* for *after*).

In this illustrative case, two (isolated) business activities are fundamentally reconfigured using IT capabilities. Specifically, the tasks of stage 3 are redesigned with greater exploitation of IT capabilities (e.g., CAD/CAM), while in stage 6, both the operations and administration are impacted by the application of a new IT-based system (e.g., customer support system and/or order entry system). Alternatively,

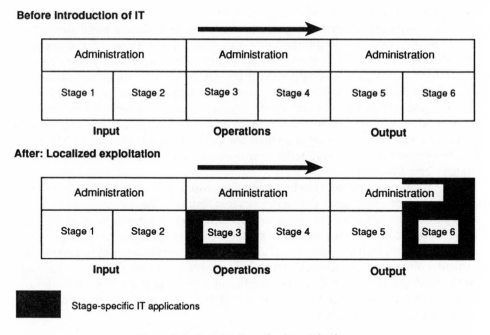

Figure 5-4. Level 1: Localized exploitation.

stage 3 could be the original loan application processing function of a credit-card company, while stage 6 could be the authorization of credit (purchases or cash advances). Both these stages could benefit from specific IT applications that could improve the operating efficiency of tasks. It is fairly straightforward to conceptualize and assess the benefits—efficiency and, in some cases, even effectiveness.

This level is very likely to be familiar to many (if not all) readers. Indeed, a significant proportion of managers is likely to claim that their business could long be characterized in this level. The discussion of this level is intended only as the referent for later levels.

Benefits of Localized Exploitation

An obvious question relates to the expected benefits of localized exploitations of IT. Following a general classification of benefits in terms of efficiency and effectiveness, our research indicates that the benefits at this level are more related to efficiency than effectiveness. However, the growing interest in this level of exploitation for strategists lies in the possibility that some applications have resulted in effectiveness, or more popularly termed as *strategic benefits.*

Over the last decade, we have observed a steady increase in applications we term here as localized exploitation across many business activities. The popular examples include order entry systems, customer support systems, computer-integrated design and manufacturing, reservation systems, just-in-time inventory systems, and so on. Indeed, the use and benefits of these systems have been so pervasive that they have been loosely termed *strategic information systems or competitive information systems.*

We argue that no system in its generic form is strategic. Our position is that there is no such thing as a generic strategic information system, since a particular system derives its role, meaning, and importance only in a given business context—embedded by its organizational and market environments. Thus, not all order entry systems are strategic, although some could provide critical sources of competitive advantages that are best understood and assessed against the backdrop of specific organizational, strategic, and competitive contexts. Similarly, not all airline reservation systems are strategic, although there are strong reasons to believe that American and United have leveraged them more effectively than their competitors, such as Frontier or TWA (see Chapter 4); and all automatic teller machines (ATMs) do not generically provide strategic benefits at all times.

It is the unique relationship between an organization's strategic thrusts, distinctive competence, and market characteristics that results in the realization of IT-based strategic benefits and not in the mere deployment of a generic system or application. This follows from a simple axiom that strategic benefits occur because of a favorable asymmetry in the marketplace, and if all competitors are equally positioned along a particular dimension, no distinctive set of advantages can accrue. Thus, the challenge for the strategist is to identify those activities of a business that are most promising for exploiting IT capabilities given specific strategies pursued and the competitive conditions in the marketplace.

Enablers and Inhibitors

Although we believe that several organizations are already at the level of localized exploitation with some experimental activities to exploit IT capabilities, a relevant question is, what are the major enablers and inhibitors at this level? The identification of these enablers and inhibitors also provides a referent for the later levels. For the purpose of discussion across levels, these are classified into technological and organizational.

For level one, the technological enablers are the favorable cost-performance trends and aggressive push by the IT vendors in terms of offering system solutions, thus minimizing the effort required to introduce the new technology. The organizational enablers are ease of assessing cost benefits in terms of efficiency in relatively narrow, well-defined areas of operations, and the relatively localized impact resulting in minimal disturbance to existing operations. In contrast, the technological inhibitors are the likelihood of obsolescence of the present generation of technology and expected further reductions in cost-performance trends in the future. The organizational inhibitors include the lack of a strategic vision for IT (i.e., no shifts in role definition for IT away from a support role) and an unwillingness on the part of senior management to treat IT as a potential source of realizing marketplace advantages. On balance, we have observed that enablers have a stronger impact, resulting in increased localization exploitation of IT within business. Figure 5-5 summarizes the major enablers and inhibitors for this level of reconfiguration.

Implications

Three managerial implications emerge for this level, namely:

Identification of high-leverage activities. Although some activities have greater scope for exploiting IT capabilities than others (e.g., customer service, order

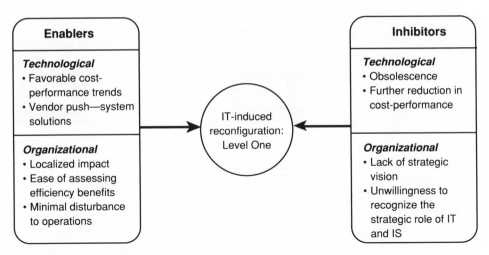

Figure 5-5. Localized exploitation: Enablers and inhibitors.

entry, etc.), the degree of leverage from specific IT applications varies considerably. Thus, while localized exploitation may appear to be simple and routine, the realization of effectiveness (or strategic benefits) requires a careful analysis of competitive and organizational conditions and the articulation of strategic thrusts.

Rejection of generic strategic information systems. While analysis of successful cases of realization of significant benefits (not only efficiency but also effectiveness) could provide insights into potential areas of application in other instances, it is a serious mistake to conceptualize systems in generically strategic terms across different contexts. Thus, it is important to identify systems that provide maximal benefits to a given organzation and not simply adopt systems that have been used by others in the marketplace. The latter may be necessary to reduce areas of inadequacy, but such systems do not provide any significant source of differential advantage.

Recognition of the scope of transformation. Localized exploitation of IT is only a starting point for IT-induced business reconfiguration; it is not an end in itself. Thus, while it is useful to conceptualize and design applications within narrow domains, their potential scope and direction of extensions should be formally recognized.

Level Two: Internal Integration

The next level of transformation recognizes the centrality of an IT platform in the integration of the entire business process. It is a logical extension of the first level in the sense that every activity exploits relevant IT capabilities given a common IT infrastructure. However, it is more than level one with all the activities exploiting their isolated IT applications, since the integration of business activities through an IT platform is a central, distinctive feature at this level. Thus, it is best viewed as a

Before: Localized exploitation

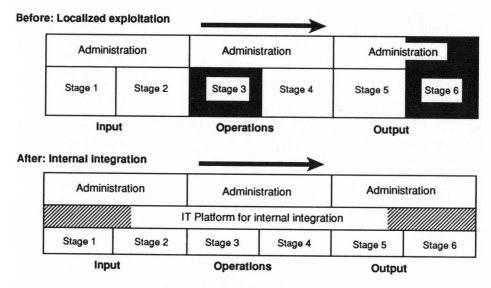

Figure 5-6. Internal integration.

combination of two types of integration—technological and organizational. The technological integration may be relatively easier to conceptualize and achieve than the organizational integration that exploits the capabilities of technological integration. While a large percentage of managers are likely to identify themselves with level one, our research indicates that a much smaller proportion are likely to conclude that they have already reached level two. Indeed, our research indicates that a major initiative among leading corporations is the creation of an IT platform that could permit organizational integration of their business processes. Figure 5-6 highlights the role of IT at this level, using the before-versus-after representations—where the central issue is the IT platform that interconnects the business activities. The before representation reflects the localized exploitation mode (level one) as it is a realistic referent for comparison.

IT Platform for Internal Integration as a Strategic Choice

It is critical to recognize that the deployment of an IT platform is not a technological solution independent of an organization's strategic context. We believe that there is no generic platform that is appropriate for all organizations even within the same industry. Thus, each organization should design and deploy an appropriate IT platform to interconnect its business activities along a chosen direction (e.g., increased interdependence between marketing and R&D or between marketing and manufacturing). The expectation is that such a platform will permit the exploitation of efficiency-related benefits of compression of time and distance as well as effectiveness-related benefits of information sharing across the business process. This platform will also provide the backdrop for organizational integration of activities. Thus, the movement to level two reflects a strategic decision to exploit benefits of integrating the distinct business activities and the deployment of an IT platform that serves as the basis for such an integration.

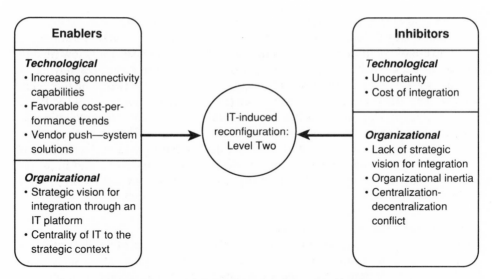

Figure 5-7. Internal integration: Enablers and inhibitors.

Figure 5-7 summarizes the key enablers and inhibitors. The major technological enablers are the increasing connectivity capabilities, the availability of integrated system solutions, and the favorable cost-performance trends. While the technological enablers are more widely applicable, the organizational inhibitors, by their very nature, are more idiosyncratic. The major enabler is the managerial recognition of the role and benefits of IT-induced integration, which emerges from a fundamental acceptance of the centrality of IT to the organization's strategic context. In contrast, the technological inhibitors—where applicable—stem from increased uncertainty of future developments as well as high costs of integration. The organizational inhibitors include general inertia and resistance to change as well as the associated conflicts pertaining to centralization versus decentralization of the critical IT platform. We believe that the necessary technology for internal integration is already available (with steadily decreasing costs of technology), and the critical inhibitors are organization-related. Our research indicates that the movement toward level two is characterized by an organizational belief and commitment to integrate the business processes through an IT platform.

Individual Income Tax Return Preparation Business as a Case of Internal Integration

In the United States, there exists a market for providing services (at a fee) to taxpayers in the preparation of their annual income tax returns, and approximately 50 percent of individual returns are filed using a paid preparer. It is a once-a-year service activity fulfilled by a range of players—individual accountants/CPAs, small tax return preparation firms, large return preparation firms (such as H&R Block), and the Big Eight accounting firms. These firms compete through such factors as adequate knowledge to interpret the tax codes for the submission of accurate and valid tax returns, convenient locations for access by consumers, brand name or personal contacts, reasonable fees, and efficient and courteous service. The market has been fairly stable with very modest growth in demand and negligible shifts in relative market positions.

The use of computers in this business process has been historically low (mainly limited to back-office data processing), with many smaller businesses relying on external service bureaus. The task of transmitting the returns between the individual taxpayer and the Internal Revenue Service (IRS) is carried out by the U.S. Postal Service (USPS). This situation can be best described as localized exploitation. In 1985 the IRS decided to introduce the concept of electronic filing of individual tax returns with the primary motive of receiving the tax return data in digitized form. For the IRS, this initiative has obvious implications for cost savings and improved accuracy, but let us analyze the emerging impact on the tax return preparation business.

Comparison of Business Processes

Figure 5-8 is a schematic representaion of the business process of an illustrative tax return preparation organization before and after electronic filing. More specifically, the first representation is localized exploitation, while the second highlights the potential role of an IT platform in integrating the business activities in the postelectronic filing era. In the first representation, the benefits of IT are at best efficiency-related and are applicable only to some specific activity such as preliminary data processing or return preparation. In contrast, a common IT platform provides the opportunity not only to realize efficiency-related benefits (i.e., lower unit cost of return preparation) but also to offer new value-added activities that are fundamentally interconnected with computerized tax return preparation activities.

Consider the volume of refund transactions between the taxpayers and the IRS. In a given tax year, 75 million taxpayers receive refunds, with an average refund of $900, resulting in approximately $67.5 billion of transactions. Prior to electronic filing (and the consequent possibility of direct deposit of refunds), there was no systematic mechanism to leverage this level of refund transactions. Thus, localized exploitation of IT was not only adequate but also most appropriate. However, electronic integration between the return filers (either stand-alone electronic filing firms or return preparers who also file electronically) and the IRS offers the necessary mechanisms to leverage the filing activity for other value-added services, such as "rapid refunds" or "refund-anticipated loans" through strategic alliances with financial service firms. The change is occurring because of the creation of a new "value-adding" role, namely, electronic filing of returns—which was traditionally carried out by the USPS with no mechanism for adding value. But electronic filing with direct deposit allows the electronic filer to develop electronic gateways to financial institutions that result in additional loan products (and other financial services) based on the knowledge that the tax forms have been accurately prepared and transmitted to the IRS (with virtual assurance of receiving the refund electronically to the designated direct deposit account). Suddenly, loans can be offered against the "collateral" of tax refunds, which is virtually assured (except in exceptional, complicated cases) with accurate preparation and transmission of tax returns.

Further, armed with valuables data (with prior approval of the taxpayer) on an individual's financial status, it is possible to offer specially tailored financial products. An interesting case in point is provided by American Express, IDS Tax Services,

Before: Localized exploitation

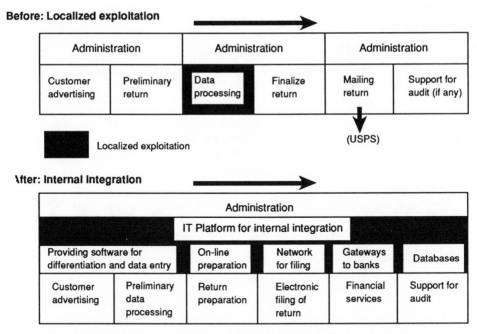

Figure 5-8. From localized exploitation to internal integration: The tax return preparation business.

which has recently launched a new company—AmeriTax—centrally rooted in the concept of exploiting electronic filing for competitive advantage. Using the electronic filing concept, they not only offer return preparation services but also develop a conduit for offering a larger set of financial products and services. Several other financial services firms are considering "leveraging" the return preparation activity for their products and services. However, this requires a common IT platform rather than isolated uses of IT-based applications. The basic business process has not been changed, but the availability of a common IT-platform offers the scope to realize strategic benefits that are otherwise not possible. Figure 5-9 is a summary of enablers and inhibitors in the specific context of the tax return preparation case.

Benefits of Internal Integration
In this level, the benefits relate to both efficiency and effectiveness. The former includes benefits resulting from compression of time and distance, leading to cost savings; the latter focuses on the opportunity to develop new competitive weapons or value-added services. Efficiency benefits may be viewed as the aggregates of benefits of the individual activities, while sources of effectiveness emerge primarily through integration. Thus, Merrill Lynch's Cash Management Account (CMA) is an example of successful exploitation of IT for strategic benefits, not because of an isolated IT application within one business activity but because of the organization's ability to interrelate its set of activites using a common IT platform to offer an "integrated product." Similarly, the now famous systems such as the Baxter–American Hospital Supply (ASAP System) and the McKesson (Economost) are not strategic

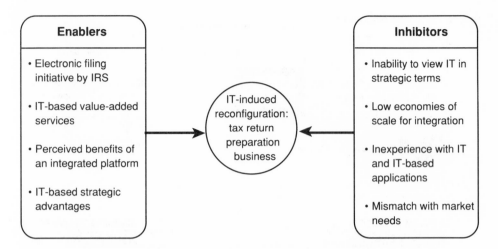

Figure 5-9. IT-induced business reconfiguration in level 2: Enablers and inhibitors in the tax return preparation business.

order entry systems because of localized exploitation of IT within order-receiving or order-processing activities. Their strategic nature is a result of the integration of business processes supported by these systems, which were different from the systems of their competitors at that time.

Our conclusion, therefore, is that while localized exploitation may provide strategic benefits in some select cases, they are invariably short-lived and can be successfully erased by competitive imitations. The real, longer-term, potentially sustainable advantage accrues to an organization because of internal integration of business activities designed to exploit IT-enabled business opportunities differently from its competitors.

Implications

Two key managerial implications at this level are:

Articulation of the logic and rationale for internal integration. While conceptually elegant and intuitively appealing, it is important that each firm develops its own rationale and criteria for internal integration of business processes using the IT platform. The articulation of the vision serves as the basis for developing detailed technological and organizational decisions to achieve integration. This vision reflects the particular mode of leveraging IT to support the strategic context.

Recognition of the dynamics of integration. Given the turbulent marketplace, the logic and the basis of integration are not static. Constant review and reassessment of the requirements of business integration through the IT platform are necessary as business conditions and technological developments evolve over time.

Before: Internal integration

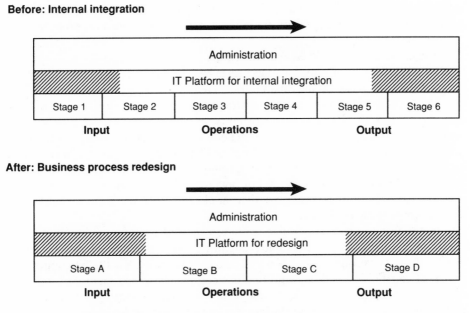

Figure 5-10. Level 3: Business process redesign.

Level Three: Business Process Redesign

The first two levels are evolutionary—requiring relatively incremental changes in the business processes to exploit IT capabilities. In contrast, the other three levels are revolutionary—requiring radical changes in business practices. The central premise at this level is that IT is a lever for designing business processes and that it should not be simply overlaid on the existing organizational context as viewed earlier. Instead of simply treating the existing business processes as a constraint in the design and development of an optimum IT infrastructure, the basic logic for configuring the business activities itself is questioned. Thus, a business process that maximally exploits the available IT capabilities is developed, and we begin to see an evolving alignment between technology and organization as opposed to the previous levels that may be best described as technology imperatives.

Figure 5-10 is a schematic representation of level three with before-versus-after representations. For the purpose of comparisons, the before representation is the level of internal integration (level two). The key is the reconfiguration of the sequence of tasks to better exploit IT capabilities. In this illustrative representation, the new stage (A) is a reconfiguration of tasks previously contained in stages 1, 2, and 3; stage B is a reconfiguration of stages 2, 3, and 4, and so on. For example, stage A may be a redesigned, more self-contained manufacturing stage which now accommodates parts of previous stages 1 and 2. It is important to recognize that it is not a simple consolidation of the stages but a redesign of relevant processes supported by not only an IT platform but also respecification of organizational roles, reporting relationships, and managerial responsibilities. A movement toward level three calls for a reassessment of the fundamental logic of the business process requiring streamlining of not merely the adjoining stages or activities but the entire business process.

The Logic of Business Process Redesign

Currently, the design of business processes is based on a set of principles of organization developed to exploit the capabilities offered by the Industrial Revolution. Concepts such as centralization versus decentralization, span of control, line vesus staff, and balancing authority versus responsibility, as well as mechanisms for coordination and control, are derived from this general set of principles. Although these are generally valid even today, it appears that the IT revolution could significantly alter some of these principles—thus rendering some modes of organizing relatively inefficient. While a new set of principles of organizing has not yet emerged, it is clear that the basics for business process design should at least be reassessed in light of the new capabilities offered by IT.

In the few selected cases where we have observed business process redesign, a common feature is an unmistakable recognition that revolutionary changes in the design of organizational processes are necessary to best exploit the emerging technological capabilities. Although no one has completely transformed their business process, we are beginning to see leading-edge companies initiating radical business process redesigns to be not only efficient but also competitive. More importantly, the logic of redesign appears to be intertwined with the strategic thrusts in the marketplace.

Batterymarch Financial Management Corporation as a Case of Business Process Redesign

Batterymarch Financial Management is a leading financial investment management firm that in 1986 managed more than $12 billion in pension funds. Its basic strategy as articulated by its chief executive follows the "contrarian philosophy," namely, "finding those stocks that are out of favor or neglected by other portfolio managers." In the words of the founder, Dean LeBaron, "The investment firm of the future will be a few senior people and one big machine." Thus, the business process for implementing such a strategy is likely to be different from the corresponding process of a traditional pension fund firm. In Figure 5-11, the business process of Batterymarch is compared with a typical pension fund firm including the personnel requirement for each, normalized for the size of operations. It is worth noting that the representations of the two business processes are significantly different. Further, this comparison indicates that Batterymarch is able to leverage its personnel more effectively: 36 for the traditional model versus 18 for Batterymarch, and 108 support personnel versus 17 for Batterymarch. This implies not only lower operating costs for managing pension funds but also significantly higher leverage of information pertaining to stock movement contained in their database and supporting system infrastructure.

The implication from the Batterymarch example can be summarized as (1) a contrarian approach to investment management, a strategy that is inherently anchored in the power and capability of IT because of the heavy demand for data, and (2) the redesign of its business processes (relative to the industry) that best exploits its investments in IT. Thus, it is not that the traditional pension fund firm does not use IT, but its use is either localized exploitation (level one) or internal

Traditional pension fund management firm

Support	13	36	4	55
Professionals	9	24	3	--
	Stock analysis	Strategy	Portfolio management	Trading	Record keeping

Batterymarch

Support	9		8
Professionals	12 investment people and 3 systems		3
	Strategy development	Portfolio construction	Trading	Account administration

Figure 5-11. Business process redesign: The case of Batterymarch Financial Management Co.

integration (level two). Batterymarch, in contrast, represents business process redesign (level three) and an attempt to attain strategy—IT alignment.

Enablers and Inhibitors

Figure 5-12 summarizes the major set of enablers and inhibitors for level three. The technological enablers continue to be cost-performance trends and the availability of new and powerful IT applications that permit process redesign. The organizational enablers are not only the awareness of the power and capabilities of IT but also the willingness on the part of the top management to make quantum revolutionary changes to fully exploit IT power. Further, in this level, a new class of enablers—marketplace characteristics—emerges. We expect competitive pressures to play a significant role in the redesign. In some cases, strong market positions may trigger innovative patterns of process redesigns, while in other instances, weak players might proactively use IT-based process redesign to differentiate their operations and outperform their competitors.

With reference to the inhibitors, the technological inhibitors relate to the uncertainty as well as the cost of redesign, while organizational inhibitors are more critical. These include the lack of a strategic vision of the role and power of IT, organizational inertia, and the costs (direct and indirect) of achieving the business transformation.

Implications

The managerial implications at this level are:

Recognition of the nature and impact of business process redesign. The single most important implication relates to the recognition and understanding of the scope and impact of potential IT-enabled process redesign. Often, managers are able to conceptualize the first two levels but not this level. If managers can systematically analyze and arrive at an IT-enabled alternative process and compare

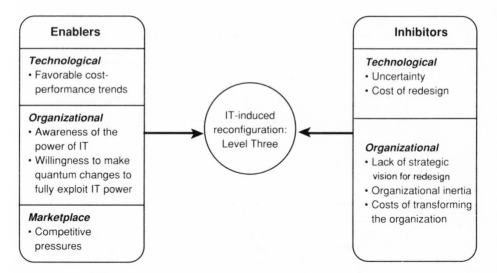

Figure 5-12. Business process redesign: Enablers and inhibitors.

the relative benefits (even approximately), the scope of impact can be better understood. However, it is important to understand that the articulation of the desired state of process redesign is only the starting point for organizational transformation. Effective formulation and implementation of redesign strategies involve carefully and constantly managed programs.

The role of strategy in business process redesign. Effective redesign—while balancing technological and organizational capabilities—should fundamentally be guided by the organization's strategic thrust and direction. There is no optimal or generic approach to business redesign independent of the goals and strategies of the business.

Level Four: Business Network Redesign

Thus far, we have seen IT-induced reconfiguration within a single organization. In contrast, this level represents the use of IT for redesigning the nature of exchange among multiple participants in a business network. Perhaps the most significant challenge from IT lies in the redesign of business networks to create new capabilities and skills as well as favorable asymmetries in the marketplace. Given its importance, we define this strategy as *electronic integration.* This needs to be distinguished from other popular terms such as *electronic data interchange* (EDI) or *interorganizational information systems* (IOIS). For the purpose of discussion here, EDI refers to the technical features of the networks, involving important issue of standards for information exchange, and IOIS refers to the characteristics of the specific system such as the nature of input/output, protocols for transaction and use, connectivity, reliability, and safety. In contrast, strategies for electronic integration address business issues involving the relative authority and responsibilities of the different participants and the consequent implications for obtaining differential benefits in the marketplace.

Our focus here is not on the issues central to technical standards (EDI) or on the features of the system (IOIS) but on the strategies for electronic integration that have a fundamental bearing on the redesign of business networks.

The Rationale for Business Network Redesign

The fundamental rationale for the consideration of business network redesign here is as follows. Given that businesses operate within a larger network of suppliers, buyers, intermediaries, and competitors, the sources of competitive advantage lie partly within a given organization and partly in the larger business network. Thus, sources of efficiency and effectiveness need to be exploited through integration of activities in the larger network. This has been traditionally carried out through vertical integration (redefinition or enlargement of the firm's boundaries and the articulation of the exchange mechanisms with the critical players at the ends of the value chain) or horizontal integration (across different business units in a diversified organization or acquisition of similar capability in the marketplace). Electronic integration is positioned here as a serious alternative to the strategic options of vertical and horizontal integration in the sense that the required capabilities are exploited through creative mechanisms of information exchange and control without necessarily their full ownership. Stated differently, electronic integration can be considered as a quasi-firm or a quasi-market mechanism that is fundamentally designed and operated through the capabilities offered by information technology. This issue is elaborated below.

Strategic Options in Business Network Redesign

At a basic level, there are two considerations in the design of business networks:

Strategies for business governance. This is the approach adopted to develop relationships with key participants in the marketplace. This is conceptualized along a continuum from loosely coupled (arm's-length, standard relationship like the classic market transactions with relatively low cost to switch from one participant to another) to tightly coupled (unique, specialized relationships with high cost to switch from one to another). The specific mode of functioning is dictated by the idiosyncratic nature of the exchange (i.e., products or services) and its criticality, which are dictated by the business strategic thrusts and independent of the IT.

Strategies for IT governance. This is the approach adopted to govern the IT network across the multiple participants. This is conceptualized along a continuum ranging from a common role (i.e., the position occupied by any given player is no different from the position occupied by other players in the network, as in the case of the adoption of a common EDI standard) to a unique role (i.e., the positions occupied by the different players are different because of either their use of a dedicated, proprietary network or their offering of specialized, value-added software or other services on the standard communications network). This continuum reflects the specific strategy adopted to exploit IT capabilities to support or shape the business governance decisions.

Figure 5-13 represents these two dimensions in a framework that highlights the four key strategic positions involving the integration of business governance thrusts and IT governance thrusts. The four positions are briefly discussed below.

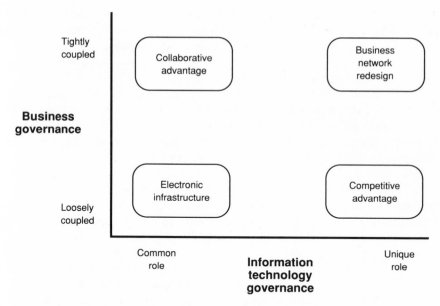

Figure 5-13. Strategic options for business network redesign.

The position defined by loosely coupled business governance and a common role for the IT governance is termed *electronic infrastructure.* In this position, there is no particular strategic advantage to any firm since none has distinctive capabilities through its position in the IT governance, and the business relationships are loosely coupled with low costs of switching. This represents the "standard mode of functioning," perhaps involving barriers for new entrants but relatively few sources of asymmetry among existing players. As we move along the horizontal axis, the next position is defined by unique positions in the IT governance with loosely coupled business relationships, and is termed *competitive advantage.* In this position, those that occupy the unique position in the IT governance structure are able to attain competitive advantage (albeit only for the short term). The sources of advantage in this position lie either in the proprietary linkage (such as the Baxter-ASAP system or the CIGNA-TED system) or through value-added services such as the airline reservation systems. Our argument is that the advantages are likely to be only in the short term since competitors will react to neutralize the benefits, especially if the benefits are significant. Thus, the advantages offered by the ATMs have been slowly neutralized to such an extent that they are now being considered as sources of incremental revenue rather than tools for strategic advantage.

The third position is given by the common IT role and tightly coupled business relationships, termed *collaborative advantage.* In this position, the opportunities exist for mutual collaborative advantage between participants. The IT network serves to improve the efficiency levels of the interconnected participants with minimal opportunity for any given player to realize differential advantage, in view of the criticality of the business relationship. Finally, the fourth position is defined by unique role and a tightly coupled business relationship, termed *business network redesign.*

The position offers opportunities for creatively exploiting IT capabilities to strengthen and modify the nature of the relationships with the key players in the marketplace. The opportunities for redesign of the nature of the relationship lie in the scope of electronic integration with differing roles, as discussed below.

Roles

Our premise is that the redesign of the nature of exchange among the players in a business network involves changing the roles or scope of electronic integration beyond information exchange or transactions. Based on our research, it appears that four distinct (and hierarchically related) roles exist:

Transactions. The network serves to exchange structured data between organizations using a prespecified, mutually accepted format (e.g., EDI). Common examples include electronic payments, order entry, and order-tracing systems—where transactions rooted in data transfer across organizations are conducted using computers and communications systems, and without any routine human interventions.

Inventory. The network is designed to make inventory "available and visable" from one party to another without excessive time delay. The critical distinction is that in addition to streamlined exchange of transaction data, it is possible to ascertain the "status" of inventory and trigger the "movement of goods." For example, in the manufacturing sector, electronic integration across buyers and suppliers enables the efficient implementation of just-in-time inventory systems and procedures. Similarly in the airline industry, the reservation systems make the inventory of seats visible and availabile to thousands of travel agents. Human intervention is more than what is required for transaction processing.

Process. A specific set of organizations integrate their business processes through electronic links (using a mutually acceptable format) for enhancing common benefits. This extends beyond making the inventory visible to the partners to include other arrangements, such as multiparty integrated manufacturing systems (e.g., design activities of one organization integrated with the manufacturing processes of another in a seamless manner), or a project that involves using components and services from multiple organizations. The distinctive feature is that a specific business network is created such that the relevant information is appropriately shared across various parts of the network to exploit both efficiency and effectiveness. This can be viewed as a logical extension of level two (internal integration) given that the integration is across distinct formal organizations for the creation of a virtual business network. The expectation is that the different parties would integrate their distinct activities in a symbiotic mode given certain commonly understood objectives. This subsumes the other two roles in the sense that some participants within the network may have a predominantly transaction role, while others manifest inventory or process roles. Further, the level of unstructuredness of information transfer is higher than that of the previous two roles.

Expertise. Specialized skills and expertise are shared using an appropriately designed business network. This role is characterized by unstructured information sharing and reflects the creation of a virtual intellectual network across physical and organizational boundaries. For example, it is possible to assess and interpret complex data (e.g., technical, managerial, legal, or medical) across different participants in a network before arriving at a final interpretation and conclusion. The challenge here is not information-based transaction but the effective interpretation and understanding of the complex meanings through the deployment of "knowledge networks."

These roles can be ordered along a continuum of unstructuredness of information—low (transactions) to high (knowledge).

Benefits

The range of potential benefits from electronic integration across these different roles can be parsimoniously classified as follows:

Operational efficiency. This reflects savings in operating cost (reduced errors and more efficient mode of information exchange) and time (quicker access to information) because of electronic transactions. While operating efficiency benefits are obvious and could be shared mutually across the different participants, the required capital costs could be asymmetrical. For example, with inventory movements using just-in-time inventory system, the upstream supplier may be required to carry a higher level of inventory than before. Although these costs could also be negotiated, it appears that in most cases the supplier is burdened with this additional cost.

Market positioning. This indicates the benefits that accrue by virtue of occupying certain positions in the marketplace. For example, the first mover could have benefits in the transaciton role with opportunities for specifying the standards, while it could provide some opportunities for differentiation in the short term in the inventory role.

Partnership conditions. These specify the scope of the business network in terms of the characteristics of the partners. For example, a focal organization may begin with selective inclusion of partners in the transaction exchange, but over a period of time it could adopt a policy of open exchange provided it has been able to establish itself as a standard. In other roles such as process or knowledge, the defintion and selection of partners is critical for deriving benefits from the network.

Strategic capabilities. These indicate the extent to which innovative mechanisms can be deployed in each role. For instance, it is relatively difficult to leverage the transaction role to realize strategic benefits, but the opportunities are relatively greater for the other roles.

Figure 5-14 combines these two dimensions—roles and benefits—to present a classificatory framework to conceptualize the nature of business network redesign enabled by IT. Figure 5-15 highlights the characteristics of the networks along these four roles. It is striking that much of the prior discussion on this topic has focused on the first two roles—transaction (e.g., order entry system) and inventory (e.g., airline res-

Roles	Operational efficiency	Market positioning	Partnership conditions	Strategic capabilities
Transactions	Operating cost savings	First-mover advantage; possibility of creating industry standard	Generally unrestricted	Low
Inventory	Benefits drift downstream	Opportunities for weak differentiation	Restricted through standard contracts	Low to medium
Process	Accelerates downstream drift	Opportunities for stronger differentiation	Restricted through specialized contracts (strategic alliances)	Medium
Expertise	Savings in time and costs are secondary	Opportunities for unique relationships	Specialized cooperative network arrangements	High

Figure 5-14. Business networks: Roles and benefits.

Roles	Nature of Information exchange	Number of partners	Network characteristics
Transactions	Structured	Unlimited	Biased → Unbiased
Inventory	Relatively structured	Limited by business scope	Biased → Unbiased market or hierarchies
Process	Relatively unstructured	Limited by business choice	Electronic integration across limited hierarchies
Expertise	Unstructured	Selective	Electronic Integration across selected hierarchies

Figure 5-15. Business networks: Roles and characteristics.

ervation system)—and on the first two classes of benefits. As noted in Figure 5-14, and discussed elsewhere in the literature, these two roles offer minimal opportunities to realize fundamental advantages in the marketplace. This has led to calling these systems a strategic necessity or electronic infrastructure (Fig. 5-13) rather than sources of competitive advantage. However, our position is that the real benefits would accrue when business networks are designed to reallocate the production and service operations (for instance) across a set of chosen partners to realize benefits from strategic alliances. Alternatively, knowledge-sharing networks that create unique cliques are another illustration of the type of benefits that can be realized from such networks. This reinforces the notion that simply automating existing operations provides only operational efficiency, but the real payoff occurs in exploiting the systems for market positional gains or reconceptualizing the business network. This is a major challenge for the strategists. Figure 5-16 is a comprehensive framework that positions business network redesign using three dimensions discussed here—business governance, IT governance, and the scope (roles) of electronic integration.

Figure 5-17 summarizes the major set of enablers and inhibitors at this level.

Implications

The managerial implications at this level are:

Conceptualizing strategies for electronic integration in terms of the intersection of three key decisions. It is critical to view electronic integration in terms of business governance decisions (the degree of coupling with different participants in the marketplace); IT governance decisions (the mode of differentiating the role and position in the IT network); and the scope (role) of integration—ranging from transactions to knowledge.

Conceptualizing organizational boundary in virtual terms. Business networks using the available and emerging connectivity capabilities strongly suggest the conceptualization of a virtual organization rather than a classical view of organizations and markets. Indeed, the creation of innovative virtual organizations (using various types of strategic alliances and cooperative mechanisms) that are interconnected using an IT platform would be an attractive source of advantage in the marketplace.

Level Five: Business Scope Redefinition

Strategy analysis typically starts with the proverbial question, "What business(es) are we in?"—with an attempt to define an organization's positions in terms of products, markets, and technologies. The aim is to explicate the logic underlying the composition of its portfolio of businesses, to identify differential strategic thrusts, and to develop criteria for allocation of scarce resources among the businesses. Considerations of business scope dictate major strategic activities such as diversification, divestment, consolidation, and mergers and acquisitions.

The final level assesses the potential role of IT in the redefinition of business scope. Two specific issues are considered: (1) business scope enlargement and (2) business scope shifts.

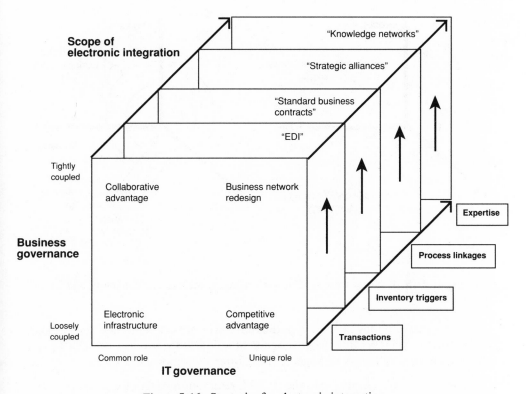

Figure 5-16. Strategies for electronic integration.

Business Scope Enlargement

As depicted schematically in Figure 5-18, it appears that IT offers some opportunities to expand the business scope, by such means as (1) selling information (repackaged and specially analyzed) as a new product and (2) offering value-added services related to the original business. Selling data is related to the value of information that varies

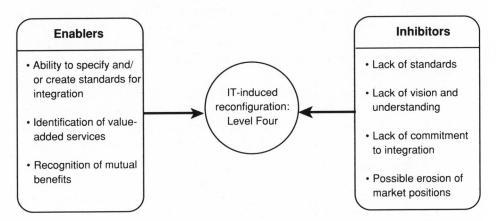

Figure 5-17. Business network redesign: Enablers and inhibitors.

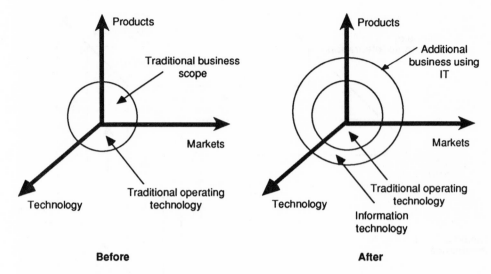

Figure 5-18. Business scope redefinition: Enlarging the business domain using IT.

across contexts and may be limited to those in the information business such as Dun & Bradstreet or TRW. But the emergence of value-added services through IT has wider applicability. This is highlighted using three well-known examples:

American Airlines. Its use of the SABRE reservation system for obtaining a significant edge in the competitive marketplace is legendary. However, what is often overlooked is the revenue-generating capability of SABRE from its hosts and cohosts in the United States and elsewhere. As it moved away from a biased electronic market toward an unbiased market, SABRE accepted several cohosts, and it is not insignificant that the subsidiary that is responsible for SABRE is the most profitable unit of American Airlines; more recently, SABRE accepted Delta as a partner for a payment of several hundred million dollars.

Otis Elevator. Their deployment of OTISLINE not only provided them with a competitive edge in terms of superior service capability but has also opened up a potentially new market for servicing non-Otis elevators. If they can differentiate their capability to service non-Otis elevators through their superior IT infrastructure, then it could signal another classic example of enlarging the business domain through IT.

McKesson. The use of the Economist system enabled McKesson to create new services such as management reports that are cost-effectively produced as a by-product of the order entry system, third-party claims processing as a peripheral activity using the same dataset, and drugstore credit-card systems.

In all these cases the additional businesses—by themselves—may not have been viable as stand-alone businesses, but as an integrated package that shares largely the same information set, they become cost-effective and provide an attractive basis for expanding the scope of business.

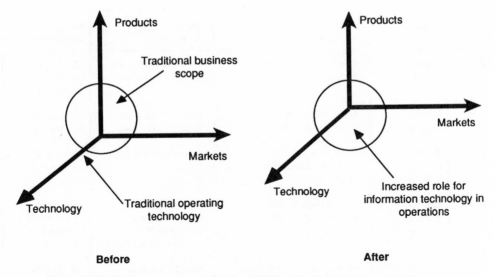

Figure 5-19. Business scope redefinition: Shifting the business domain using IT.

Shifting the Business Scope
Figure 5-19 depicts the shift in the business scope caused by information technology, which should be viewed as complementary to the enlargement of business domain (see Figure 5-18). A major task for strategists is to ensure that the functionalities offered by their "core technologies" are not made obsolete by emerging newer, substitute technologies. The importance of IT from a strategic management perspective lies in its potential to render many of the traditional tasks and skills obsolete. Because of improved functionality and superior cost-performance economies, it is now possible to redesign many operations more efficiently and effectively. For example, the traditional typesetting tasks and skills are rendered costly and ineffective by desktop publishing. And American Express has radically transformed the handling of its receipts from a paper form toward electronic imaging, thereby ushering in a new quality standard for its marketplace. Thus, in relation to Figure 5-19, the implication is that the core technology of the firms is shifting at a fast rate with an increased IT component in many industries, thus requiring appropriate strategic responses. Given the broad conceptualization of IT adopted in this book, it appears that nearly every major skill and task is likely to be affected by IT, although the degree of impact will vary. Hence, our view is that if firms proactively consider and adopt IT-based functionalities, they are more likely than otherwise to succeed in the long run.

The Individual Tax Preparation Market
as a Case in Point
It appears that electronic filing offers the potential to leverage the filing activity for additional value-added activities, while downplaying the relative importance of the preparation activity for certain type of returns. This is because the tax professionals—who primarily relied on their knowledge of tax codes for their sources of reve-

Level	Theme	Potential Impacts	Major objectives	Management Implications
One	Localized exploitation	Potentially high savings in narrow areas of business	Reduced costs and/ or improved service	Identify firm-specific areas for exploitation
Two	Internal integration	Integration offers both efficiency and effectiveness	Elevate IT as a strategic resource	Articulate the logic for integration
Three	Business process redesign	Powerful in creating differential capabilities in the marketplace	Reengineer the business with IT lever	Strategy—IT alignment
Four	Business network redesign	Opportunities for creatively exploiting capabilities	Create a virtual organization and occupy a central position in the network	Articulate the logic of network redesign for the focal firm
Five	Business scope redefinition	Altering the business scope both proactively and reactively	Identify new business as well as potential threats	Identification of new scope of business

Figure 5-20. Five levels of transformation: A summary.

nue—now are faced with the prospect of some competitors using return preparation software as viable substitutes for simpler returns. The ability to codify commonly used tax codes into standard (or modular) tax preparation software offers the potential to reduce the variable cost of operations and thus provide a larger set of services without proportional increase in operating cost.

It is important to note that the redefinition of business scope enabled by IT in the tax preparation market is neither unique nor significantly colored by the fact that a governmental agency was involved in the context. The transformation is enabled by the creation of new business roles (e.g., tax filing) that are fundamentally rooted in IT capabilities. It is perhaps accelerated by the favorable stance taken by the dominant player in the market, the IRS. Similarly, we believe that the potential that exists for enlarging the domain as well as proactively shifting the domain is not limited to the contexts described by the popular cases such as McKesson, Merrill Lynch, and *USA Today* but are more pervasive. Thus, the challenge for professional strategists is to identify and respond appropriately to these unmistakable trends.

Figure 5-20 summarizes the five levels of transformation through IT.

THE MANAGEMENT CHALLENGE

The discussion thus far has delineated five levels of IT-enabled business transformations. Not all levels may be relevant or critical to every organization, although it is worthwhile to evaluate each for its potential in different organizational settings.

Throughout this chapter, specific management implications have been enumerated for each level of transformation, but it appears worthwhile to synthesize the key management challenges here.

We synthesize the management challenge in terms of two issues: (1) the need to treat the IT infrastructure as a strategic resource and (2) the evolving alignment between the strategic context and IT—reflected in a framework termed the Strategic Alignment Model.

IT Infrastructure as a Strategic Resource

It is becoming increasingly clear that the successful exploitation of IT stems from a coalignment between the strategic context and the IT infrastructure of a business. Recall the popular examples of IT-enabled strategic benefits in the literature: Baxter–American Hospital Supply's ASAP System; McKesson's Order-Entry System; Merrill Lynch's Cash Management System; American Airlines' SABRE system; and United Airlines' APOLLO system. It is true that many of them were designed and deployed as specific responses to operational problems and bottlenecks, but they now play a central role in not only supporting but also shaping the respective organizational strategies. Indeed, a major reason why these are still touted as classic examples is that these organizations—having realized the strategic potential of their IT infrastructure—have continually ensured that their IT infrastructure serves as a cornerstone of their strategy. In all the successful cases, the characteristics of the present infrastructure are significantly different from the original infrastructure, and each successive generational change has been predicated on the role of IT to enable new strategic thrusts in the marketplace.

Our research indicates that the treatment of IT infrastructure can be categorized into three types, as follows:

I. Independent. In this type, the development of IT infrastructure takes place outside the organization's strategic context. Thus, design and modifications to the IT infrastructure are independent of the strategies pursued, implying a minimal role for the IT infrastructure in either shaping or implementing strategies. This reflects the traditional "support" role for IT as a "utility." The rationale for resource allocation reflects an administrative expense view.

II. Reactive. In this type, the organizations have sensed the importance of IT, with the result that there is increased awareness of IT as a possible conduit for implementing the chosen business strategy. Consequently, the design and development of IT infrastructure takes place given a particular strategic thrust. It is reactive in the sense that the chosen strategy directs the shape of IT architecture, but not vice versa.

III. Interdependent. In this type, the development and modifications to the IT infrastructure are in constant coalignment with the strategic context. Thus, modifications in the IT infrastructure signal implications for possible changes and improvements in strategies, while modifications in strategic thrusts trigger appropriate changes in the IT infrastructure. It truly reflects a bidirectional inter-

Distinctive characteristics	Type I "Independent"	Type II "Reactive"	Type III "Interdependent"
Description	Design of IT infrastructure is independent of the strategic	Design of IT infrastructure is derived from strategic context	Aims at a dynamic coalignment between the strategic context and the IT infrastructure
Leading indicators			
Structure	Relatively low level of the IS function	Recent trend toward increasing stature	IS/IT function viewed as a critical function within the organization
Systems	IT planning is operational, and is independent of strategic planning	IT/IS planning is derived from business plans	Strategic IS/IT planning identifies and responds to business opportunities
Resources	Treated as an "administrative expense"	Treated as a "business expense"	Treated as a "business investment"

Figure 5-21. Rearticulation of IT vision: Three dominant types.

dependent state, where the rationale for resource allocation reflects a business investment perspective.

Based on the preceding discussion, it is obvious that the IT infrastructure offers significant potential for not only supporting but also shaping the business strategies. Thus, while many organizations may belong to the first two types, it is clear that many successful organizations are moving toward the third type. Figure 5-21 compares these three types along some critical characteristics.

Movement toward Type Three: A Case Example
Consider the TED (Total Electronic Distribution) system of the CIGNA Companies—a leading insurance firm. Recently, they have deployed an electronic integration system (level four) in their property and casualty business to provide timely response to agents' requests on policy quotes. This is an example of type II, serving as a mechanism for implementing their business strategy. In simple terms, the functionality is similar to American Hospital Supply's ASAP system, in the sense that it is a dedicated system that connects the independent agent to CIGNA's operations only and is a simple form of business network redesign (level four). The expectation is that the agents would, at minimum, request a quote from CIGNA and, at maximum, channel more business to CIGNA, given its ability to respond more quickly than competitors to various detailed information during the course of finalizing a particular transaction.

If TED is viewed only as an electronic distribution channel for existing products, then it remains type II. On the other hand, if they could leverage their IT infrastructure to noncomplementary insurance products from "partners" in their business net-

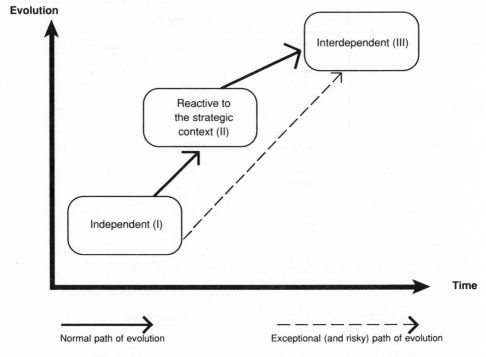

Figure 5-22. IT infrastructure vision: movement from type I to type III.

work (enlarged view of level four) or carry financial products other than insurance (level five), then it reflects a move toward type III. Thus, while they are expected to benefit in terms of efficiency gains as well as increases in volume through the deployment of an electronic integration system for their current strategy (type II), quantum strategic benefits are likely to accrue when they successfully move toward type III for leveraging the IT infrastructure for competitive differentiation.

Based on our research, it appears that it is dysfunctional to be type I, with no real linkage between strategy and the IT infrastructure, as it implies that potential gains in efficiency and effectiveness are sacrificed. Type II represents an adequate intermediate solution but has the danger that competitive benefits may be eroded as others imitate and adopt similar strategies. On the other hand, type III signals a more dynamic and constantly changing mode—with creative tensions between the strategic managers and the technologists with the common goal of exploiting technology for competitive benefits. Figure 5-22 depicts an evolutionary model which highlights the fact that it is logical to move from type I to III through II. For organizations of type I, it is tempting to move directly from type I to type III, but such a move may be risky given the absence of IT infrastructure linked to the strategic context. However, such a move may be appropriate when organizations are contemplating major strategic redirection rooted in IT capabilities.

Figure 5-23 is a summary of the emerging view in the treatment of IT infrastructure for strategic management.

Characteristic	Emerging view		
Focus	IT platform	NOT	Isolated systems
Investment vision	Business transformation	NOT	Technological sophistication
Investment criteria	Business criteria	NOT	Cost-benefit criteria alone
Scope of impact	Business domain	NOT	IT or IS domains
Executive responsibility	Strategic (line) manager	NOT	IT manager
Guiding principle	Strategy—IT alignment	NOT	IT for implementation

Figure 5-23. The emerging view of IT infrastructure.

Achieving Strategic Alignment between Business and IT Strategies

The major management challenge lies in the development of a dynamic alignment between the business strategic context and the IT strategic context. While this may be implicitly understood, there is a glaring lack of frameworks to conceptualize the nature of alignment in operational terms.

We argue that the alignment perspective should—at minimum—involve four domains: business strategy, organization infrastructure and processes, IT strategy, and IS infrastructure and processes. The model is represented in Figure 5-24, and the underlying dimensions are described below.

Business strategy is defined in terms of choices pertaining to the positioning of the business in the competitive product-market arena. It is defined in terms of three basic dimensions: business scope (articulated in terms of products and markets); distinctive competencies (articulated in terms of the salient characteristics that distinguished the firm in the competitive marketplace, such as superior service or product design); and business governance (articulated in terms of the nature of cooperative relationships, such as joint ventures and strategic alliances in the business arena).

Organization infrastructure and processes is defined in terms of the choices pertaining to the particular internal arrangements and configurations that support the organization's chosen position in the market. More specifically, it is defined in terms of three basic dimensions: administrative infrastructure (articulated in terms of the organization structure, roles and responsibilities, and reporting relationships); processes (articulated in terms of the management processes and activities to implement the strategy); and skills (articulated in terms of the key organizational skills possessed or required to implement the business strategy).

IT strategy is defined in terms of choices pertaining to the positioning of the business in the IT marketplace and is analogous to the business strategy. It is defined

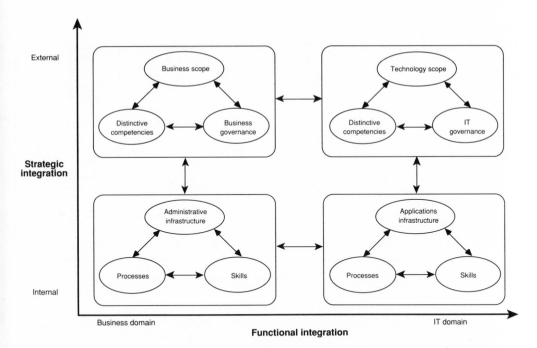

Figure 5-24. The strategic alignment model.

in terms of three basic dimensions: technology scope (articulated in terms of the range of IT capabilities of the organization, such as image processing, global banking networks, or electronic gateways); distinctive competencies (articulated in terms of the salient characteristics in the IT arena that distinguished the firm in the IT marketplace, such as connectivity capabilities, cost-performance, reliability, and safety); and IT governance (articulated in terms of the nature of cooperative relationships, such as joint ventures and strategic alliances in the IT arena).

  IS infrastructure and processes is defined in terms of choices pertaining to the internal arrangements that determine the data, applications, and technology infrastructure to deliver the required IT products and services. It is defined in terms of three basic dimensions: applications infrastructure (articulated in terms of the configurations of hardware, software, and communications); processes (articulated in terms of systems design, development processes, and related activities to implement the IT strategy); and skills (articulated in terms of the key organizational skills within the IS function possessed or required to implement the IT strategy).

Beyond Linkage
Within this general model, the classic view is to consider the linkage between any two domains at a time. For instance, the link between IT strategy (ITS) and business strategy (BS) reflects the potential of IT to influence business strategy (ITS → BS) as well as the articulation of IT strategy given business strategy (BS → ITS). But such a linkage fails to recognize the important internal domains of organization and management processes as well as the IS architecture, which play important roles in the

Four Dominant Patterns of Alignments

Characteristics	Competitive potential	Technology potential	Business value	Service level
Domain anchor	Product-market arena	IT arena	Organizational domain	IS products and services
Management focus	Reengineer business processes	Adapting the IT platform	Transforming work and organization	Redesigning IS portfolio
Analytical frameworks	Competitive strategy frameworks	Technology scan and forecasting, scenarios	Business process analysis	Portfolio analysis of applications
Measures	Business measures relative to competitors	Measures of IT capability and flexibility	Organizational efficiency	Service levels

Figure 5-25. Comparison of alternative patterns of alignments.

translation of strategies into actions. In contrast, considerations of two sets of linkages highlight critical cross-domain linkages. For example, linkage among business strategy, IT strategy, and organization and management processes (O) reflect not only considerations of strategy formulation (BS ↔ ITS) but also issues of strategy implementation (BS → O). Given the benefits of interdependence between strategy formulation and implementation, we argue that the evolving alignment among these four domains can be conceptualized as four triads or coalignments (among three domains each).

This offers four patterns of alignments—each with some distinctive characteristics and manifestations. Specifically, the coalignment among the business strategy, IT platform, and organization is termed competitive potential. The coalignment among IT platform, IT strategy, and business strategy reflects technology potential, while the coalignment among business strategy, organization, and IT strategy is termed business value. The final coalignment is among IT platform, IT strategy, and organization, which is termed service level. Figure 5-25 compares these four patterns of alignments. Our research indicates that organizations—in general—have been successful in achieving one (or two) of these patterns of alignments, but not necessarily blending these four into a coherent and consistent framework to guide decisions and actions. Although each organization may choose to focus on one or more of these coalignments depending on its organizational and competitive contexts, it is clear that consistent attention to these four enhances an organization's ability to leverage IT for sustained success in the marketplace. Thus, it is necessary to move beyond the consideration of any two domains toward recognizing the interplay among the four.

Our purpose in arguing for an alignment perspective is to position the management challenge as a critical issue requiring some serious analysis and assessments—which cannot be addressed through any quick-fix rules or structured procedures. An alignment perspective implicitly reflects dynamism, which is central to the management challenge. It is hoped that this section has stimulated managers to conceptualize the role of IT in creative ways. We hope that managers will rise to the challenge and develop efficient modes of achieving the dynamic alignment among the constituent dimensions.

CONCLUSIONS

It is a truism that IT will have an influence on business organizations in the next decade. It is also a truism that the potential impact will be significant. The business operations of the leading organizations in the next decade will be marked by a significant departure from the present modes of functioning with increasing roles accorded to the capabilities and opportunities offered by IT. In this section, we identified five levels of business transformation that are fundamentally enabled by IT. While not all levels may be equally relevant and important for all organizations, it may be worthwhile to evaluate their specific role in different settings. We do not want to be overly prescriptive in arguing that a particular level may be inappropriate based on some classificatory scheme. Instead, we urge managers to critically evaluate their present positions along these levels and identify sources of opportunities relative to competitors.

Further, it is essential to note that the real strategy lesson is the recognition and understanding that the real benefits from IT accrue only with fundamental transformation of business strategy choices, internal processes (organization structure and processes), the IT platform, and the IS architectures. The Strategic Alignment Model serves as a framework not only to conceptualize the interdependence but also to identify attractive and appropriate courses of actions to achieve the organization's goals.

REFERENCES

Barrett, S. and B. Konsynski. 1982. "Inter-organization Information Sharing Systems." *MIS Quarterly,* special issue.

Benjamin, R. I. 1982. "Information Technology in the 1990s: A Long Range Planning Scenario." *MIS Quarterly* 6, 11–32.

Benjamin, R. I., and M. S. Scott Morton. 1986. "Information Technology, Integration, and Organizational Change." Management in the 1990s Working Paper 96-017.

Benjamin, R. I., J. F. Rockart, M. S. Scott Morton, and J. Wyman. 1984. "Information Technology: A Strategic Opportunity." *Sloan Management Review* 25, no. 3, 3–10.

Clemons, E. K., and M. Row. 1988. "McKesson Drug Company: A Case Study of Economost—A Strategic Information System." *Journal of Management Information Systems* 5, no. 1.

Diebold, J. 1984. "Six Issues That Will Affect the Future of Information Management." *Data Management.*

Henderson, J. C., and N. Venkatraman. 1989. "Strategic Alignment: A Framework for Strategic Information Technology Management." Management in the 1990s Working Paper 89-076.

"Information Business." *Business Week,* August 25, 1986, pp. 82–90.

"Information Power." *Business Week,* October 14, 1985.

Ives, S., and G. P. Learmonth. 1984. "The Information System as a Competitive Weapon." *Communications of the ACM* 27, no. 12, 1193–1201.

Keen, P.G.W. 1981. "Communications in the 21st Century: Telecommunications and Business Policy." *Organizational Dynamics.*

Keen, P.G.W. 1986. *Competing in Time: Using Telecommunications for Competitive Advantage.* Cambridge, Ballinger.

King, W. R. 1978. "Strategic Planning for Management Information Systems." *Management Information Systems Quarterly* 2, no. 1, 27–37.

McFarlan, F. W. 1984. "Information Technology Changes the Way You Compete." *Harvard Business Review* 62, no. 3, 98–103.

McFarlan, F. W., and J. L. McKenney. 1988. "The Information Archipelago—Governing the New World." *Harvard Business Review* 61, no. 4, 91–99.

Malone, T. W., J. Yates, and R. I. Benjamin. 1987. "Electronic Markets and Electronic Hierarchies." *Communications of the ACM,* 484–97.

Porter, M. E., and V. E. Millar. 1985. "How Information Gives You Competitive Advantage." *Harvard Business Review* 63, no. 4, 149–60.

Rockart, J. F., and M. S. Scott Morton. 1984. "Implications of Changes in Information Technology for Corporate Strategy." *Interfaces* 14, no. 10, 84–95.

Rockart, J. F., and J. Short. 1989. "IT in the 1990s: Managing Organizational Interdependence." *Sloan Management Review* 30, no. 2, 7–18.

Wiseman, C. 1985. *Strategy and Computers: Information Systems as Competitive Weapons.* Homewood, Ill.: Dow Jones–Irwin.

CHAPTER 6

Business Strategy Development, Alignment, and Redesign

K. HUGH MACDONALD

Part II of this book arguably contains the core of the results from the Management in the 1990s Research Program. The availability of new, powerful information technology is expanding the strategic options open to organizations. The nature of these new options has been discovered and reported upon by Rotemberg and Saloner in Chapter 4 and by Venkatraman in Chapter 5. Their findings are the result of fundamental research. It seemed useful to add the practitioners' perspective, which is done in this chapter.

This chapter and the related appendices (C, D, and E) were written by K. Hugh Macdonald, sponsor representative to the 1990s program from ICL. He was assisted by five other sponsors in developing the implications of the academic work as put forth in Chapters 4 and 5. In essence, this chapter lays out the practitioners' interpretation of the practical implications of the underlying fundamental research. As such, it is not research but rather reaction to research by knowledgeable practitioners.

Not only are some of the practical implications laid out, but considerable attention is paid to the difficult task of spelling out the kinds of process steps practitioners have found effective in moving from general principles to concrete action steps tailored to making specific changes in an organization. Such management processes are often much more robust when they emerge from the hands of practitioners used to dealing with the complexities of the ongoing business world.

At a different level, this chapter shows the rich implications of the research developed earlier. The same kind of practical development can be done for all the other chapters of this book. It takes enormous effort and the concentrated attention of a talented member of the organization who knows his or her own organization and industry well and who also deeply understands the research. This takes time, effort, and an unusual ability to bridge across two worlds. It is precisely the kind of effort that has to be made if an organization is to set about the process of transformation that will be required to succeed in the 1990s and beyond.

CONTEXT

Part II of this book addresses a range of issues in the domain of *business strategy,* in terms of new approaches to competition and collaboration, and in terms of major changes to business processes and business relationships that can be enabled by information technology. This chapter addresses some possible approaches to using those ideas.

A definition of *strategy* is likely to generate argument. For our purposes here it is sufficient to regard strategy as a mixture of knowledge and assumptions about the organization, goals, objectives, actions, milestones, budgets, and plans, all based on a foundation of knowledge about customers, suppliers, the general environment (political, social, economic, etc.), the actions of competitors, and a number of internal organization factors. It primarily reflects external factors, positioning, and actions to meet the organization's goals. Formulation and implementation of strategy is the prime task of organization leadership.

The general subject of developing and implementing strategy does not suffer from any lack of literature. There is a vast array of strategy processes that are promoted or implemented by educators and consultants. What is proposed here is not in competition with these approaches and is not proposed as a total substitute for any comprehensive strategy development process that may be in productive use. This is not a primer on strategy. What is offered is a number of process components that recognize the role of IT and that can be included in wider strategy development processes. These process components embody some of the concepts discussed in Chapters 4 and 5.

IT is recognized by advanced organizations as an essential part of the infrastructure of the organization—"IT as a strategic resource" is widely acknowledged although less widely applied. Increasingly, IT is becoming a part of the business itself, part of the services provided or part of the products supplied, as well as being the foundation on which the business processes of the organization, both internal and external, depend. In many cases, these business processes would not be possible without IT, at least for economic reasons but in many cases because of procedural complexity or because information processing time scales would be excessive and the business processes would be irrelevant if IT were not used.

The limited vision of an "administrative expense" role for IT is clearly insufficient, but shifting this vision to one of "business investment" requires some new understanding. That IT can change competitive relationships, can enable a complete redesign of internal processes, can alter interorganizational relationships, can extend the "reach" of the organization toward suppliers and customers, and can even change the fundamental scope of the business are all difficult concepts to absorb. Translating these ideas into the changes that are necessary to make them happen adds to the problem.

The issue is not to demonstrate that changes that have occurred in other organizations can be explained by relating them to these concepts, but rather to create a "strategy climate" within an organization so that the relevance of these concepts to one's own organization can be explored.

Experience in applying these concepts have suggested approaches to such questions as:

Who needs to be involved?

What preparation is needed? Particularly, what information is required to illuminate the issues and allow the conclusions to be tested?

What related issues should be addressed?

What form should conclusions take?

How can the apparently huge potential of IT be matched to the organization's strategy?

What changes to the organization's structure and processes are needed?

What supporting capabilities are needed to implement the changes?

The question of who needs to be involved can be the subject of great debate, involving issues of confidentiality, centralization and decentralization, staff and line relationships, roles of headquarters staff, and many other factors. Our experience suggests that it really is much simpler than this. Good strategies are only good because they have been implemented by the organization and their value has become evident. Cases of success or failure in developing and implementing strategies have not come about just because of "good" or "bad" strategy development processes but because management made the strategies happen. Good strategy processes will achieve very little without the active support of organization leadership, and this implies more than just a "blessing." Unfortunately, the passive approach has led to failures, and in turn to the fallacy that turbulence in the environment makes strategy irrelevant.

Good processes provide an umbrella under which a number of important issues can be addressed and conclusions reached. These include, among others:

Understanding of trends and forces that apply within an industry.

Examination of various options and the testing of the sensitivity of business results to a variety of scenarios that may unfold.

Preparation, through a combination of understanding and specific actions, for a variety of futures, including the determination of the "trip wires" that will indicate which particular scenarios may be unfolding.

Because of the relevance of IT to strategy, as both an internal and external enabler and even as a significant component in an organization's manifestation of competitive differentiation, senior management must understand the capability of IT. This does not imply that senior management requires the skills of the "bit pickers." Some deep technical understanding of IT needs to be represented at high management levels. What generally seems to be essential is a deep appreciation of the capabilities and potential, combined with a balanced view of the implementation problems as they relate to the organization, its processes, and the IT applications themselves.

In the end, a "strategy culture" involves a balancing act—the alignment of desires and realities, directed toward capturing a desired future.

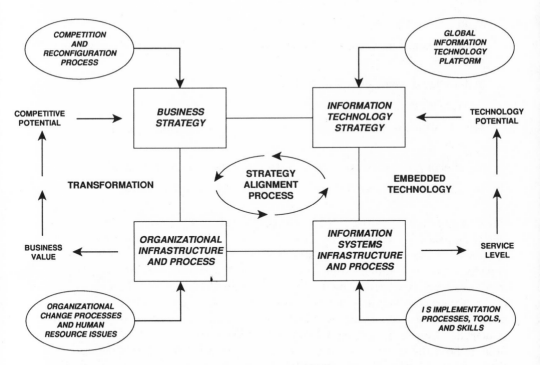

Figure 6-1. The expanded strategic alignment process.

A RESEARCH FRAMEWORK AND A PROCESS FRAMEWORK

The Management in the 1990s Research Framework was introduced in Chapter 1, Figure 1-2. This framework, besides illuminating the interrelationships and the balancing acts that constitute the successful organization, also provides a valuable problem model. The problem has two elements: (1) what to put in the boxes, and (2) what is implied by the linkages.

Chapters 4 and 5 contain a number of theories and research results that illuminate parts of these problems, but these results need to be transformed into processes that exploit these theories and results. One such process model, the Strategic Alignment Process (SAP), derived from the Strategic Alignment Model (SAM), is described in Appendix E. The SAM introduced in Chapter 5 has been expanded to reflect the supporting processes that are required "behind" each element of SAM. This expanded form is shown in Figure 6-1.

The SAP establishes the coalignment of business strategy with information systems architecture and processes, and IT strategy with organization and management processes, and between these two axes. But business strategy does not arise spontaneously—it derives from considerations of how the business is to be operated internally or externally, or relationships with competitors, of reflections of changing customer needs, supplier opportunities, industry trends, and so on. IT strategy is derived from selections from a global technology platform which reflects the full panoply of IT capability that can be obtained. Information systems architecture derives from the internal adoption of processes and the provision of skills in the building of the application systems that support the organization and management processes. The organization and management processes reflect the current organizational and human resources that may exist and their deployment, and these resources may need to be changed, in terms of skills and scale.

Our experience suggests that creating business strategy, particularly when taking account of the impact of IT, includes at least the following four considerations:

1. The impact of industry and competitive changes, particularly under the influence of IT, and the generic strategies in the strategy portfolio.
2. Strategic changes induced by IT that affect the reengineering of the internal value chain which reflects the business operations of the organization.
3. Strategic changes induced by IT that affect the restructuring of the external value system of which the organization is a part and may affect the internal value chain as well.
4. IT capabilities shifting and/or expanding the business domain and scope.

These must all precede alignment of business strategies, IT strategy, information systems architecture, and organization and management processes. While the processes and interconnections described above relate to IT, with some slight changes of wording, the general argument and the processes seem to apply equally well to other technologies.

"ROADMAP"

This chapter comprises a number of subsections. The first subsection discusses the implications of changing patterns of interfirm competition and collaboration. Appendix C describes some approaches to considering the competitive environment through basic checklists of the attributes of organizations in different parts of the competitive domain. Suggestions are made that illustrate the generic strategies that such positioning implies, together with concomitant threats to which organizations are susceptible.

Historical changes in the competitive environment in a number of industries suggest that there are a number of patterns of migrations of organizations between different positions in the competitive matrix outlined in Chapter 4. Considering these patterns of migration, favorable and unfavorable, provides additional contributions to selecting the generic strategies and addressing the threats that are applicable.

The next two subsections address IT-induced business reconfiguration. Of the five levels discussed in Chapter 5, the first two "evolutionary" levels are not considered further, as these are well covered in other literature. The "revolutionary" levels relating to business process redesign (level 3) and business network redesign (level 4) are examined in these two subsections. Outline processes to explore the potential and application of these changes are described in Appendix D.

The next subsection discusses briefly some of the considerations involved in level 5, business scope redefinition. The subject is also covered (although not explicitly) in other subsections.

There is considerable interplay between the processes discussed in all these subsections. It is clear that business network redesign will probably require internal business process redesign. As the alignment process is pursued, it may be necessary to invoke other processes, either to review or reconfirm strategies or to accommodate limitations in capabilities. No overall strict process is essential, although this chapter assumes that the processes are invoked serially.

Once the basic positions are established as a prerequisite for strategic alignment, then the SAP can be invoked, as in Appendix E.

The processes are only discussed in outline. For implementation, it will be necessary to develop forms ("planning frameworks") that are appropriate to the strategic planning context of the implementing organization, and a "process manual."

THE MIT90s RESEARCH FRAMEWORK AND
THE STRATEGIC ALIGNMENT PROCESS

It is clear that the "words" and the "linkages" on the MIT90s Research Framework that was produced in 1984 are reflected in the SAP. In fact, the SAP provides a considerable contribution to the "problems" posed by the research framework.

It is suggested that the SAP can be regarded as a process expression of the framework. The latter reflects the "balancing act" that must be achieved, while the SAP provides a process model that contributes to establishing "balance."

THE APPLICATION OF INTERRELATEDNESS
AND EXPLOITABILITY

The concepts of interrelatedness and exploitability apply to IT products, suppliers and markets, and also to the application of IT itself. However, the idea of interrelatedness is not restricted to IT; it applies as much to small independent breweries and large-scale automobile manufacturers as it does to the market for personal computers.

The relevance of interrelatedness is increasing with the development and ubiquity of IT. While the issues are clearly applicable to IT itself, these considerations are appearing in many other industries as IT, or an "information component," becomes a significant element of the industry's products and services.

In what follows, Figure 4-2 is the "base frame" into which other information is inserted to create a number of further frameworks. The general characteristics of the four quadrants are reflected in the descriptive names applied to each quadrant: "Barroom Brawl," "Clash of the Titans," "Chaotic Proliferation," and "Preemptive Penetration." As a convenient shorthand, organizations that are occupants of the quadrants are described as "Brawlers," "Titans," "Proliferators," and "Penetrators," and no critical sentiment associated with these terms is implied.

Having considered the interplay of interrelatedness and exploitability, and the general characteristics of markets (and the firms in those markets) that derive from that interplay, a distillation of attributes and implications is required. This is intended to assist diagnosis of positioning of an organization and industry in the framework and derivation of the implications for development of strategy.

The composite concept of exploitability, combining the attributes of the competitive environment (whether it is insulated or exposed) and the attractiveness of the market (based on its size, insulation, growth, ease of supply, margin, etc.), does not yield a simple boundary between "low" and "high" conditions. A market may exhibit high exploitability and hence appear attractive, but the benefits will depend on a combination of scale, positioning, market segment insulation, and so on.

While the difference between markets that exhibit interrelatedness and those that do not can be more readily recognized, it is important to appreciate that for this to be significant, the attributes that give interrelatedness must be differentiating factors rather than existence factors. It may seem that facsimile machines exhibit interrelatedness in the sense that they must be compatible with local telephone standards. This is important for the facsimile machine to be useful, but it does not imply interrelatedness any more than does the use of the local electricity supply; neither of them is a useful discriminator. The unique features of one facsimile machine compared to another relate to local convenience of users rather than to attributes that affect the nature of the interrelationships between suppliers and between users.

Attributes of Quadrant Occupants

The positioning of an industry or an organization in the interrelatedness/exploitability framework may be obvious from the definitions of the terms. This positioning can be tested by comparing the attributes of the subject industry or organization with a checklist of attributes exhibited by industries or organizations in the different quadrants. Some of these attributes are shown in Figure 6-2.

Generic Strategies

To occupy a quadrant in the framework, with the industry or organization attributes exhibited in Figure 6-2, implies that certain general strategies and organizational behavior are required if an organization is to be successful. (Success may imply "promotion" to another quadrant, or survival may demand "migration" to another quadrant.) Figure 6-3 shows some of the relevant behavior and strategies that should be expected from occupants of each quadrant.

A successful Brawler will need to search for differentiation to sustain a niche position: the essential strategy is one of differentiation. Close contact with customers is required to obtain early warning of changing customer needs. Successful Brawlers will probably be in a permanent state of innovation.

Titans must be concerned to protect and enhance the high exploitability they are pursuing, either by improving margins through investments in production efficiency or by tactics aimed at protecting and improving market share, enhancing volumes, and thus spreading overheads.

Proliferators should be searching for bandwagons that can be exploited. Because customers desire fewer, more coherent, offerings, a number of competitors may seek relationships with one another to increase the coherence of the market and hence improve the opportunities for one another.

Penetrators are concerned to pursue major opportunities, either as single large organizations or through combinations of firms banding together. Market share is an

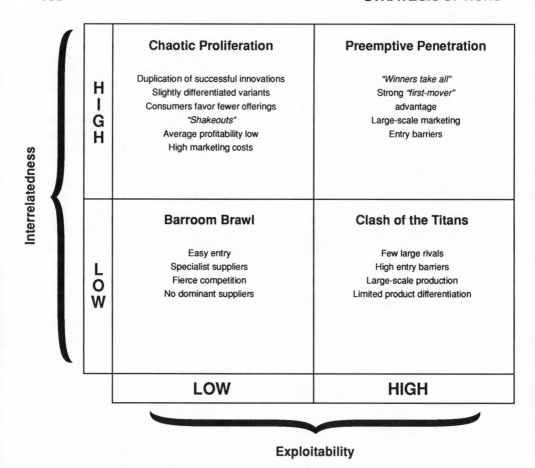

Figure 6-2. Attributes of framework quadrant occupants.

important factor, with marketing strategies related to the building of market share. The erection of entry barriers may also be possible.

The list is certainly not complete but is intended to illustrate the kinds of strategies we would expect to find in the strategy portfolios of organizations that are effective in their quadrant.

Threats to Quadrant Occupants

While pursuing the behavior/strategies shown in Figure 6-3, occupants of each quadrant are also vulnerable to threats resulting from actions of other competitors or changes in market characteristics brought about by the collective behavior of customers or competitors. Figure 6-4 summarizes some major threats.

Brawlers that lose efficiency or expertise (and thus miss changed needs) will suffer. Complacency will lead to failure.

Titans, if they lose market share, may find that their access to the exploitable margin is reduced, and they may be forced to concentrate on niche markets (and

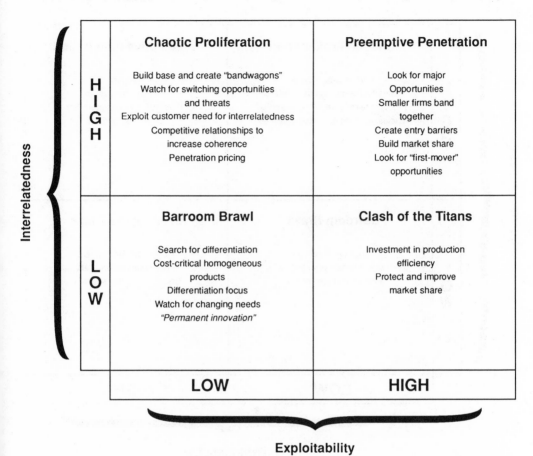

Figure 6-3. Behavior/strategies of quadrant occupants.

thus become Brawlers). Changes in the structure of the market (particularly if rivals and/or customers create or demand interrelatedness) will seriously undermine the position of a Titan.

Proliferators who fail to build a customer base, or assume that some minor product variant will protect their competitiveness when it has become irrelevant, or fail to create or follow a bandwagon, or are excluded from large-scale alliances may find profitability elusive. In such circumstances, interrelatedness may prove to be more of a hindrance than a help.

A Penetrator who fails to spot major changes in requirements or opportunities, or is preempted by a dominant firm, will suffer because catch-up is extremely difficult. Its position as a Penetrator may not be sustainable.

Quadrant Dynamics

From the discussion of behavior/strategies and threats, it will be clear that organizations can find that their customers adopt attitudes that shift their requirements (the

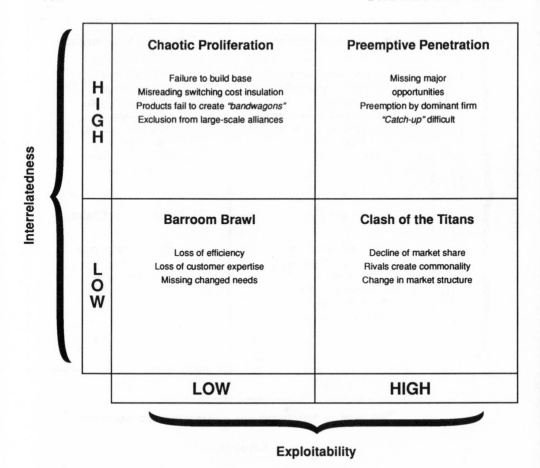

Figure 6-4. Threats faced by quadrant occupants.

"industry") into another quadrant. A supplier must therefore follow and occupy the new quadrant, including adoption of new behavior and strategies. An organization occupying a quadrant may fail to apply the relevant behavior/strategies and have no choice but to retreat to another quadrant, perhaps as a survival tactic or as a preliminary to more serious (even terminal) failure.

It is necessary to differentiate between industries and segments. An industry may generally exhibit the attributes of one quadrant, while small segments of that industry may occupy another quadrant. It may appear that some organizations exhibit behavior typical of low-exploitability quadrants, while other organizations in the same industry appear to be occupying high-exploitability quadrants. This may be a segment effect, but it may be a defensive action by an unsuccessful organization and consequently is an unstable situation.

Changes occur in industries over time, caused by actions of both customers and suppliers. The positioning of the industry within the framework may change. The personal computer market demonstrates this well. Originally, PCs had low interrelatedness and low exploitability; there were many competitors and little similarity or compatibility between models from different suppliers. Undoubtedly this was a Brawl. With the introduction of the IBM PC, one supplier showed signs of becoming a Titan. As PC-compatibles appeared, interrelatedness developed, and the market exhibited the characteristics of chaotic proliferation—with some signs of temporary preemptive penetration on the way. Some vendors are now establishing standards as a preliminary to creating more enduring penetration, while other vendors have been concentrating on major niches and remaining Brawlers, albeit big ones, perhaps aspiring to become Titans.

Theoretically, any movement between quadrants in the framework is possible. In practice, it seems that most movements tend to be either horizontal or vertical, although they can, in most cases, be in either direction. No evidence of a high-exploitability and high-interrelatedness situation surrendering interrelatedness has been found (from Penetrator to Titan, although this might be attractive to a near-monopoly Penetrator). Surrendering both interrelatedness and exploitability at the same time, and changing from penetration to brawling, seems to imply too extreme a catastrophe, and change from brawling to penetration appears too revolutionary. Some cases of apparent movement from the Titan quadrant to the Proliferation quadrant have been noted, although it could be that this diagonal movement was really a two-stage process, with the short-term existence of a penetration state. Observations suggest that changes can readily occur to either interrelatedness or exploitability, but simultaneous changes to both are too extreme.

Horizontal movement from left to the right, toward higher exploitability, can be regarded as a direction of increased advantage to the industry and the participants. A movement in the opposite direction, toward lower exploitability, would appear to be disadvantageous, unless it is associated with the exploitation of a stable niche.

Changes to increase interrelatedness may be provoked by an industry or demanded by customers, with "push" more common than "pull." In a sense, such a movement toward higher interrelatedness may be viewed as advantageous. Retreat from a market defined by high interrelatedness seems less likely, although if some significant niche remains, it would seem possible to retreat from high to low interrelatedness to secure a niche position, from proliferation to brawling.

If exploitability is high, then an appropriate strategy for a Titan may be to build interrelatedness and thus become a Penetrator, leaving others who have failed to exploit interrelatedness to a loss of exploitability and hence forced retreat to brawling. A dominant Penetrator might consider removing interrelatedness, but this would appear to be a significant redefinition of the market, and unattractive to customers, so movement from Penetrator to Titan seems unlikely.

As organizations and industries change exploitability and interrelatedness over time, or are subject to changes, they are engaged in a serious competitive business dynamic. The quadrant-to-quadrant movements that seem most likely to occur are shown in Figure 6-5. This competitive framework provides some perspective on the movements to which one can be subjected. The application of the diagnosis, and the selecting of strategic options, are discussed in Appendix C.

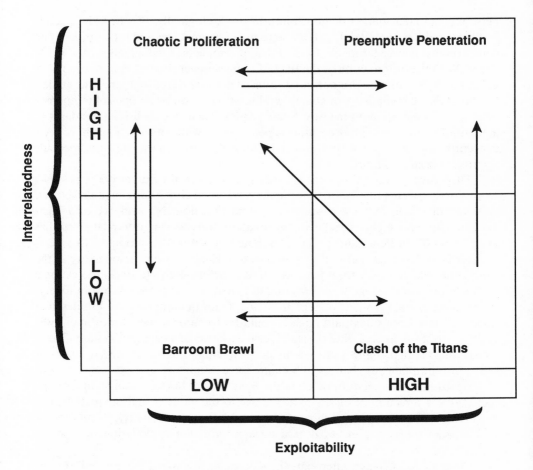

Figure 6-5. Most likely quadrant-to-quadrant movement.

IT-INDUCED BUSINESS PROCESS REDESIGN

Chapter 5 discussed the role of information technology in the reconfiguration, or transformation, of organizations. As IT assumes a strategic role, five levels of transformation were identified, with higher levels of business transformation also associated with more extensive potential benefits.

The two "evolutionary" levels (level 1, localized exploitation; and level 2, internal integration, involving the development of an integrated IT platform) are both well understood and are not discussed further in this chapter because the implementation issues are well covered in the literature (see Chapters 1 and 9 of this book). However, it should be appreciated that, for an organization whose IT development plans are concerned with implementation at either of these levels, the Strategic Alignment Model is still relevant, and the Strategic Alignment Process can be applied.

The three "revolutionary" levels (level 3, business process redesign; level 4, business network redesign; and level 5, business scope redefinition) all represent a larger challenge, both in terms of conceptualizing the changes and in the subsequent implementation. Particularly for an organization with a "burden of history" in established processes, practices, and relationships (and especially if these process traditions have become institutionalized within an industry), major issues in the "management of change and transformation" are involved. Process and network redesign are the focus of Chapter 5 of this book. Frequently it may seem that examining these issues involves thinking about the unthinkable. The technical aspects of the transformation may be trivial in comparison with the human resource management issues. These issues are the focus of Chapters 8 and 9 of this book.

Much of the preparatory work that is essential if addressing the issues of business process redesign is to be productive is equally applicable to levels 4 and 5. Furthermore, when addressing these "higher" levels, there will almost inevitably be issues that emerge that provoke business process redesign. Therefore, an understanding of business process redesign is relevant to the issues discussed in previous subsections, and the outcome is an important set of inputs to the activities covered later. The underlying ideas for business process redesign that were found to be most helpful were those that were built on extensions from the original concept of the Value Chain (Porter, 1985). The extension we have found to be most useful we have chosen to call the Value Process Model. Our Value Process Model is presented in Appendix D and has proved to be an effective way to think through the choices for action.

BUSINESS NETWORK REDESIGN

Rather than repeat the material in Appendix D, additional ideas are recorded, covering the extensions of information requirements and processes needed to address business network redesign. Some of the concepts described in Chapter 5 are expanded.

At first sight, business networks would appear to be an extended manifestation of electronic data interchange (EDI), better expressed as electronic data integration. Much more is implied. The potential for IT to be applied across the full range of communication between organizations affects not just the exchange of transactions, or the substitution of an electronic connection for a variety of traditional "paper interfaces," but many other relationships as well. The electronic link can alter the relative "power" of the participants, both shifting the balance and expanding the joint capability of the organizations.

The backbone of the subject is the interplay of various roles (forms) of business networks and the benefits that accrue to the participants, together with the sustainability of those benefits. Throughout this subsection, benefits are assumed to be useful only if they are differential, if they provide a competitive advantage to one or more participants in the network. If creating a business network provides some non-differential benefits, such as saving operations costs, but as others emulate the system the newcomers can establish parity of performance (cost, in this case), then we regard such a business network as having a neutral effect. Although the cost saving may be useful, it is available to all players. No lasting competitive advantage is obtained, although a first mover may be able to use the cost savings to create a longer-term advantage of a more sustainable nature.

The aim is to develop strategies around the creation of or participation in various forms of IT-based business networks, in which the organization matches its role in the networks and roles of the networks to achieve and sustain competitive advantage. In addition, forms of participation where advantage cannot easily be achieved or sustained must be recognized and opportunities sought to shift the form of participation to minimize disadvantage and develop advantage. It is necessary to recognize that the decision about participation may not be possible—the business network may be the way business in an industry or with major organizations must be done, and participation may be a survival issue. If the role of the organization in the business network is potentially disadvantageous, then this needs to be recognized and opportunities for internal business process redesign sought in order to compensate for the changes in competitive power that participation in the business network may imply.

Business networks are defined as systematic relationships between various individuals, organizations, or enterprises, normally paired in "seller and buyer" relationships, in a value system. The phrase is used to imply commercial relationships rather than electronic connections. In practice, whether for efficiency or convenience, business networks are supported by technical (communications) networks used for exchanging information. We are concerned with the relationships and their implications and not with the technicalities of the interconnections or (electronic) communications networks that transmit or receive messages.

We have found that many case studies suggest the following:

1. "Strong" organizations can "force" participation in business networks as the way in which they wish to do business. The strong organization is using its buyer/seller power to establish preferred administration methods. Others may have to choose whether or not they wish to trade with the strong organization.
2. With a few exceptions, the initial justification for IT-supported business networks (where serious justification in advance has been attempted) seems to have been based on operational (administrative) cost savings, or on assumptions about enhanced "binding" provided by the IT systems—presuming that the system will provide a path of least resistance for customers placing orders, or a form of significant convenience, speed, accuracy, and so on. Wider strategic impact has been recognized later.
3. There is some evidence of recognition or disappointment that initial benefits have not been, or may not be, sustained—particularly in the differential sense.
4. There are strong forces for standardization in IT-supported business networks, beyond the levels of connection standards, and extending to message standards and others. As seen in Chapter 4, standardization can be a reflection of interrelatedness, and all the implications of the proliferation and penetration quadrants of the interrelationship/exploitability framework apply. As standards are established, competitive business networks can emerge easily, new organizations can join a network, and shifts in relative buyer/seller power will occur. Initial binding advantages may evaporate.
5. Some organizations participating in such relationships have been surprised by the redistribution of capital within the business network. These systems facilitate the implementation of "just-in-time" approaches to inventory management, with the consequence that the "supplier" can carry the inventory (and hence the capital,

cost of capital, and other inventory costs) for delivery at short notice, rather than "selling" the inventory (and the obligations for the inventory costs) to the customers. The customers can reduce the time inventory is carried. Unless the supplier modifies internal processes to provide quicker production response, or introduces inducements (such as better quantity discounts) to move inventory to customers, the supplier can find inventories expanding.

6. There is some evidence of "regret" about participation in IT-supported business networks, but usually at a time when this has become "the way business is now done." Escape from the system may not be a viable commercial option.

These horror stories usually seem to relate to organizations that did not understand the strategic implications of participating in IT-based business networks. There are some spectacular success stories, ranging from airline reservation systems through a range of customer/supplier systems to advanced systems in which considerable integration of complex processes has occurred across organization boundaries and new collaborative capabilities have enhanced the competitive strength of the participants. Some systems have served not only to enhance the performance of participants but to enlarge the opportunities available to the participants. "Win-win" situations are common.

However, rather than leave the consequences (and benefits) to chance, it is suggested that an understanding of the roles and benefits of business networks can be explored in advance to allow an organization to recognize the benefits and their sustainability and to prepare strategies to maintain advantage or to compensate for the possible disadvantages. The real issue is probably not whether an organization participates in such business networks, but how and when it participates.

What is also apparent from many cases is that where competitive advantage was established and sustained, this was frequently accompanied by imaginative enhancements to the original functions performed in the IT systems supporting the business network and by extensions of the network to handle additional business processes. For example, comprehensive exploitation of the technical potential of IT has been combined with the conversion of a simple electronic connection (or EDI system) into a "marketing channel" through which customers are introduced to new products and services by the IT system, thus speeding up new product introductions, new pricing, and terms. It certainly appears that the "winners" were organizations that (1) had sufficient mastery of IT that they could rapidly exploit additional ideas and extend the scope of the system, and (2) possessed an imaginative management that perceived opportunities to extend the scope of the network and more deeply "penetrate" their suppliers or customers—in many cases, it seems that one of the organizations has "invaded" the value processes of the other organization.

What is discussed below is not a simple solution to the problem of finding the spark of genius on demand but rather some approaches that will create an environment that will help to stimulate this spark.

Some Basic Principles

In considering business network opportunities, the value chain or Value Process Model (as discussed in Appendix D) provides a convenient tool for the exploration and assessment of opportunities. This approach requires that the models be developed for both the organization itself and the other parties in the business network. The more that is known about the other parties in the value systems, the greater the potential for determining linkage and integration opportunities, implications, and implementation issues. It may be necessary to start with very simple models and little cost information; but even a primitive understanding of the broad processes is useful and can be refined as the exercise proceeds and discussions with the other parties occur.

A number of factors need to be considered:

1. Business relationships range from loose/open relationships (between a large number of organizations) to tight/closed relationships (between a limited number of organizations).
2. Technology considerations are based on connections and applications and depend on whether these are standardized (and potentially widely available) or unique and proprietary (and available to a small or controlled population).
3. Strategic options derive from the interplay of business relationships and technology considerations.
4. Integration scope is the depth of penetration of the system into the internal processes of the participants in the business network.
5. Participant roles are related to the IT systems used or shared.

As an aid to the conceptualization of IT-supported business networks, it is observed that many exhibit the characteristics of a hub-and-spoke structure. An example of a hub might be a chain of do-it-yourself retailers, and the spokes might be the various suppliers of tools, paint, wood, fittings, and so on. In general, both hubs and spokes can be buyers or sellers. While hubs are generally surrounded by spokes, in some circumstances the business network may involve the interconnection of hubs in peer-to-peer relationships.

Business Relationships

An important point is the extent to which the parties in a business network are biased, whether by the systems/business processes or by commercial agreements. Hubs may wish to operate "electronic markets" among competing suppliers, the spokes (a loose relationship), or they may wish to build close relationships with the spokes to ensure that suppliers are operating to standards of quality (with supporting internal quality processes) that avoid large-scale quality functions being performed by the hubs when goods are received. In an electronic business network, hubs may invite competitive bids from spokes (a loose relationship) or may share marketing information and volume expectations and requirements with chosen suppliers, and use the network to negotiate a supply program (a tight relationship).

Technology Considerations

At one extreme we find highly standardized applications systems, based on both standard interfaces and standard applications, and at the other extreme are proprietary links and applications systems. In practice, mixes of standard or proprietary elements